PRAISE FOR
UNDER THE BRIDGE

Winner of the Arthur Ellis Award for Best Nonfiction Book of 2006

"Chilling . . . Godfrey applies the *In Cold Blood* treatment to the 1997 murder of a 14-year-old Canadian girl, allegedly at the hands of seven teenage girls and one boy. . . . The book reads like a breezy bestseller, but it's Godfrey's in-depth reporting—she spent six years following the case—that gets under your skin. She will make you understand why a girl would kick another in the head—and why a parent would deny what is before her eyes. . . . Lipstick, platform shoes, and braces have never felt more menacing."

—*GQ*

"Godfrey skillfully blends hard-nosed journalism with a literary lyricism that far and away transcends that of her true-crime colleagues."

—Elle.com

"A tour-de-force of true crime reportage."

—*Kirkus Reviews* (starred review)

"Will keep anybody with a brain and a heart reading into the night."

—*Knoxville News-Sentinel* (TN)

"A stunning book that manages to terrify and enlighten at the same time. No one understands the teenage mind like Rebecca Godfrey. And no one can penetrate its darkest recesses with such insight and compassion."

—Gary Shteyngart,
author of *Absurdistan*

"Hypnotic, obsessive, wonderfully transformative."

—John Guare,
author of *Six Degrees of Separation*

"*Under the Bridge* is a fine piece of reportage and a shocking rendering of the tragic end of one young life and the dark and sinister beginnings of others. Godfrey writes with stinging insight and an urgency that moves the story from teenage hush and whisper to the reality of the coroner's office and sad, fatigued cops. The principals are all victims—of schools and communities and families that don't care—and perpetrators—harming one another and themselves in this startling fall from innocence."

—Anthony Swofford,
author of *Jarhead*

"A skilled and emotionally compelling investigation into the dark heart of adolescent society, both in isolation and in the context of our culture. Godfrey . . . combines a storyteller's skills with a journalist's keen eye for detail to create a complex interwoven narrative

of the events that is at once intimate and detached. . . .
A keen-edged and heart-rending account."

—*The National Post* (Canada)

"Godfrey's portraits are complex and unsentimental. . . .
A homicide is best told as a story, and this marvelous
book makes this very clear."

—*The Globe and Mail* (Canada)

"Easily one of the most harrowing non-fiction books of
the year. . . . Godfrey cannily shifts perspectives, which
allows for insights not only into the legalities of the case
but also into the minds of the teens involved. This is a
dark ride."

—*The Vancouver Sun* (British Columbia)

"Haunting . . . phenomenal cinematic raw material."

—*The Hollywood Reporter*

"*Under the Bridge* is a prodigiously researched and carefully observed account of a senseless murder and its
aftermath. Rebecca Godfrey brings a sympathetic imagination and a finely tuned ear for language to bear on a
dark subject, with spectacular results."

—Evan Cornog, publisher,
Columbia Journalism Review

Also by Rebecca Godfrey

The Torn Skirt

UNDER
THE
BRIDGE

Rebecca Godfrey

POCKET STAR BOOKS

NEW YORK   LONDON   TORONTO   SYDNEY

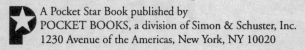 A Pocket Star Book published by
POCKET BOOKS, a division of Simon & Schuster, Inc.
1230 Avenue of the Americas, New York, NY 10020

Copyright © 2005 by Rebecca Godfrey

Orginally published in hardcover in 2005 by Simon & Schuster, Inc.

ISBN-13: 978-1-4165-3156-2
ISBN-10:   1-4165-3156-4

This Pocket Books paperback edition March 2007

10 9 8 7 6 5 4 3 2 1

POCKET STAR BOOKS and colophon are registered
trademarks of Simon & Schuster, Inc.

Cover design by Claudine Mansour
Front cover photo © age Fotostock/Superstock

Manufactured in the United States of America

For information about special discounts for bulk
purchases, please contact Simon & Schuster Special Sales
at 1-800-456-6798 or business@simonandschuster.com

AUTHOR'S NOTE

The material in this book is derived from author interviews and observations, official records, and court proceedings. Certain conversations have been re-created based on these sources and some names and details have been changed.

"Never again are you the same. The longing is to be pure. What you get is to be changed."

—*Prayer,* Jorie Graham

PROLOGUE

Carefully Floated

You can't see anything. In the dark waters of a saltwater inlet known as the Gorge, Sergeant Bob Wall was underwater, searching for the body of a girl. Though he had been a member of the elite Dive Unit for twelve years and was properly and fully equipped with full scuba gear, insulated underwear, neoprene gloves, a buoyancy compensator, and a twenty-five-pound air tank on his back, his search for the girl was frustrating and difficult because underwater, everything was so dark. His eyes were open as he moved forward, yet he could see only blackness. He would have to look for the girl by feeling alone, feeling and touching the darkness that surrounded him, a cold, black depth below the surface of the world.

Concealed in his black wet suit, Bob Wall moved slowly, twelve inches at a time, while the other men held the rope taut and firm. Under water, he touched the detritus of suburbia. Bicycles, so many bikes. He touched beer bottles and rusted nails and shopping carts. "There's so much junk in the Gorge," the men of the Dive Unit say; they speak of the water as if it is their enemy. "The visibility's awful. The water's crap." *You can't see anything.*

When you're searching, you like to sink to the bottom, the men say.

You have to use your buoyancy compensator, make yourself "negatively buoyant," so you're almost prone on the bottom. It looks as if you're doing a push-up. You're as far down as you could possibly be.

Blind and feeling everything, Bob Wall touched the sand with a single hand. His other hand held tight to the rope. Two members of the Dive Unit sank with him, keeping the rope as taut as they possibly could, holding on with both hands, holding tight.

The girl who was missing was fourteen years old.

The girl, she'd been missing for over a week.

If the terrible rumor were true, she would have sunk to the bottom of the Gorge by now. Sergeant Rick "Gos" Gosling was glad he was holding the line and not the one doing the physical search. The "anticipation of finding a body is so stressful," he explains. "You always have that nightmare of finding the face looming up against you, like that scene in *Jaws.*" You'd be pushing yourself against the dark water and knowing you might see a face, lifeless and still. You'd come up against the horror of death, right there, literally, before your eyes. Gos remembered the time he'd found an old woman trapped in her sunken Chevrolet. Her eyes met his; the old lady, she looked right at him and he jumped back, feeling nausea and sadness. The old lady's eyes were blue and her mouth was open, as if she'd died in the midst of a roar or a song.

Sometimes under water, there would be these strange moments of beauty, a light that would crack through the blackness and the sandstorms. In the darkness, the men say, sometimes, "You get swirls, a pale green, a glimmer."

It was a strange occupation—looking for something you didn't really want to find. And on this pale, blurry day in November, the men really didn't want to find the fourteen-year-old girl because it would mean the rumors of murder were true. "You've got to be kidding," Gos said when he heard about who was alleged to have killed the girl. His partners scoffed as well, for the story of her supposed killers seemed such an absurd and impossible tale.

The absence in the water seemed to confirm their disbelief.

If you asked the men why they didn't believe the story, they would answer quite logically. This was Victoria, British Columbia, a small island in the Pacific Northwest famed for its natural beauty and easygoing lifestyle. Young girls did not get murdered in Victoria. Girls in this town, they grew up unharmed. They shopped at Hillside Mall, attended schools named after politicians and war heroes. Girls lived safely on streets named after trees and explorers. Girls may have been murdered in the closest big cities of Vancouver and Seattle; in these cities murders were common and no one would be surprised to hear the story of a young girl brutally murdered. But girls did not die young here on this idyllic island, a sheltered paradise. Gos never before had been asked to investigate the murder of a young girl.

Bob Wall reached the end of the line. Still nothing. The girl was supposed to have been killed right on the sandy shore, near the old white schoolhouse, now covered by lurid yellow crime scene tape.

Gos wished he could look at the sun, get a sense of the time of day. He did not know it was 11:15. He knew only that they'd been underwater for almost an hour. He wanted to lift the seaweed, which was clammy and cold against his cheek, but to remove his hands from the rope would cause the line to flail, cause his partner to drift off his path.

Suddenly, this: a tug on the rope. One tug, then another, then a third. Three tugs was the code for discovery.

All three men rose and left the dark below.

In the eelgrass, Bob Wall had seen something, a pale white strip of fabric. As he moved closer, he reached for the fabric, retrieving it from the rough stalks tinged with a color like ivory. His hands reached in; they found the fabric was a pair of girl's underwear. "Panties," he would later write in the Dive Unit Operation Log, "were retrieved from the eelgrass."

Using a camera floated out to him, Bob Wall photographed the underwear. He then marked the spot with a wooden stick known as a pelican marker. He kicked back to shore and placed the underwear inside a sterile Ziploc bag. Wall flinched slightly as water fell from the bag and as he touched the wet fabric and saw the label, so ordinary and familiar: Fruit of the Loom.

Several minutes later, at 11:29, Bob Wall made a second discovery.

The men holding the rope felt a sudden, sharp pull and thought together and silently, we found her. The young missing girl. She would be there, on the bottom of the Gorge.

But when Bob Wall rose, his left hand held something smaller than a body. In his hands, he held only a pair of blue jeans. The jeans were covered in silt as gray as ash.

Bob Wall photographed the jeans, stuck the pelican marker in, placed the jeans in the plastic bag, sealed the bag, returned to the marker, and went down again.

"We *knew* we were close now," Gos recalls. "We were expecting to find the whole package," Gos says. "We've got the clothing. *She should be right there*. That really did confuse us."

The men moved along westward more slowly, feeling every inch of the sand and the black water.

The line search continued until they had covered every inch of their planned path. The area under the bridge was still to be searched, but this search would require a new plan, for there were pillars to be navigated and the route was not as clear.

The men surfaced, kicking back toward the small Zodiac boat. They climbed aboard, lifted their goggles, and wiped seaweed away. A light mist fell on the surface of the water, and the air smelled like autumn bonfires. Near the schoolhouse, reporters, photographers, and onlookers gathered, all drawn to the scene by the obvious presence of *something major going on.* The men in black, the yellow crime scene tape, and this unusual site as well: in the sky, a red Coast Guard helicopter hovered over the Gorge.

The Dive Unit were slightly cynical about the presence of the helicopter. The Coast Guard was not trained to deal with *evidence,* and besides, what could you really see when you were so far above? To really find anything, you had to dive down.

The men drank coffee.

"We will do this," they said. "We will find her."

At 12:22, static came over Gosling's radio. The men shivered and drank their coffee. On the radio, a distraught voice said: "We've got something."

The vagueness, the Dive Unit knew, was meant to deter journalists. On the radio, searchers never say they've found a body. The men knew the code. And then the helicopter above them, on the other side of the Gorge, near lavish and proud homes, the helicopter suddenly started to descend.

When they received the oblique message, the four men jumped into their van without bothering to take off their wet suits. They drove quickly through the quiet streets of a suburb named View Royal, past homes still decorated with Halloween images of ghosts and falling spiders and lanky goblins. On reaching the home at 2814 Murray Street, they parked the van crookedly and ran past the stone pillars and scarlet foliage and through the backyard down toward the silver water. "It was a big frenzy there," Gosling recalls. "Everybody converged. The coroner, some journalists, investigators, there was everybody."

And there was the girl, who'd been found not by the men underwater but by the men up above.

She was floating in the reeds, her body hidden by the stalks, which were dry and close to the color of cinnamon. Her long, black hair floated like a velvet path, and the naked part of her body was covered by the cold rise of water.

In the water, the girl was floating while the men stood upright. They surrounded her in a circle, and the scene might have seemed like a baptism in reverse, a girl lifted from the water and placed on a gurney, her body in a black T-shirt instead of a white dress.

The body was carefully floated to the wharf by the men of the Dive Unit. *Carefully floated* was the term Bob Wall would choose for his police report. *Carefully floated.* The phrase, like the gesture, was poetic and kind, an act that might have been the only poetry and kindness shown to the murdered girl.

The men lifted her out of the Gorge, away from the spot of her secret grave.

PART ONE

The Youth of View Royal

COLIN JONES

The girls liked Colin Jones. He could not get rid of the girls. In the months before the murder, the girls were always coming over to his house at 14 Marton Place. Colin Jones was *that* guy. Sixteen and laid back. Handsome and easygoing, with sandy freckles, a slim face, and a casual and constant grin. He was not the type of guy to become involved in a murder or the dreams of a murder. He was the kind of guy who lives in every small town—a boy at the end of boyhood who dreamed of new cars and the next raging party. Colin Jones describes himself like this: "I had long hair, nice long curly hair. All the girls liked it. I listened to Guns N' Roses. I was a party animal."

"Those girls hung around me," he recalls.

Hung around me. Those girls.

Colin Jones noticed Nevada the minute she moved onto his street. She was long-legged and gawky, and her face was framed by ringlets the color of flames. She chewed bubble gum and wore tight jeans. When he said her name, he thought of American casinos, of rodeos, of cheerleaders and of gasoline. Nevada. Her front tooth was chipped and when she smiled, it seemed like she was winking at him.

Nevada lied, smiling shyly; she said she was seventeen.

• • •

In View Royal, everybody knew everybody. The suburb was a village of fewer than eight thousand persons, a village full of cousins and old sweethearts and drinking buddies and lifelong friends. There were no bachelors in View Royal. There were no women called Ms. There were only families. Children went first to View Royal elementary, then to Shoreline Junior Secondary, and then to Spectrum Senior Secondary. College and travel were rarely considered. Men worked at the mills and the dockyards, and when the mills and dockyards closed, their sons worked at the Costco and the Wal-Mart and the lumber stores. Women worked at the nearby Helmcken Road Hospital, and their daughters worked at the many stores in the Tillicum Mall.

Colin Jones himself knew practically everybody in the town and could offer quick dismissals ("he's a little puke") or nods of respect ("that guy's hilarious"). He knew the older brothers of Nevada's two best friends, and he knew Nevada's dad rode bulls in the rodeo. Above all, he knew beauty and innocence, and Nevada—okay, he'd admit it: he had a crush on her, but he lost interest when he found out she lied to him.

Nevada was, in truth, only fourteen.

Often, in the months before the murder, late at night, Nevada and her two best friends would sneak out of Nevada's home and walk down the lane, shaded and hidden by the high boughs of oak trees. The girls would sit on the curb of the cul-de-sac, under a street lamp, and they would smoke cigarettes and stare restlessly at parked SUVs and closed white doors. Autumn on Vancouver Island always is a gray, bleak season. That autumn the fog and rain were even more present. During the murder trial, James Stevenson MacDuff, an expert weather "interpreter," testified that in November 1997, "many days had no sunshine or less than one hour of sunshine a day."

The three girls would throw rocks at Colin Jones's window. Josephine flung the pebble to the glass. Josephine, like Nevada, was fourteen, and her features were as classic and delicate as those of a new doll. Her eyes were round and an icy blue; her lips resembled a full and perfect heart. Yet Josephine could be reckless and cruel, and her heroes included Al Capone and John Gotti. She longed to be a gangster. This longing was not the idle dream of an adolescent teenage girl but a fervent and heart-felt ambition.

Although he did not know of her ardent affection for the mafia, Colin Jones was nonetheless unsettled by Josephine right from the start. He did not share the infatuation of his friend Paul who thought Josephine was "the bomb." Colin Jones was not fooled by the porcelain skin and sultry lips. Josephine, he said to himself, was "a twisted little troublemaker."

Kelly Ellard, on the other hand, was cute and awkward and seemingly ordinary. Her brown hair flipped up just below her tiny ears. Her manner was reminiscent of the little sister, annoying and desperate for her older brother's company. In fact, Colin had gone to school with Kelly's older brother and thought he was "quite the dick." He could gleefully recall the time her brother's obnoxious bravado resulted in a harsh beating from the notorious Barker brothers. ("He got beat up bad!") He knew that Kelly's brother owned a "sweet" Monte Carlo, with tinted windows and an "awesome" sound system. And he knew Kelly's stepfather, George Pakos, was a former soccer star, who had scored, according to the Victoria Sports Hall of Fame, "two of the most important goals in the history of Canadian soccer." During the 1986 World Cup, while playing for Team Canada, he'd stunned 50,000 Honduran fans with his winning kick, bringing victory to the Canadian underdog team. Everyone in View Royal knew George and said he was "a great guy." These were the notable and distinct facts to a boy like Colin Jones: fights, triumphs, and cars. As for Kelly herself, he knew little about the young girl, though she seemed more polite and less lascivious than Josephine. He could only later explain her fate by saying, with some sympathy: "She's been picked on most of her life by her brother. Her mother couldn't control her, but her brother could."

Kelly was not a troublemaker, he says. "She just seemed lost all the time."

• • •

"They're like lost puppies," he thought as the girls came up the stairs and into his bedroom. Pillow creases marked Josephine's pale cheek, and her blonde hair was wild with static electricity. He was not sure if they came to him for company or weed. Nevada lay down on his bed, and her scarlet curls fell across the clean cotton of his pillow case.

Josephine seated herself before his mirror, her back perfectly erect. "Can we have some of your weed, Colin?"

"Yeah, Colin, please," Kelly begged.

Josephine stared into the mirror, and Kelly gazed at Josephine as one looks at a map.

"Pass me that joint, slut," Josephine said to Nevada.

Hey, Colin wanted to say, *Don't talk to Nevada like that.* But he was lazy and high, and he felt subdued by the onslaught of perfume and giggling.

Colin Jones had posters on his bedroom wall, posters of Metallica and a Ferrari and a Mach 1. Best of all, he had eight speakers. *Awesome,* he thought, gazing about his domain. Awesome cars, awesome speakers. The girls were ruining his reverie. Giggle, giggle.

The girls wanted to listen to Tupac Shakur, but Colin Jones possessed none of that "gangster shit." He did not listen to rap, and he scoffed at the younger boys of View Royal with their saggy pants and backward baseball caps, fronting like they were from the ghetto.

"Why are you such a headbanger, Colin?" Josephine said, giggling.

"You're like one of those guys in *Wayne's World,*" Kelly said, looking up at Josephine to see if her remark garnered a laugh.

"Give me some of that Bacardi," Josephine said. As she took the bottle from Nevada's purse, she boasted to Colin that she had "jacked" it from Nevada's mother.

What kind of girl calls her friend a slut? Colin wondered. What kind of girl steals liquor from her friend's mother? Answer: a twisted little troublemaker.

Colin Jones knew then that Nevada was too far gone.

"Basically, Josephine corrupted Nevada," he would later say. Though he was often high and always easygoing, he observed the corruption and felt concerned to witness this: the fall of the girl next door.

"Bring some women," his friend Tommy told him. Tommy had just moved into his own apartment and wanted to have a tequila party. Colin couldn't find any women, and so, as a "last resort," he brought the girls—a decision he would later regret. The girls seemed so happy when he invited them. *Awesome! Colin, you're the best!* Josephine's smile was sincere, and her face was luminous. Nevada sat on his lap as they drove to the party in his friend Paul's station wagon. Kelly handed her last cigarette to Josephine, and as she did so, Colin observed the red dots above her eyes, on the skin where she'd plucked at her eyebrows. Josephine's eyebrows were thin and overly arched, and her skin was white and pure, without the slightest mark. Kelly, he thought, just doesn't really have the act of artifice down pat yet, and he remembered then that he'd heard the boys at her school teased her and called her "Grubnut."

"Hey," Josephine said to Paul, draping herself over the driver's seat. "Did you know that I'm going to New York? I'm going to join the mob. I'm gonna be a hit man!"

"They let girls do that?" Paul asked.

"Hell, yeah. They like women in the mob. They don't have to serve any time if they get caught."

"Well, good for you," Paul said, feigning support. In

the backseat, Colin Jones shook his head, and it occurred to him then that most girls Josephine's age were watching *Cinderella,* but Josephine, here she was, abandoning dreams of princes and preferring the narrative of *Scarface.*

"The party was a total disaster," Colin Jones would later recall. "The girls said they were snorting speed, but I think it was just caffeine because Kelly started falling all over the place. Nevada looked really sick and I thought I better get them back to View Royal, so I had to leave the party and drive them all home."

It seemed an omen of sorts to him: the three ill girls.

He dropped them off at Nevada's house, vowing that he would never invite them to another party.

And then, only half an hour later, he heard the sound of a pebble chucked at his window. He ran down the stairs, eager to tell the girls to get lost and leave him alone.

But there was only one girl.

Josephine stood there, dressed as she had been dressed for the disastrous party. Barely dressed. A short black skirt, skinny legs, the rise of her black platform heels.

"We got kicked out of Nevada's house," she said, morosely.

Good, he thought, *finally.* He looked up the street and saw Kelly in her father's arms, being carried into her father's car.

"I've got nowhere to go, Colin," Josephine said.

"Why don't you go home?"

She looked intently at her blue fingernails. "I got in trouble at home, and my mom kicked me out and now I'm living at this group home and they lock the doors at 11:00. Can I just stay here?"

From the light affixed above the number 14, he could see Josephine's stomach, her belly button, and he knew she was a twisted little troublemaker and she'd want something from him eventually. If he did not give it to her, she would take it—steal a CD or weed or his iguana named Steve.

For two seconds, she stood there silently. She did not swear or beg, but he knew she was waiting for him to take her in.

He looked away, over her thin shoulder, above her blonde head, toward the suburb, the ranch houses and bungalows, now unlit and closed. He shook his head, but she just stood there, and he thought he might never get rid of Josephine. She might be there at his window or door for the rest of his life, like a constant reminder of the soft and lost part of himself.

For some reason, he watched her, later, after he'd refused to let her in and gone back upstairs to his bedroom. She sat for a while on the curb in the cul-de-sac. He could not make out her expression, but he imagined it was hostile. Nevada was in bed, tucked under her down comforter, and Kelly was at her father's home, with the hot tub in the backyard and her brother's Monte Carlo all agleam. Josephine might muster herself forward by imagining she was possessed of the soul and bravery of John Gotti. Really, she was so wraithlike, dragging her feet as she began her slow walk away from

Marton Place. He imagined she might look up and give him the finger. *Fuck you Colin Jones.* But she did not, and he put on his headphones and stared at the pulsing black net of his eight speakers, while Josephine walked away, into the darkness of the night, which was becoming darker and quieter still.

WARREN G.

Many people on the paradise-like island of Victoria refer to View Royal as "the place near the hospital" or "the wrong side of the tracks," but to Warren, View Royal was "heaven." For as long as he could remember, he'd moved around, and the list of places would take up the length of his left arm: Medicine Hat, Regina, Nanaimo, South Wellington, Castlegar, Trail, Estevan, and back to Nanaimo. He thought the constant moves were the reason his father wanted to live in a trailer, for as far as he could tell, his dad made a lot of money and Warren would later say, "I didn't want for anything." After a life of moving, Warren grew used to packing up all his possessions in a duffel bag and not holding on to anything. Luckily, he made friends easily and could let go of them just as easily as his last address. Well, actually, letting go was harder. Letting go, starting again. Warren was getting pretty sick of it in the year of the murder, the year he would turn sixteen. In the fall of this year, around the same time neighborhood girls were pestering Colin Jones, Warren's dad announced he was moving once more, this time to California.

Warren's father was moving to live with a rich widow he'd met in a Vegas casino called Circus-Circus. He wasn't taking the trailer this time. He was moving into the widow's home, where there was a collection of art and a view of palm trees. Though he'd never traveled outside Canada, Warren knew a few things about California. He knew his namesake, Warren G., as well as Dr. Dre and Ice Cube, lived in the cities of Long Beach and Compton. He knew those Mexican gangsters, *cholos,* roamed the streets, and he thought *cholos* were pretty cool ever since he saw them in the movie *Once Upon a Time in America.* ("I liked the way they wore Virgin Mary's around their neck.") Yet View Royal had this and mainly and truly this: Syreeta.

For six months, he'd spent every day with her, or as he put it, "Me and Syreeta, we were together 24/7." *First love, true love.* He believed these were the words to capture the experience of always, always, forever wanting to be by her side. First love. True love. So when his dad offered the information about the move to California (which was perhaps more information than invitation), Warren said, "I think I'll stay here."

Him and his dad, they didn't have much of a relationship anyway. His dad was the strong, silent type. He looked the part, kind of like Clint Eastwood. You wouldn't want to mess with him. He wore tight jeans and cowboy boots and tinted shades, and his hair slicked up just slightly on his forehead in the shape of a treble clef. Warren's mom, she liked those kinds of guys—she liked men like Charles Bronson and Clint Eastwood. ("She had a huge crush on Dwight Yoakam.")

Warren knew this: he wasn't supposed to be born. Not that he wasn't wanted, but his parents weren't married and they both already had a couple of kids and bad marriages in their history. Warren's mom, she'd had it with motherhood, gone so far as to get her tubes tied, and still, somehow, he was born. How could that be? "You must have been one strong kid," his mother told him.

The surprising birth of Warren occurred on April 26, 1981, in a town called Medicine Hat. His parents tried to stay together, for him, though they didn't get married and didn't really like each other at all. It was a disaster right from the start. Maybe they'd been in love once. Yet he couldn't imagine they loved each other, and he knew in his heart he was the son who caused all their fights.

• • •

In 1996, Warren's father moved his family to Nanaimo, to the last place the three would reside before their familial demise. Nanaimo, on the far end of Vancouver Island, was a town of strip malls and the Harmac Mill, where Warren's father worked as a welder from 7:30 A.M. to 6:00 or 8:00 or 10:00 P.M. Some Sundays, he'd take Warren to the swap meet, and he'd look for welding equipment while Warren wandered around looking at the chipped dishes and toasters, and once his father bought him a hockey net.

In Nanaimo, at the age of fourteen, Warren discovered on his own: acid, how to drive, the collected works of Too $hort. Clara, an older neighborhood girl, taken, as the girls often were and might always be, by the sight of Warren's large eyes and hopeful smile, introduced him to gangster rap, while Laura gave him his first tab of acid one night when they sat on the steps of the Silver City Theater. Clara would pinch his cheeks and tell him how cute he was, and he'd blush but enjoy the affection because he knew it so rarely.

He learned to drive because his mom was always begging him to get her cigarettes. His mom wore tasseled moccasins and spandex pants, and because of her predilection for almost ceaseless inebriation, Warren never invited Clara or Laura into his home. He'd dress his mother in the morning, when she was dizzy from drink. He'd get her some food, drive off to get her cigarettes, and then return to the trailer, make her some coffee, and tell her to take it easy with the booze. Nights, he'd sleep on the couch knowing he shouldn't have to and didn't want to hear the fighting from the bed behind the thin wall. When school was over for the summer, he decided to go off on his own to visit his older brother in the prairie town of Estevan. It wasn't that he was unwanted, he would later say, it was just he wanted to give his parents some peace of mind.

During his summer stay in Estevan, Warren always appeared happy-go-lucky ("I put on a false face, smiled"), but quite frankly, "Estevan sucked. I just didn't feel comfortable there. I didn't feel right. I was younger, smaller." Later, after everything that happened "with the murder and everything," one memory of that summer would emerge to Warren as if it had been an unheeded warning.

"Me and my brother were driving to a party, and this cop pulls us over, and he asks me my last name. When I told him Glowatski, he kind of smirked, and he said, 'Another *Glowatski*, huh?' and he shook his head. I didn't want that stigma."

Warren asked his dad about their heritage, and his

dad just said something quick about Poland, but he didn't want to talk about it much, as if he had no interest in traditions and legacy.

All summer, he saw violence and parties. There were fights at the parties, and parties at the fights. "I was too young to be in that scene," he admitted, and his only good memory was of an older pretty neighborhood girl who pinched his cheek and called him "little cutie." Otherwise he learned of neither art nor philosophy, and only of how it felt to be an outcast, which to him meant, "I didn't feel comfortable. I didn't feel right." There were bonfires in the gravel pits and he got high, and stared at the flames and the dust. His mom called him and said she missed him and she was so lonely and could he please come home? He felt guilty and loved, and in this way, he went back to Nanaimo.

His absence had not seemed to improve relations between his parents, and shortly after his return, they fought loudly and cruelly over the happenstance of laundry. His mother did not want to do his father's laundry, and his father screamed prophetically: "I'm going to Vegas. I'm going to meet a rich widow. And you won't be seeing me and Warren ever again."

The next morning, Warren and his father left in the trailer and moved to the Fort Victoria Park in View Royal, not far from the train tracks. Warren didn't mind leaving Nanaimo because it was "quite a dump," just doughnut shops and movie theaters and huge malls and nothing much at all. Warren loved View Royal right away, for there was the Gorge, silvery and blue, and the mountains, which seemed to float in the sky as if suspended, their snow-topped peaks rising from the clouds. On his own, he went to Shoreline School and registered himself. ("Teachers are a bunch of yammering idiots," his father often said.) A tall and pretty girl with curls down to her shoulders told him, "I'll show you the ropes." She told him he was such a little cutie. He met Rich and Erik, two handsome boys, who said they were members of the Crips, the Los Angeles gang often sung about in songs by Too $hort and Snoop Dogg and Spice 1. Though the boys in View Royal had never met Crips from Los Angeles, the gang was part fantasy, part dream, as alluring as the mafia was to Josephine. To be a Crip meant you carried a certain menace and, more importantly, a private elite membership in a respected tribe. Rich and Erik showed Warren the black "C" tattoos on their hands. ("I've had the tattoo since I was twelve," Rich would later say, while testifying at a murder trial.)

Girls at Shoreline said Rich looked like L.L. Cool J. They called him Richie D., and around that time, Warren began to call himself Warren G. Erik wore his baseball cap just tilted perfectly to the side and also knew every song by Too $hort and was impressed that Warren knew the lyrics so well. Rich and Erik and D'Arcy beat him into the Crips and, after this initiation by pummeling, they said, "You're part of the family now."

Though older boys in View Royal may have scoffed at Warren G. and "his whole gangster act," older boys were unaware of the care and attention he brought to his outfits, which were, perhaps, both costume and disguise. He favored white. The color was distinctly his own, and it set him apart from his fellow gangsters, the members of the CMC (Crip Mafia Cartel). For the members of the CMC, blue was mandatory, red forbidden. White was Warren's personal choice, and an unlikely one, for black may have better created the look of a badass he aspired to. At 5'4 and 115 pounds, Warren was far from a thug, and in fact could not have been cuter and, despite his knowledge of lewd song lyrics and his tempestuous domestic situation, innocent. Never has a boy looked more as if he wandered out of a fairy tale. His eyes were immense, and his eyelashes were long, and his expression was earnest and longing and always, always hopeful. He was possessed of the certain androgynous beauty that appeals so strongly to girls who have not yet turned sixteen. Like heartthrobs of past and present (that year it was Leonardo DiCaprio), Warren G. appeared neither manly nor mean, and in fact, his soft beauty suggested he might really need to be saved.

"Hey, little cutie," the girls all said, the pretty girls of Shoreline. They teased him and called him Little Romeo. While his father spent weekends gambling in Las Vegas, Warren hung out in View Royal, and all the pretty girls gave him their wallet-sized school photographs and on the back of their portraits, they drew hearts and wrote of love forever. He was given photos by Felicity and Angie and Katie and Willow and Chelsea, Oressa, Maya, Tara, Brandy, and Marissa, but Syreeta was the one he would fall in love with, almost right away.

She was younger, in the ninth grade. He saw her in the hallway. He gazed at her as she walked away. At

Diana Davis's fourteenth birthday party, he spoke to her for the first time. On the porch, he asked her politely if she would like to go out with him.

Syreeta replied: "As long as you don't mind that I'm getting braces in the morning."

He'd laughed, said he didn't mind at all, and they'd kissed on the porch, and in the morning, she called him, and she made him laugh again.

"You remember who I am?" she said.

"Of course."

"You remember that we're going out?" she asked. How could he forget? He'd thought she might not have wanted to go out with him because Syreeta was considered to be the most beautiful girl at Shoreline School. ("I liked her smile, I liked her shiny hair, I liked her smooth skin.")

On the day his father moved to California, Warren G. packed his few possessions into his duffel bag. Among those few possessions were his Spice 1 and Too $hort and Geto Boys CDs, and his three pairs of white baggy jeans—one given to him by his new friend, a tall and earnest basketball player named Dimitri. He packed his sweater with the Mossimo logo. He'd asked Syreeta to bleach the sweater for him because the sweater was cream and he thought cream was an "ugly" color and he wanted the Mossimo sweater to be white.

Syreeta thought it was mean of his father to not even ask Warren if he wanted to go to California. His dad said he was getting married to a nice lady he'd met in Vegas, and she lived in the town of San Clemente or San something. Later, no one could remember the town of the rich widow, only that Warren's dad had left his son to go live with her there. Syreeta thought Warren's dad just grunted out the invitation rather half-heartedly, like this: "I'm going. You comin'?" but Warren didn't see it that way, and he hugged his dad and told him he'd come and visit him at Christmas, after school was done, and he told his dad again that he didn't really want to leave Syreeta and he was "comfortable" in View Royal.

When he packed his duffel bag, he felt a momentary sensation of fright. He wished suddenly he was moving into Syreeta's home, for if View Royal was heaven, the home of Syreeta Hartley was the highest part of heaven. Her house was all white. The rugs were white and the walls were white and the sofa was white. The whole place seemed to shine and illuminate him when he walked in, onto the white carpets and past the Marc Chagall print where a man seemed to float in the sky holding on to a cello. He found her house "relaxing" and "peaceful." He'd asked Syreeta if it would be possible for him to move in with her, just for a while, just until he got his own place, but she told him her mom thought this was "not a good idea." Warren did not tell Syreeta that he was disappointed. He just packed his duffel bag and prepared to leave the couch of the trailer where he had slept for almost every year of his life.

When his dad left for California, he said to Warren what he always said when he left.

"See you in the movies." That's what he always said.

SYREETA

Syreeta was born blind in her right eye, but the doctors didn't notice right away. Her mother named her after Stevie Wonder's wife. There was no correlation there, in the way her mother named her after a blind man's wife. Syreeta's mother owned an album by Stevie Wonder's wife in 1982, and she just really liked the name. She found it romantic.

By the time the doctor noticed her eye's flaw, Syreeta was used to seeing the world differently from others. Her vision could be brighter, clearer, depending on the tilt of her head. Her eye wandered too. They called it a lazy eye. But this too, the wandering of her pupil, she was not bothered by, and the truth was, by the time she was a young woman, she was so startling to strangers, with her full lips and dark hair, the Spanish blood, that no one teased her, or even noticed her different eye, and she sometimes even forgot that she did not see the world as others did.

The "Spanish blood" came from her father, who now lived not in View Royal, but in a town named Squamish where he raced Monster Trucks. He married her mother too young. In their wedding picture, they looked as if they were just kids. Syreeta screamed in surprise when her mother showed her the photo. *My*

God, she thought, *my mother looks so much like me,* with her rippling black hair and her brown eyes and her dimpled chin. But her mother resembled a child bride, just nineteen, in her white dress with lace trim on the neck. *No way I'm marrying that young,* Syreeta thought, though her boyfriend, Warren, he had asked her several times to marry him, and though she was only fourteen, she imagined they would be together always.

Her mother and she often looked at pictures together. This wasn't vanity so much as the photos were pleasing, and captured all the beauty that surrounded them: their own, their friends', the island where they lived. Syreeta and her mother kept their photos in boxes rather than albums. Syreeta had started a new box for photos of her boyfriend, and on the top of the box, she wrote in her schoolgirl hand, Warren G.

On the days when she picked up new photos from the shop beside Brady's Fish and Chips (where she worked after school), she would wait eagerly for her mother to get home from work. While her mother cooked their dinner, she would spread her photographs over the kitchen table so her mother could see. The snapshots weren't careful portraits, just these fleeting moments that she wanted her mother to be part of, to know. A new photo: Diana, Tara, Marissa, Felicity, and her at a sleepover, all in their pajamas. Another one: her and Marissa in the back of a blue pickup truck. "Look at Diana," her mom would say. "She's so cute!"

"I know. She looks like a little bunny or something," Syreeta said. A third new photo: the boys. "Here, that's

Erik Cash. Remember I told you about him? I want him and Diana to get together."

"What a baby face."

"I know."

"He's got his father's eyes. His dad looked just like that, exactly."

"Really?" Syreeta would always listen carefully to her mother's observations, as she had found her mother's observations precise, though never judgmental or cruel. It pleased her that her mother liked Warren. "He's so polite and well spoken," her mother observed. Syreeta knew Warren wanted to make a good impression, but his politeness was not forced or false. He was besotted with her mother, in an innocent way, and whenever he came to her house, he would be sure to take off his Crip baseball cap and he would never swear. Always, he would always greet her mother warmly, shaking her hand, and asking her about her day, and once she found him sweeping the leaves off the driveway.

She could understand why Warren always wanted to come over to her place, especially after she saw the trailer where he lived, and his "mean" dad who just seemed "so angry."

"I just feel really comfortable here," Warren would say, and Syreeta would nod her head, because that's what others said as well. Her mother's competence was comforting, and the house revealed a quiet instinct for order and beauty. They hadn't always lived so well. When Syreeta was a little girl, after the divorce, she and her mother lived in rentals, in basement rooms. But her mother soon became manager at Pacific Coast Savings and brought them to a better home. Sometimes her mother would hug her out of the blue. "Rita," she'd say, tousling her hair. And sometimes when they were shopping together in the mall, the salesgirls asked if they were sisters.

Though she loved her mother, she loved her friends as well. The Five. "There was always us five," she'd later recall. She could see her life as before and after. Before was the year when she got braces, when she met Warren, when there were always "us five." She could almost rhyme the names off, for each name was melodic and sweet. Syreeta, Tara, Marissa, Diana, and Felicity. The Five were the prettiest girls at Shoreline, though they did not see themselves as possessed of the greatest beauty or perched atop a hierarchy. ("We were friends with everybody," they'd insist. "If I can show someone that I'm a good-looking person on the inside, it's more important than showing it on the outside," Syreeta would say.) Still, the boys at Shoreline marked them in a certain way. In their yearbooks, around Syreeta and Tara and Marissa and Diana and Felicity, boys drew rays like those that surround children's drawings of the sun, and above each girl's photo, they wrote HOTTIE.

Of the five, there was no leader. When they were all in grade 5, Tara had been the leader of one clique, Syreeta the leader of the other. At some point, Syreeta wasn't even sure when, the two leaders had formed an alliance, a slightly uneasy friendship. But in the fall, when neighborhood girls were bothering Colin Jones and Warren was looking for a new place to live, Syreeta and Tara were growing suddenly close and loyal. They worked together at Brady's Fish and Chips after school. Brady's was owned by Diana's parents and was in a little strip mall just off the highway, next to a store that sold saris, and a street named Earl Grey. Marissa was the smallest of the group. She was born in December, born later, and was barely five feet tall, barely one hundred pounds. Her smallness suited her, for she giggled constantly and was neither rude nor hard, just possessed of a childlike giddiness. Warren nicknamed her "the little munchkin."

Marissa had cried the night Warren asked Syreeta out. ("She just started bawling her face off because she had such a crush on Warren.") Now Marissa was going out with the basketball player Dimitri. She still loved Warren, but "like a big brother." Felicity was the "rowdy" one. Tara had the assured manner of the leader, for she was very tall, and like a *Seventeen* cover girl, with lovely bright eyes and straight blonde hair. The Five were together for sleepovers, shopping on Saturdays, reading fashion magazines. What were their interests? "Laughing," Syreeta would later say. "I was always interested in just laughing and having fun."

Her real dad wasn't around much because he lived up in Squamish and really didn't have much to do with her life. When she was a little girl, they had spent more time together. He used to ask her to sit in the front seat when he drove his truck at the Monster Races. When she started talking of a boyfriend, he seemed to change toward her and became unnecessarily stern and wary. As in the time he saw the red marks on her neck left there by kisses from Warren. Her father said: "You tell that boy to watch out, or I'll skin him like a raccoon."

She told Warren this, and Warren looked quite frightened, and then slowly appreciated the humor of it, because she was laughing and she wished she could be a mimic, and imitate her gruff and burly father, saying: "I'll skin him like a raccoon."

Gregory Green, her stepfather, wasn't around so much because he was a logger, and so he was in the forests for weeks at a time. But when he came back from the forests, her mother would sing to herself and wear her nicest dress, with a silk belt around the waist, and white flowers on the burgundy.

Warren was always over for dinner, and after they'd eaten, he would sit out on the porch with Gregory Green. Syreeta noticed the way Warren's face just lit up when Gregory asked him to come out on the porch, and she knew he wasn't used to spending time with an older man who was good-natured and not so angry all the time. Gregory kicked his feet up onto the porch railing, and Warren did the same. Gregory lit a cigarette by flicking a match on his zipper, and Warren did the same. Warren smiled at Gregory, hopefully, and then said, "Well, I guess I should go help Wendy with the dishes."

"Oh, let the women do the dishes," Gregory said. "That's what women are for."

Warren was kind of surprised to hear that, but it made him feel good, a little, like when a rapper asserted his challenge to a foe. Warren stayed on the porch and did not move when Syreeta's mom came out with one hand on her hip, the other on a dishrag. Although he didn't *really* have a crush on Syreeta's mom, Warren, nonetheless, thought she was beautiful and glamorous and out of reach and shimmering. Standing there, long legged, her black hair loose on her shoulders, she said, not cruelly, but surely, as if there were to be no dispute—"If you want to eat another meal here, Greg, don't talk like that in my house."

When she was back inside, Warren thought Gregory might offer up a retort, but he only looked a little stunned and chagrined. Warren couldn't help but smile. He thought to himself, *So that's where Syreeta gets her spark.* (Syreeta's "cheeky," he often said, admiringly.)

But later, when she would reflect upon the girl she'd been, Syreeta wouldn't describe herself as cheeky or sassy or bold. Harsh words would soon be used about her, published in newspapers and magazines, spoken by judges, cops, and attorneys. And yet she never thought much about her personality. She really had no idea what she was like. Naive, she guessed. "I was probably like any other teenager. I was carefree. For us, life was great," she recalls, not using the word *murder* or *death,* because these words still seem almost impossible to say, as if they don't belong to her life, which was wonderful when she was loved and fourteen. "Life was great," she says, "but then it all just changed in a flash, without any control over it."

SLIVERS AND SAWDUST

At Punjab University in India, Manjit Virk spent the late 1970s studying for his master's degree in English literature. He read the Romantic poets—Lord Byron, Wordsworth. He specialized in Shakespearean drama. "I liked the tragedies best," he would later recall, without irony.

His older sister had moved to Victoria, and she mailed him a magazine called *Beautiful British Columbia*. He looked at the photos of the West Coast landscape. "I couldn't believe a place like Vancouver Island really exists with all the rocks, the trees, and the mountains. Everything looked freshly washed. There was no dirt." He teased his sister. "No way," he said. "That's not a real place! I can't believe it's real." She invited him to visit, and in 1979, when he was twenty-three, he took Pan Am Airlines to Delhi and then to England and then to Seattle. And he saw the real town of Victoria was even more wondrous, "very beautiful, *so* green." On this trip, he met his future wife, a young woman named Suman Pallan. "She had a very calm composure. She was polite, soft—a good listener." Falling in love was unexpected. He had never foreseen that he would stay forever in the place of photographs.

After they married, there were some "hurt feelings,"

for the marriage had not been arranged, and there was some concern among their elders that an unarranged marriage would not last. He looked into teaching, but found out his MA was not recognized as complete. His credits from India could not be transferred, and, to become a professor, he would have to spend another four years in college. He considered becoming a pharmaceutical salesman, but this meant he would have to travel, and his wife was pregnant, and he did not want her to be alone. "And so, I became a lumberjack," he says, rather surprised at the strange fate. "You have to survive." He worked at the local mill, and earned $4.50 an hour, and he missed the heat and religion of his home. He learned first aid. In the mills, the workers found slivers in their fingers or pieces of sawdust in their throat, and he became skilled at taking away the slivers and the sawdust.

When his daughter was born, he became revived, grateful, full of joy. She was named Reena, which is the Punjabi word for mirror, "like a looking glass."

Soon after Reena was born, the family moved to View Royal for the parks and the schools that were near their new home. After they bought the house, "we realized it was not a high-end area, that there were a lot of rentals and single mothers, but I never felt we needed to stay in the top neighborhood, like Oak Bay. We are humble. We don't need to be proud, and say, 'We're stuck-up and better than other people.'" Later, it would seem to him as though the presence of evil was in the neighborhood, in the most unlikely shapes and forms. Yet for many years, he was not aware of the dangers, and he would watch *The Muppet Show* with Reena, and then put her on his shoulders and walk with her to Gorge Park, where white lilies and bluebells bloomed. Gorge Park looked like the places he had seen in the magazines his sister sent to India. The places he once believed too clean to exist. Gorge Park was his firstborn daughter's favorite place to play.

• • •

In the months before the murder, Reena did not yet know that her name meant "the mirror," nor did she know that in ancient languages, Reena also meant "the queen."

Later, words like *misfit* and *outcast* would be used to describe Reena, but these words don't capture her as she was at fourteen, a girl with the rare combination of boldness and innocence.

Reena attended Colquitz Junior Secondary, so she did not know Syreeta or Warren G. She had never met Marissa or Dimitri. Often, at her school, she was teased and ignored, for she was an uneasy loner, with her broad hips and nervous eyes. She was dark skinned and heavy in a town and time that valued the thin and the blonde. Taunted, left out, she started to skip classes. Starla, her neighbor, recalls that one day Reena said in her giddy and sudden way, "All your problems go away when you die."

And then, just before Halloween, a momentous event occurred. Reena found a place where she wanted to be. She'd been wandering to a site near her home on Irma Place. Irma Place was around the corner from Brady's Fish and Chips, but Reena did not find herself in that part of View Royal. Instead she found a park where unloved and unwanted kids smoked cigarettes and talked of dangers and sin. Reena began to smoke. She fought with her parents and missed family dinners and sermons and ultimately left her house for, as Suman recalls, "she would not abide by the rules of the home."

A girl from the park told her about the Kiwanis group home, and it was there she met Dusty and Josephine. Her adoration for these two girls was instant, if not mutual, an adoration both fierce and doomed. Leaves fell from the sturdy trees. The fog became constant. Eerie Halloween decorations were placed on windows and walls. And Reena, seeing her possible self reflected in the badass girls, emerged and no longer wanted to die.

In Kiwanis, Dusty was called "Miss Tough Girl" and Josephine was called "Princess," but Reena was called nothing, for other girls did not notice her and she was only in the lonely home for a few days before she went to stay at her grandparents'. But, in the few days of her residency, she heard talk of Crips and gangsters and crazy basement parties. She watched Josephine moving through the halls, elevated by her black platform shoes, seemingly never nervous, only delicate and sure. Josephine boasted of becoming a hit man. She stole Reena's hairdryer. She might have stolen Reena's mascara, but Reena was too afraid to confront her, and instead hovered nervously near the entrance to Josephine's room. After a few minutes, maybe hours, Josephine and Dusty said to their desperate and hopeful admirer, "Okay, Reena, you can come in."

• • •

Reena's grandmother, Tarsem, a woman with white hair and a soft, warm body, noticed Reena's blue nail polish.

"Why are your nails that color?" she asked her granddaughter.

Reena was cuddling next to her grandmother, and they were watching Bollywood movies. On the screen, the girl was running from pursuers, and she ran and ran until she reached a park where a chorus of adoring men broke into song, dancing behind her. Reena sang along with the chorus: *Mainay Pyor Kiya*.

She did not answer her grandmother about the blue nails, or tell her grandmother that Josephine's nails were blue and Josephine was her new friend. On the screen, the girl was on a mountaintop and there seemed to be stars on her sari; she shimmered and shone, and then Reena's favorite part of the movie took place. The girl was hoisted up by a magical presence. She appeared to float on the clouds, and beneath her, a group of girls in white dresses sang: *Mainay Pyor Kiya*. The girl sang: "I am in love."

Though Reena's grandmother had once believed in the Hindu faith, she'd spent the past thirty years as a believer in the prophet Jehovah. Soon after her arrival in Canada, two smiling visitors had knocked on her door and greeted her warmly, and did not look, as others often did, with discomfort or disdain at her sari. She invited the strangers into her home, brought them tea and cookies. Her English was faltering, but they did not mind. They told her about the Watchtower. They spoke slowly and left her books with pictures of the world in flames. She phoned them and asked them to come over for tea again next Sunday. And they came, unlike the neighbors, who declined her invitations because they said they were going camping or were working on Sunday. The ladies were very friendly to her, and she enjoyed their stories, and slowly learned to read English through warnings and promises contained in their brochures.

When the movie was over, Reena went down to the basement where Raj was living. Raj was her uncle, and he was young and handsome, at loose ends, having graduated from college and gone into real estate development. But real estate was tricky. You could never predict the desires of newcomers. Reena woke him up and begged him for a ride.

"Come on," he said, though he had this sudden pain in his left leg. He wasn't sure why. It shot through his knee and up to his hip. He drove a yellow Karmann Ghia, one of a kind. Reena asked him if he would mind driving through View Royal, because she was hoping Josephine Bell would see her in this amazing sports car. There was no one in View Royal with a Karmann Ghia. The little car was like a rare bird, and they moved from a suburb high on the green hills. They drove past the highway and the hospital and the railroad tracks and then drove down. There is a noticeable and sudden descent on entering the community of View Royal. The town, built around the Gorge, is on a lower level. They drove past the Fort Victoria trailer park, past Syreeta's house, past the home of Colin Jones.

"That's where Colin Jones lives," Reena said. "He's friends with Josephine."

Raj noticed Reena's blue nails and asked her why she had painted them that color. She waved her fingers; she said, "I like blue," and as he often did since her brief stay in Kiwanis, he worried about her. So much, he thought his worry might be causing the tremor in his leg.

"Reena," he said, but she did not hear him because she had unrolled her window and her head was turned, hopefully, to the streets.

"Why do you listen to Bryan Adams?" Reena said, laughing. "He's so lame."

"You used to like it."

"No, I didn't! I never did!"

He'd bought the CDs she had asked for. Puff Daddy and the Notorious B.I.G. He just bought them last week, and the purchase was one he regretted. The Notorious B.I.G. CD was called *Life After Death*. On the cover, an obese man posed beside a hearse. Gunshots were interspersed with the obscene chants.

Reena leaned forward, pressed Eject, inserted the Puff Daddy CD. She found a song, and began singing along, as she had sung earlier to the Bollywood film.

Raj recognized the song, as one Sting used to sing, only now sung by some low-voiced guy mumbling unintelligibly.

"Do you like this song?" Reena said. "It's my favorite." She sang along with the sweet-voiced girl, who was now singing a new chorus that wasn't in the Sting song. She was singing, "Come back, baby, come back."

Reena explained to Raj how the girl singing was Biggie's wife, and she sounded so sad because she missed Biggie so much. Biggie had been murdered! "Someone capped his ass," Reena said.

"Sting sang this better," Raj said, and he laughed, because he did not want her to think he was critical of her. He knew Reena had run away because her mother, Raj's sister, wouldn't let her smoke or wear makeup or tight clothes. Even worse, Reena had announced that she did not want to be a Jehovah's Witness any longer. "I'm tired of this JW shit," Reena said. She wanted a birthday party. She wanted to celebrate, and JWs believed celebrations should be subdued, if not obliterated. There'd been some talk of excommunication. Raj himself was not a JW, and he tried to be a kind of haven for his niece.

"Sting's version is not better!" Reena said. She leaned forward to turn up the volume. They drove past Shoreline School and over a bridge that crossed the Gorge. There was the white schoolhouse called the Craigflower Colonial school, which was now a museum. Raj wondered what the schools were like in Canada in colonial times, in the year the schoolhouse was built: 1845. Surely the kids did not walk around talking of guns and murder. Even when he was a kid, he didn't hear about such nihilistic things, though high school was far from idyllic for him. He was skinny and quiet, and almost every day some athlete would bump into him and say, "Get the fuck out of my way, Paki." He felt the tremor through his leg again. He wanted to ask Reena how Colquitz was because he hoped she'd returned to the unfriendly classrooms. The tremor moved to his heart, he could feel it, so tangible now, there was no doubt: something was wrong with his body.

"Reena," he said, "can we listen to some other song? How about a compromise? R. Kelly."

She had put on some song called "Return of the Mack." This too was nihilistic, he thought, listening to the lyrics. "You lied to me." A fourteen-year-old girl should not know of these things.

"Please," Reena said, "If we bump into my friends, I'll be embarrassed if we're listening to R. Kelly."

He thought then that he was too hard on her. He knew what it was like being fourteen, and caring so much about what your friends thought. He knew that when you were that age, acceptance was everything. And how could a girl like Reena be accepted? She could try to be like the others, paint her nails blue, listen to the same songs as her friends, stop with the "JW shit," and after a few years, she'd move on and fall in love and find her own family.

He reached over to put his arm around her, and as he did so, he noticed the word on her skin.

Crip.

"Reena," he said suddenly, though he tried to be gentle and never criticize her, as so many did, constantly.

"Reena, what is that on your hand?"

She smiled. "It's a gang," she said.

"I know what it is," he said. "Why are you even writing that word down?"

"I think they want me to be in the gang," she said. "My new friends . . ."

"Look," he said sternly. "You get involved with that, you're either going to end up dead or in jail."

She didn't seem to hear him, for she was staring so intently at the homes of View Royal. They drove past the homes where the killers still slept, their plan for murder neither conceived nor yet acted on, and Josephine was not anywhere to be seen, though Reena wished she could see her because Josephine was her new friend now. Josephine Bell, a girl so slim and mercurial, so blonde and white and heartless, though of the last quality, Reena was not yet fully apprised.

SHE'S LIKE MY SISTER

Josephine's nails were blue as well, but unlike Reena, she drove herself through View Royal in a brand-new white Neon.

Josephine may have lacked empathy and a pure heart, but she was possessed of a certain drive and ambition. She had so many goals. She was listening to a song called "Somebody's Gotta Die." She sang along, then switched to the Seattle hip-hop station where they would soon play the song about how "mothafuckin' power" meant "mothafuckin' respect."

And as she drove in her new car, she reflected on her progress. Truth be told, and she would tell it, immodestly yet constantly: she was becoming legendary! Colin Jones may have thought of her as a "twisted little troublemaker," but who was he? A white guy with long hair (very uncool) in a ponytail (even uncooler) in straight jeans (uncoolest) and a dull suburban life (uncool, obviously). By the time she was in New York and working for John Gotti, Colin Jones would merely be a mechanic or a sales clerk. If he was lucky, he'd become floor manager at Wal-Mart.

As she drove by the field behind Shoreline School, Josephine recalled a recent event of which she was most proud. The conversation went like this:

Warren, a curly-haired boy, with eyes rapt and wet: "I've heard so much about you."

Josephine Bell: "Yeah, what did you hear?"

Warren: "All the guys said you were good looking. It's so cool that I finally get to meet you."

Josephine Bell: "Yeah, whatever. That's nice."

She'd taken a cigarette some girl handed to her. She tilted her dimpled chin. Everybody was talking to her.

Everybody: "I can't believe you're back! It's so cool! Where have you been?"

And she'd smiled mysteriously, not revealing the grim fact that she'd been on a tour of foster homes, dull, stupid homes with dull, stupid people, who asked her to leave after they found new children, better children, their own children. Warren asked her if she'd like to go to a party with him. He said something about his girlfriend, Syreeta. She sunned in the words of praise. *Oh my God, that's Josephine Bell! Josephine Bell!!! I can't believe I finally get to meet you.*

"I felt like a celebrity," she would later recall. "I thought somebody was gonna ask me for my autograph."

• • •

Had Josephine known Reena was hoping to find her, she would not have cared. She would not have driven in search of the besotted girl in the Karmann Ghia. Josephine would not have been impressed by the car's subtle elegance. The loving uncle would have seemed too protective and his concerns about nihilism in contemporary culture not worthy of a debate. She had no desire to meet Reena's father, for his knowledge of Chaucerian motifs was, to her, utterly irrelevant.

She drove toward the home of Kelly Ellard. She wasn't sure if Kelly would be able to hang out tonight, for Kelly was "actually a pretty good girl." ("Like if I go and hang out with her, and stuff, she'd say, 'Oh shit. I've got to call my parents.' She'd always be worried about that, whereas, me, I don't care. I'd say, 'Let's skip our curfew. Let's be badasses.' But Kelly would say, 'Oh no, I'll be grounded.'") Josephine thought it was "kind of funny" the way Kelly would "actually listen to her parents and stuff."

Nevada was grounded, so Josephine drove down the street to see if Colin Jones was home.

She thought of Kelly some more, wishing she could see her and go for a drive in the new car. She and Kelly had always been best friends, ever since they were both eleven. When she'd been living in those stupid homes far away from View Royal, she'd kept Kelly's picture on her wall. She hadn't written her letters. That would have been too much. But she'd missed Kelly, and she realized as she drove that Kelly was her "loyalest" friend. *She's like a sister to me,* she thought.

Some girls would be jealous of Josephine Bell, but not Kelly. Some girls would think Josephine Bell was a slut just because she was gorgeous. ("That always pissed me off when girls would say, 'Maybe she's a slut,' just because some girl is pretty. I'm not a slut. I'm not at all.")

Kelly wasn't like that, Josephine thought to herself. Kelly never got jealous of anybody.

• • •

Ping. Ping. She was back, the twisted little trouble-maker. Colin Jones looked out on the street and saw

Josephine leaning imperially against a shiny white car. He went outside and stared at the white Neon, brand new, with smooth white doors and a curved roof and windows without streaks of rain.

"Nice car," he said, feeling a slight longing for the immaculate vehicle.

"I've got it for a few days," she said, staring him right in the eyes.

He nodded. He was on to her.

After he'd ditched her, she'd started hanging out with Donovan and Khalil, two brothers who lived over by View Royal Video. Their mother was away a lot and so they had basement parties. Donovan and Khalil were minor celebrities in View Royal, and in the neighboring towns of Langford and Esquimalt. For one thing, they were both black, and therefore of the highest and most elite pedigree. To be black in Victoria was to be infused with an aura of indescribable glamor. It meant, regardless of your real personality, that you were just like, you had to be, must be, just like the glamorous and dangerous black men on TV. Tupac and Biggie and Too $hort and Ice Cube, and those black men from America who had guns and big cars and mansions and champagne and diamonds and Jeeps and low-riders and their own clothing lines and names of secret solidarity like Ruff Ryders and Eastsiders and big cars and mansions and champagne and ghettoes and pit bulls and sexy women in stilettos and anthems like, "Fuck with me, you fucking die, motherfucker."

Donovan and Khalil, Colin thought, probably taught Josephine how to steal her new car. They did it with hairdressers' scissors, sticking the long shears into the lock and then into the ignition.

"I have it for a few days," Josephine said, and she lit a cigarette, ran her hand through her blonde hair, and she seemed to him to be waiting for an invitation or a compliment.

He went inside his house and called 911.

"There's a car on 14 Marton Place," he said to the dispatcher. "A white Neon. I'm not going to say who. I'm not going to say how. But it's stolen and you might want to come and get it."

But by the time the police arrived, Josephine was gone. It would not be the last time she would know when to leave, know how to avoid the cops. But not knowing of her future misdeeds, Colin Jones found himself both admiring and greatly irritated by her smooth escape.

Later, on the phone, Josephine and Kelly discussed the stolen car.

Kelly promised her, "If you get caught, I'll take some of the blame. If the cops come and take you in, just tell them I stole the car."

"Kel, I would never do that!"

"But you could."

And Josephine thought: *yes, I could, because Kelly is a true friend, like a sister, and Kelly,* she thought, *Kelly would do* anything *for me.*

"A VERY DANGEROUS YOUNG LADY"

Once there was a woman named Dinah who had six daughters: Diamond, Donna, Deanna, Dahlia, and Destiny. Dusty was the youngest daughter, a girl in View Royal, who was, she would later say, "totally out of control."

Dinah, her mother, was first to kick her out. ("Dusty's trouble. I couldn't handle her.") For a few difficult months, she'd lived with Destiny, but then Destiny kicked her out. So she went to Kiwanis. Then she got in some trouble, and so Kiwanis kicked her out, and in the fall, she went to live in Alberta with her oldest sister, Dahlia.

Destiny warned Dahlia, "Dusty will cause nothing but trouble." Yet Dahlia believed she could be the one to help Dusty. "I love my little sister. She has a good heart."

• • •

Dusty moved like a boxer, with a kind of gait both ungainly and purposeful. She wore her hair pulled back in a ponytail, and her lips and eyes were broad and brash. Dusty's most unusual, and unnerving, feature was her voice, which contrasted so greatly with her physique. Her voice was full of melody and quite charming, and if you heard her speak, you would think, as Dahlia insisted, that Dusty had "a good heart."

Dusty had met a boy just before she left Victoria. The boy's name was Jack Batley. She wrote it five hundred times on the piece of paper her probation officer had handed her. ("Change is possible. Change is up to YOU!") Jack might have been described by others in View Royal as "rat-faced," but Dusty liked his rough eyes, and she liked the way he looked in his black and white Adidas jacket.

Perhaps her separation from Jack was the reason Dusty made such a disastrous au pair. Dahlia had several young children, and a full-time job as a truck driver, so when she invited Dusty to live with her, the invitation was not wholly one of charity. When Dahlia went away on her four-day drives to Yellowknife, Dusty would be in charge of babysitting, cooking meals, cleaning the house, picking the kids up from school, and putting the children to bed.

Yet Dusty played music very loud and slept in and once wrote "Niggers rule" on the wall with strawberry jam.

"Living with Dusty was a living hell," Dahlia's daughter would later recall. "She would make crank phone calls telling people to lick her cunt and threatening to kill them."

While in Alberta, Dusty received some very distressing news. Jack Batley had a new girlfriend, and the new girlfriend was Reena Virk.

"It's true. I saw her wearing his jacket," Dusty was told. "His Adidas jacket!"

Dusty flung herself across the carpeted floor and then thought of Reena. Reena!

The little kids were on the couch watching *Saved by*

the Bell. Dusty picked up the phone and called a number in Victoria. In her sweet voice, she threatened. "The Crips are coming to your house to cap your ass!"

She then asked a boy on the couch, a boy of twelve, a friend of her niece, to help her. After Dusty gave orders to the young boy, she dialed the number and handed the phone to him.

"I'm coming down there tonight to KILL YOU!" the boy said, though his voice was not deep or menacing, and he was far away from View Royal and only twelve years old.

• • •

Dusty became reckless in her days as an au pair, and she wondered if she would ever see Josephine again. She knew that Josephine, like her, was shuttled about to homes all over the place. She wanted so to tell Josephine of Reena's betrayal. Josephine would understand, for when they were all together at Kiwanis, Josephine was always saying that Reena was the jealous type and Reena was jealous of her beauty.

The way he'd strolled around the trail by the Tillicum Mall. . . . His arm around her. . . . His name, Jack, just like the boy in *Titanic* who had no money and was a noble thief and died for the love of the girl named Rose. . . .

Dusty crashed her sister's car into the curb. Dahlia was evicted, for the landlord did not appreciate the loud music or the "Niggers rule" graffiti. "Dusty was totally destroying my life," Dahlia later said to police. "But I just couldn't send her back to View Royal. I kept threatening to, but I didn't have the heart to do it. I thought she just needed a little direction. I didn't want to give up on her like everyone else did. I gave her chance after chance. I bought Dusty clothes, makeup, jackets, shoes, smokes, whatever she needed."

But then one day her son took her aside and said, "Mommy, Dusty swears at me! She's mean. Please don't go back to work. I hate her!"

And her daughter said, "If Dusty stays here any longer, I'm going to run away."

Rather than sending Dusty away, Dahlia arranged for her friend Marlene, also a single mother, to move in and replace Dusty as babysitter.

Marlene told her, "Dusty is a very dangerous young lady."

On the seventh day of October, while Dahlia was on her Yellowknife run, Dusty held a steak knife to her niece's throat and threatened to kill her. Dusty denied this was true, and yet her niece's friend told police, "Dusty held the knife above her shoulders and was about a foot away from Brianna's neck. She said, 'Brianna, if you don't shut up right now, I'll stab you in the throat!'"

"That's when I started to get scared for my babies' lives," Dahlia recalls. "I kept thinking, 'She could really hurt someone.' The police did not charge Dusty. But Dahlia still called Social Services and told them to take Dusty out of her house. "I said if they didn't, I'd kick her out and she'd be living on the streets."

Despite the violent misdeed, Dahlia still loved her sister and showed her no anger. ("We all grew up angry and it has to stop somewhere.") She believed Dusty might still be redeemed. "She's a really good girl, but she has a bad temper and she needs a lot of help. My mother is a big part of all Dusty's problems. I think a big part of Dusty's problems are because she doesn't know who her father is and my mom doesn't know either. And that hurts Dusty in a big way." Then, as if her police report might be read by some benevolent and omnipotent force, Dahlia closed with a plea: "Dusty has had a life of no love and no caring. Someone has to help her. She's a hurt little girl even though she is fifteen years old."

She felt a sudden unease when Social Services came to take her little sister away.

"I knew she was going to get in trouble when she got back to Victoria," she recalls. "She thought she was all alone in the big world. I told Dusty to grow a brain and then she could come back to live with me."

A NEW HOME

Grace Fox was a nice lady, Warren thought, for she took him into her house and treated him like a son. Her true son, Chris, was a pretty good friend of Warren from Shoreline. Warren's father arranged to send Grace some money, to pay for food and clothes, that kind of thing, and there was some discussion about the "rules of the home."

Grace and her son, Chris, and now Warren as well, lived in a housing complex known as Christie Point. The homes were divided into four sections, named Elm, Pine, Spruce, and Oak. They resembled motels, two-story buildings with flat roofs and rows of identical doors, and yet Christie Point was built on the banks of the Gorge in the midst of a federal bird sanctuary.

The way to Warren's new home was paved with blue tar and pebbles, and wild geese with elaborate plumage darted by. White swans floated in the Gorge.

In the house, there was a black leather couch and a large-screen TV and a coffee table. There was a bedroom where Warren slept in the bed that had once belonged to Chris's older brother, Joel, who was now eighteen and living in Vancouver. For the first time since he was six years old, Warren slept on a bed instead of a couch, and he went out of his way to be polite and gracious around

Chris's mom. Grace adored him; she felt as if she was doing what every woman and girl wanted to do when they looked at Warren: save him.

Warren bought a navy blue baseball cap for fifteen dollars at the Tillicum Mall, and at Quik-Press he paid a few dollars more to have the logo CMC applied. Grace sewed his name on the back of his baseball cap. She used white thread and stitched *Warren G.* Grace knew this was his nickname, but she did not know, as most kids in suburbs across North America knew, that Warren G. was Snoop Dogg's cousin and a Crip and from the LBC— Long Beach, Compton. Warren G., like Warren G., had a rep for being a sweet-faced ladies' man. Grace teased him—that's how he learned of the phrase. "You're a ladies' man, aren't you?" and Warren answered, "I guess so. The girls all call me Little Romeo."

Though the Fox household was humble, their view was a beautiful and desired one. From his bedroom, Warren could see the glimmering waters of the Gorge. Across the way were the rich folks who paid millions for the view. He felt lucky having the view, the sense of living near the calm waters, near the thin and elegant arbutus and cedar trees that lingered over the water's edge. He and Chris could sit on the porch at the back of the house, next to their crazy neighbor who had all this junk—plastic parrots and those stupid little elves and geraniums and a rusted old barbecue—and they wouldn't even notice the junk because they'd be kicking back looking at the miles and miles of shining water and the fancy homes across the beautiful divide.

Soon he knew everyone in Christie Point. He knew

all the kids who lived there, and they told him the summers at Christie Point were awesome. They'd all hang out at the swimming pool, which was right behind the homes in the Spruce complex. Barbecues and skinny-dipping, a boy named D.J. told him. Summer rules!

He still called his mother, and she'd say, "Baby, my baby, I miss you. When are you coming home?" He felt guilty, and he promised her he'd come visit, and he did not tell her that he loved Grace like a mother.

Another good thing about Christie Point was that when you reached the end of the road, walking away from the Gorge, you were quite literally at Shoreline School. So, he and Chris could sleep in until 7:57, then grab their baseball caps and throw on some clothes and go running down the lane, past the ducks and the geese, and they'd be in homeroom right before the bell went off. Warren loved Shoreline. He didn't so much like the academics or even the athletics, but he liked peer counseling and Mrs. Smith. Mrs. Smith was the guidance counselor—just this big, cuddly woman, and she treated him like a son. Once he was telling her about something that happened with his mom, and Mrs. Smith started crying. "Wait a minute," he said. "Aren't I supposed to be the one who's crying?" The thing was, he never really did cry. Not even when his dad left to go to California. Life was life. You made the best of it. Every night he thanked God for Syreeta.

Mrs. Smith asked him if he'd come in with Syreeta and talk to some of her students about being a couple. A nonviolent couple. "I see you two as role models," she said.

"Really?" he asked, and he smiled. Dimitri, Marissa's boyfriend, thought being a role model was pretty lame, and he knew that Erik and Rich, his fellow Crips, would think it was lame too, but the idea appealed to him and he didn't want to let Mrs. Smith down. Syreeta really liked Mrs. Smith as well, and she said that she would like to be a counselor when she was older and be like Mrs. Smith, just there for everyone.

At lunch hour, they'd all hang out in the smoke pit. The Five did not consider themselves more popular, but would acknowledge that, in comparison, girls like Josephine and Kelly "didn't get much attention." Josephine was barely ever at Shoreline, and when she showed up, she was usually really mouthy and was considered by The Five to be "devious.'" Syreeta felt a little sorry for Kelly and Josephine, because it seemed to her that their mothers hadn't taught them to be ladies. Kelly and Josephine wore baggy pants like boys. Their lipstick was dark and garish. Boys called Kelly "Grubnut" and she was rarely, if ever, called "hottie." Syreeta felt bad for the girls, and grateful that her mother had taught her how to put on makeup and to always wear nice clothes. Sometimes her mother would say, "Rita, you're not leaving the house like that. Go brush your hair." Syreeta was, her friends agree, always "well put together."

After school, their little group would all walk the short little walk to the home of Mrs. Fox. Grace was usually working, and as Syreeta noticed, "Warren and Chris pretty much had the run of the place." Grace worked long hours at the hospital. Marissa would sit on Dimitri's lap, and Dimitri would want to watch sports because he was, at heart, a jock, and the only one to actually join a team. He was always boasting about how he was going off to join the NBA.

Sometimes they'd all start spontaneously singing when a good song came on the radio. They listened to the Seattle hip-hop station, which played commercial rap, like Puff Daddy and R. Kelly, not hard-core rap, but cooler songs than you'd hear on Victoria radio stations. Warren would look around at all his friends and know that he'd made the right choice to stay in View Royal.

Grace was a big lady, heavy, and she corresponded with men in prison. One in particular was named Reginald, and he was a member of the West Coast Players. This surprised Warren, because when Grace found out that he'd become a Crip, she got all motherly with him. In an odd coincidence, she warned him about the dangers of gangs, with the same warning Raj offered to Reena. "You're either going to end up dead or in jail."

• • •

Warren was not worried about death or prison because in his future, he imagined Syreeta as his bride. One day after school when they walked together along the beach, the swans seemed pure and bold and strange, and they gave him the courage to propose. She'd only laughed and then smiled, languidly.

He'd tried so hard to be respectful and not be in the way of Grace. He listened to her romantic worries and offered her advice. "Be careful of that guy Reggie," he said. "I saw his picture, and he looks like a crackhead.

You can do better than him." Grace just laughed. She was in love, and besides, Reginald had told her she was a very special lady. When he was away from Grace's home, Warren tried hard to please the Crips, selling a little weed on the side and acting the tough badass around Erik and those guys so they would like him. And sometimes he felt like he was living a double life, but not a false life, since the innocent schoolboy and the badass were both true and part of him. He was not acting when he was polite around Mrs. Hartley or Mrs. Smith or Mrs. Fox. He genuinely loved them all like they were his mothers. And when he was tough, like when he yanked a necklace off Erik's neck, he got this adrenaline rush and released some anger he didn't even know he had. Erik was just pissing him off, and he came up behind him and just yanked the green cross on a gold chain and from that day on, Warren wore Erik's cross around his neck and there wasn't much Erik could do, because in the rule of the ghetto, you got what you took and what you took was yours. On the day of his initiation, when Erik, Rich, and D'Arcy jumped him in, there was blood all over his face, and he came up off the concrete, blood rushing to his head, blood rushing to his heart, and he felt so alive and part of something and just for a second, when Erik gave him his hand to lift Warren up and say, "You're part of the gang now, bro," Warren wanted to kick Erik right in the gut, but that wasn't part of the ritual. Sometimes things made him angry, like when he had to ask Syreeta to do his laundry at her house because he didn't want to bother Grace for quarters, because any mistake, like asking for four quarters to wash the dirt off his white jeans, might be the mistake that led her to love him no more. *Anger* wasn't really the word, though he did not know there were words like *humiliation* or *shame,* so he thought it was maybe anger, this emotion that he felt when he did things he would later regret. Once he grabbed this dye that Chris Fox had, and he dyed his hair blonde and all the girls were "really choked." Syreeta didn't look too pleased. His hair was sort of this sunflower color, but a parched and dull sunflower. He didn't understand why he'd dyed his hair—just so suddenly, and on a whim. He wasn't exactly vain, but he kept his white jeans bleached and clean, and he folded them neatly every night and put them in his duffel bag, which he kept on the floor next to Chris Fox's dresser.

"You think I'll still be a ladies' man?" he said when he was at peer counseling, and he took off his baseball cap and showed Mrs. Smith his newly dyed curls.

"Oh no," she said, shaking her head. He smiled. "Don't worry," he said, because she looked suddenly sad. Outside Mrs. Smith's office, old Grubnut Kelly Ellard was pacing around, and he didn't know it, but Mrs. Smith wanted to speak to her about swearing at a teacher. He left the office sure he was going to go ahead and do that peer counseling role model thing with Syreeta. Mrs. Smith wanted them to talk about how they worked out their problems nonviolently.

He saw Syreeta in the distance of the hallway, leaning against his locker, dressed in a red T-shirt that matched the red laces on her white shoes. Her hair was pulled back into a ponytail, and when she saw him coming, she smiled even though she rarely smiled lately because of her braces. "Warren G," she said, and she kissed him right there, in front of everybody.

Maybe it was that day, though he blanked out the date because it was not an occasion he wanted to memorize. The occasion of his expulsion, that is. After school, he and Syreeta went down to the beach and then to her house for dinner, and he talked to Syreeta's step-dad for a while, just about man stuff, and then he went home to Christie Point, cheerful as always, past D.J. and his sister Ashley. He saw this great blue heron that lived on the bird reserve. The heron always reminded him of himself, the way he was in Estevan. The heron was all alone and strange in the bird sanctuary with the flocks of geese and swans. And so when he returned home, he was going to ask Grace what she knew about herons. She sat by the TV, a grim, determined expression on her face. She said, "Warren. . . ."

He didn't really listen to the words because the words sort of blurred, but she said something about how Reginald was getting out of prison in December and he was going to move in here, and so there wouldn't be enough room for Warren anymore. He sure didn't want to be in the way again, overhearing the bitter words of adults, so he said, "Yeah, sure." What was he going to say? He said *yeah, sure,* when she asked him to leave her home. "Don't worry, Grace," he said. "Don't worry about me."

MORE FRIENDS THAN ENEMIES

On this same day, Josephine also received some distressing news.

"Hey, I just got a phone call," a freckled boy named Justin told her. When he called, she thought he must be wanting to invite her to a party or tell her she was beautiful. Instead, he said, "Some girl just called me and told me you had AIDS!"

"What the fuck!" Josephine screamed.

Only an hour later, she was seeking comfort in the arms of a boy named Tyson Bourgeois. Tyson's friend Johnny, a BMX rider with a scarred lip, said, "Hey, Josephine. I just got a phone call."

"About me?"

"Yeah, some girl was talking shit about you. She asked me if I'd seen you lately and she said you weren't so pretty anymore."

"Are you serious?" Josephine said. Tyson and Johnny were cracking up, so amused by the pettiness of the adolescent female.

"Yeah, she said her name was Reena, I think. I have no idea who she is or how she got my number."

How could this be? How did Reena get the phone numbers of her friends? It occurred to Josephine then that she was victim of a second humiliation, as vile as the phone calls: Reena must have *stolen* her address book. Josephine was the one who stole, who took, who had. She was distraught and could not bear the thought that something had been taken from her.

And then, as Josephine recalls, "For three days, people kept coming up to me, saying, 'Did you tell Reena you hated me? Reena said you did. Some girl told me your eyebrows are fake. Reena called me and said if I slept with you I'd get AIDS.'"

Why would Reena do this to her? It did not occur to her that Reena may have been trying to show Josephine that she too was tough and badass and hard core, that she too could be a thief and a troublemaker.

Instead Josephine thought, *She is trying to make me unpopular, trying to make people think I'm not really as pretty as I seem.*

And her anger at Reena's transgression seemed to Josephine a perfectly normal response, the response John Gotti would make to such disloyalty. "She was trying to ruin my life, so I had a little problem with that. I think anybody would."

Josephine turned to her best friend for counsel.

"I can't believe she'd do that!" Kelly said.

"She's jealous," Josephine mused. "She's not doing it out of spite. She's doing it out of jealousy."

"That fucking bitch!" Kelly said.

"Well, she's not too bright. She's making all these calls and using her first name. She calls them, and says, 'Oh yeah, this is Reena calling.'"

"I can't believe she's talking shit. Who does she think she is?"

"I know. What the fuck does she think she's doing! Doesn't she know who I am? I have lots of friends and I know lots of people. I'm Josephine Bell! Nobody can fuck with me. I have more friends than enemies."

• • •

The forests around her at Seven Oaks did not still her rage. Seven Oaks was beginning to get to her. Apparently, they were having trouble finding a foster home for her, but Seven Oaks was only a temporary home, so she'd be out of there pretty soon. She did not think of herself as unwanted, though. She believed she was just not living by the rules and was doing whatever she pleased. At school, the principal brought her into the office, and said, "Josephine. We need to speak about your commitment to learning." Mrs. Olsen wanted her to try an alternative school if she would not commit to the educational environment at Shoreline Junior Secondary.

Josephine did not want to ponder the fact that she was soon to be homeless and uneducated, and so instead she turned to her collection of stolen goods. She herself had stolen a tube of Chanel mascara and Calvin Klein jeans. But her "gophers," as she called them, had brought her a Guess handbag, Christian Dior eyeshadow, and a black lace bra, size 34C. Her gophers were a group of little girls, some as young as twelve. *Go forth, young bitches!* she might as well have declared, for her minions scattered through the malls of View Royal, searching for offerings.

She spent a few hours before the mirror, enraptured by her reflection. The forests held the Dangers, and sometimes, if she stared at the trees, she could remember the man's voice and the time he. . . . She put on her new bra and several layers of eyeshadow. Her arched eyebrows were most definitely not fake, and yet they did appear as inverted smiles, drawn with a black pen. She had this 11:00 curfew, and now the night was getting darker and she no longer had her stolen car and Kelly was probably asleep and safe in View Royal.

Josephine slept in her bed at Seven Oaks. She might have felt distressed and lonely, for Seven Oaks was a bleak and desperate place. Not as bleak as Kiwanis. Kiwanis—the only good thing about that place was she met Dusty. She remembered Reena trying to tag along with her and Dusty, and trying to impress them both by telling them she had a probation officer. "For fuck's sake, Reena, you can't have a PO if you've never been arrested," Dusty said, and Reena looked so hurt and surprised.

"Leave us alone, Reena!" Dusty screamed.

When Dusty took off and disappeared, Josephine had been sad, for Dusty had the makings of a good sidekick. She knew from her studies of Gotti lore that the best sidekicks were faithful and volatile and heavy-set. Where was Dusty now? Maybe she was in jail but girls didn't usually go to jail for more than a month. If she still had her address book, she could have called around and tried to find Dusty, but fuck, her notebook now belonged to Reena. At the thought of Reena, Josephine turned in her sheets and was forced to listen to the wind through the trees. Had she known that Dusty would soon arrive at Seven Oaks, Josephine might have slept less fitfully.

A CONSTANT QUEST

Before the death, Reena's grandfather would tell her of a village called Jandiala where there was no railway station, but wheat and cotton and sugar cane. There was a single school for boys, and there, Reena's grandfather, as a young boy named Mukand Pallan, earned high grades and dreamed of his father.

His father had gone to Canada in 1906. To go to Canada or Africa or England, that was the trend for young men in Jandiala. "They left to get settled, to make a living," Mukand recalls. His father left the village and traveled by boat to Singapore and Shanghai, through Honolulu, and then to San Francisco, where he took a train to Seattle, and finally another smaller boat to Victoria.

His father worked in a famous garden in Victoria, the Butchart Gardens, where acres of rare and magnificent flowers flourished in the mild and damp climate. He worked not with the flowers, but in a quarry, loading limestone from the sunken cavern. With the white ash on his hands, he walked home past the Himalayan poppies and Dutch tulips and French forget-me-nots.

Mukand was born in 1930, the year his father returned to India. His father built a large three-story stone building in the village, and, on the ground floor, a store sold flour, grains, lentils, and sugar. He built a well for the village, and this brought the family even more respect because, as Mukand recalls, "it is a big contribution if you supply water."

Mukand was never sure why his father did not come back to the village. He left soon after Murand's birth and he did not return. Mukand thought it had something to do with the war, which ruptured all the ways of transportation. *Transportation.* The word was one of the first English words he learned and he would try to envision ships and planes, the modes of transportation that took his father away, transported him to Canada. The war made voyages home perilous, impossible. War kept his father in Victoria. Mukand missed his father and he tried to imagine Canada.

Canada. This is how he imagined it: a cold country, snow, and lots of white people.

From this country, his father sent silk, lots of silk from China. Mukand's mother would sleep with her cheek on the smooth, red gift; she would drape the gift around her body and walk through Jandiala, serious, and with heartache. His father sent Viewmasters. You could look through them and see the sights of his father's new town. The Empress Hotel, named after Queen Elizabeth and covered in ivy. The Royal Canadian Mounted Police, dressed in red, their faces stern and white and mustachioed, the horses like singular cavalry. His mother told him, "You'll go to Canada soon. When the war is over. Your father will come and get you."

But the war went on, and his father did not return. Mukand became one of the best students in Jandiala. It did not occur to him to misbehave. Rebellion was unnecessary; it was good behavior that would unburden his mother and bring his father home. In the 1930s in India, the schools were British, yet his notebooks were made of native paper and emblazoned with the seal of Haria Singh and Brothers. In his notebook, Mukand wrote the common English proverbs he was learning to memorize. He wrote:

A burnt child fears fire.
A constant quest is never welcome.
As you sow you shall reap.
A single sinner sinks the boat.

Only nine years old, he was not quite able to grasp the moral complexity, or so he thought, modestly. "I just like them," he told himself, and he would sit at the dinner table, and recite them to his mother, with the hint of Mrs. Gaitskill's accent.

"A burnt child fears fire," he would say, and he knew of fire and would think of a small child in a newsboy cap and tweed pants running from forests of flame.

"A single sinner sinks the boat," he announced gravely, though he did not know what a sinner was yet, only that a boat would soon bring him to his father, and so he must never be a sinner, he must never sink the boat. He earned high grades in math, his head covered with a turban, bent over the notebook, learning long division scrupulously. He earned the highest marks and dreamed of going to university in the city where his father was, the city named after the British queen where good men on horses wearing red uniforms rode past stone buildings covered in ivy.

He learned new sentences:

I was not aware of this danger.
It is a result of your carelessness.
The judge sentenced the culprit to two years.

And though he was very thin and solemn, with high cheekbones and narrow, wary eyes, he enjoyed singing, sometimes secretly, when he walked by the fields of cotton and sugar cane. He liked the patriotic fighting songs.

His father wrote him that "the rivers are just like two bands; it's very rare when they can meet again, but we will as the rarest river does."

He would smile when he went to the films with his mother. Outdoors, in the theater with no roof, they would watch the singing and the dancing, and he would go home, and write the songs down in his notebook. It was not that he knew he was leaving India, only he knew if he ever did, he wanted to have these notebooks in case he forgot the songs and phrases he loved as a child.

Mukand saw photographs: his father wore three-piece suits now, the vest buttoned under the blazer, the pants creased, the tie of silk. He and his father seemed alike, thin and tall, with their shoulders slightly sloping in, and their brown eyes kind and wary.

The Pallan store was popular, but his father did not want him to work there because he preferred his son to study so he would earn good grades and be accepted by a university in Canada. Of his father, Mukand would describe him succinctly: "He was a very gentle man."

He finally went to Canada in 1947. He was seventeen now, and he wore three-piece suits just like his father, suits of scratchy brown wool, with narrow pants and fitted vests and a blazer with buttons of tortoiseshell.

For the rest of his life, he would remember the journey as one remembers falling in love. It was a kind of soaring he'd never felt before. He first left Bombay in an old army boat and sailed for San Francisco. The boat was very nice, he believed, a Marine Adder, owned by President Lines. The journey was costly and revealed previously unknown hierarchies. His third-class ticket cost three hundred dollars. His sister was in second class—a five hundred dollar fare. They slept in bunk beds, his brother above him, with the small slit of a window showing the endless blue.

In first class, there were diplomats and businesspeople.

What captivated him were the students. There were hundreds of them, leaving Bombay, going to America for what they called "higher education." He would sometimes sit near them while they studied on the long tier of deck. He had brought his own book, and he would sit by the students and feel slightly kindred. He wrote on the cover, "My Trip to Canada," and inside he kept notes.

2 Feb—Singapore
7 Feb—Hong Kong

9 Feb—Shanghai/ Yokohama
22—Honolulu

He would want to write more, in English, and so he returned to the proverbs, which he had memorized nine years ago. They came back to him now, on the passage to a new country.

He wrote them as neatly as possible. There was not a letter that dangled or an ink spot or a forgotten word:

A burnt child fears fire.
A constant quest is never welcome.
As you sow you shall reap.

He knew now, at seventeen, the meaning of the proverbs, and believed in their wisdom and warnings. Fire and sin and quarrels were never welcome. They brought only sinking and fear.

On March 2, 1947, he arrived in Canada, and in his notebook, he wrote: "We were very thankful to God that we came to Victoria and that's what we had in our mind when we saw relatives and friends who we were longing to see."

All through his boyhood, he'd imagined Canada as white—the white skin of people, the white snow on the ground—and yet on the March day, there was so much green, the dark, heady green of the evergreens, the clean green of the careful lawns. The phrases left his head. "I was not aware of this danger." "It is a result of your carelessness." He forgot them, though they remained in his notebook, which he kept next to his bed.

And he would keep this notebook forever, even when he was a grandfather to eight, when he had retired and spent his days playing cards, at the temple. Sometimes he needed a respite from the Jehovah's Witnesses who came for coffee and his granddaughter with her blue nail polish and troubled heart. This notebook—he never chose to discard it, never dismissed it as juvenilia or nostalgia. It recalled both his childhood and his journey across the sea. "My Trip to Canada" would remain on the outside, and on the lined pages of the Haria Singh and Brothers notebook, were the English proverbs Mukand had memorized because as he recalls, "I just liked them."

A constant quest is never welcome.
A single sinner sinks the boat.
It takes two to make a quarrel.

THE GODDESS OF VICTORY

All around Principal Olsen was Nike. Not the goddess of victory, but the emblem of the sports corporation. Who knows why certain symbols become status symbols? Ten years ago, the Lacoste alligator on shirts with collars turned up, then the little Ralph Lauren polo player, and now this Nike swoosh. Mrs. Olsen could look into a classroom and see four swooshes. The swoosh abounded on the chests of her young charges. The swoosh on sweatshirts, on caps, on shoes. Alicia Clarkson today even wore a white Nike band around her forehead, like tennis players used to wear, and so the swoosh was on her forehead, as if a sacred object, like the bindi above the eyes.

A basketball player named Jen, unaware of the forthcoming murder, waved to Mrs. Olsen, and walked down the hall toward the foyer. In the foyer, Marissa was teasing Warren. *Speedy Gonzales.* Warren bounded from the bench in imitation of the fastest little Mexican mouse who could always dash from his pursuers and save the starving and the tiny. Warren with his white baggy pants and recently permed and dyed hair, now like a mushroom cloud of blonde curls, ran around the foyer. "Arriba! Arriba!" he cried. "Yeehah!"

Erik Cash, school heartthrob, sat on the floor in front

of his locker, just being cool. He too was unaware of the murder soon to be. Instead, he wondered about Friday night. Should he go to Brandon's birthday party? Or should he spend the night with his girlfriend? Erik wore his baseball cap like this: flap to the right, tilted ever so slightly. Other boys had tried to copy this insouciant and original style. Other boys failed. The yearbook photographer came by, and Erik Cash posed for the photo. He threw up the Westside gang sign. He looked not yet twelve.

Dimitri and Marissa walked together, hand in hand. The tallest boy in the school and the "little munchkin"—the tiniest girl at Shoreline School. The yearbook photographer asked if they would pose for a photo. Dimitri made a *W* with his fingers just like Erik and the rap stars did when they were photographed. Marissa giggled as she was wont to do. Later, in the spring, certain photographs would not appear in the pages of laughing youth. After the murder, Mrs. Olsen, Shoreline principal, decreed that no photos of the accused killers should be included in the 1997/98 Shoreline yearbook.

• • •

At Shoreline, there were no cheerleaders. With the recent cutbacks, the school could no longer afford the extravagance of uniforms. Shoreline could not even afford to provide uniforms for band members or athletes. This year, there had been some embarrassment, even shame, when the Shoreline students arrived for games or concerts at Oak Bay or Lambrick Park High School. Mrs. Olsen would explain to the other principals that her students were wearing regular clothes not out of disrespect or disobedience, but because the school simply did not have the finances for uniforms.

Despite the lack of uniforms, the basketball team would triumph. In the yearbook, the coach states, "Our team was small, but mighty. Their good enthusiasm and good sportsman-like skills carried them through a tough season. All boys demonstrated good skill and smart aggressive play throughout the year. Well done guys!"

Perhaps the lack of uniforms contributed to the attitude of a girl named Madeline, class valedictorian at a school in a wealthier district. "I just knew, pretty well for my whole life, that I would never be friends with anyone from Shoreline. I don't know why that was. I remember once Shoreline was playing against our school, and my friends scratched the *S* off the side of their bus so it said Horeline. I said, 'Hey, you idiots, *Whore* is spelled with a W,' but the guys just got mad at me, and said, 'Who cares. It's funny.' We always called the school Horeline after that, but not really to their faces or anything."

• • •

In art class, Desiree drew two elephants under palm trees. Brittoni drew the moon above the sea, with the shadows of evergreens in the corner. She used chalk for the shadows of trees and gold crayon for the shimmer on the sea. Ashley folded her knees to her chest and wrote a poem, privately. "In my dreams," she wrote, "I see a clear running stream, a sign of tranquillity." Ashley looked up, as though she might be discovered, but all her friends were busy with their own work. She wrote,

"Wherever I may be, peace will be by my side. The tears I so often cried / Will all have dried / Bringing me rays of sunshine and happiness / To fill my life with warmth / And serenity / No longer scorned by the evil of others / A road of my own that I will travel / No hills, no curves, and no gravel. Giving a clear, open way to where I belong / Showing me love and how to be strong."

Shawna was the only one that day to draw not a landscape, but an abstract of her own design. Against the backdrop of a globe, an eagle rose out of a long, narrow eye, drawn up like the eye of Tutankhamen, and beside the observant eye, the sheaf of a knife jutted up, slicing through the globe, emblazoned with adornment of a perfectly drawn butterfly.

Megan drew another scene from nature, this time a sparse and elegant tree, with thin branches, rendered in a delicate line. Yet out of place were the dark birds she added almost as an afterthought. One dark bird was nestled in the branches, slightly camouflaged, by the arch of the bough. Another emerged from behind the trunk—neither raven nor crow, but a black predatory bird rising under the pale tree toward the white moon. This was the end of October at Shoreline, and Megan could not have known that soon, under the tree by the Gorge, dark figures would commit an act of savagery. On this day, the "evil of others" was just a word, and death and grief were but minor motifs in their art and poetry.

A PHONE CALL

Hi, Colin?" There was a giggle, soft breath, and then the girl said: "Colin, hi. I have a crush on you!"

Colin glanced over at his girlfriend, who was sitting on his bed, applying pink nail polish.

"Who is this?" Colin asked. He'd never heard the girl's voice before.

She told him her name. She said, "Don't you remember me?"

No, Colin Jones thought to himself, *I don't know who the hell you are.*

Her voice was so boisterous and hopeful, without sarcasm or guile. "I've got a crush on you. Don't you remember me?"

And then she said, her voice trembling slightly, "Do you want to go out with me?"

The bold need of his secret admirer startled him. Colin Jones just hung up the phone, uneasy. He could not help feeling that a trick was being played on him, even though the girl sounded very sincere. The phone rang again.

"Colin," his mother yelled from downstairs. "It's for you."

He returned to the phone, reluctantly. She spoke

before he even said hello. She said, "Colin, I think you're really cute."

"Look," he said. "I don't know who you are."

"I met you at Mac's."

He tried to think, and his memory was often slim and dusky, perhaps from his days and nights of smoking weed, burning off brain cells. That's what the kids said, you burn brain cells, you get burned out. But *girls,* he always remembered, and he did not remember giving his phone number to any girl nor did he remember meeting a girl at the Mac's who sounded like she was maybe, at the most, thirteen.

"I like you," the girl said, "Let's get together."

"I don't think that's—"

"Come on. Please. Come on."

When she said that, *Come on, please,* she—this girl, whoever she was, this insistent, flattering girl— reminded him of the other girls: Nevada, Kelly, and Josephine. *Come on, please. Colin, please.* Both aggressive and immature, these girls who demanded, and begged, in their soft, girlish way, weak, and insistent, and highly annoying to him now.

"I'm sorry," he said, and he hung up, and just then, his girlfriend raised her blue eyes and smiled, turning her palm to show him her nails like pearls. "Who was that?" she asked.

"I don't know," he said, truthfully.

She scraped polish off her thumb.

He went downstairs.

"When's Dad home?" he asked his mom. He wanted to talk to his dad about the loan for taking a welding class. He'd been working at Scott Plastics, and it was starting to be a drag, dealing with the assembly line, and he'd rather hold that flaming gun in his hand, scorch and transform machinery.

On the 6:00 news, Murray Langdon was saying, "Stay tuned. Coming up we'll tell you why Bill Clinton will soon be in British Columbia."

The phone rang again. Colin picked it up, already sure.

The young girl giggled. She said her name was Rhea.

He remembered then. He remembered her! She'd been in the Mac's store in the rows of candy while he bought a Slurpee. She'd been with Ali, who lived up the street. She was Ali's cousin, he believed, and he couldn't remember her clearly. He had a vague impression of a chubby girl, a large nose, long, black hair down to her shoulders. She'd smiled at him shyly, and he'd said, "Hello." Certainly there had been no chemistry, no flirtation. He had picked up a pack of Export A's, and headed out to Tommy's car, and never thought again of the girl. He had never given her his number. So how did she get his number? For Christ's sake, his last name was Jones.

"I like you," she said again. "I have a crush on you," as if this was reason enough. It was the logic of a teen girl.

And it was not his way to be rude or mean, because he was laid back, and seemingly incapable of rage. He felt bad for the Rhea girl, and so he just mumbled something before hanging up the phone.

But then she wouldn't leave him alone. She must

have called him fifteen times. Her calls reminded him of the neighborhood girls, just coming over "like lost puppies." Just bothering him, hanging around him.

Please. She said *please,* and she just kept calling, and calling. Seven times, maybe seventy times, just all the time, all day and all night, all the fucking time.

And finally he said, "Okay, meet me at Mac's at 6:30."

He'd never had any intention of meeting this Rhea girl, and he felt a little bit bad about lying and setting her up for disappointment, but he didn't know what else to do. What else could he have done? He'd asked her not to call, asked politely, and she'd just kept calling, again and again and again. He thought this was the kindest way to get rid of her.

He imagined then Josephine giving his phone number to this Rhea girl. "Here," she must have said. "Call up Colin Jones. He has a crush on you." He had no idea why Josephine would do such a thing. Maybe she found out he'd ratted her out on the stolen car. Maybe she'd found out he'd told Nevada to stop hanging out with such an untrustworthy girl. Maybe she just thought it was funny. Certainly she was a twisted little troublemaker. He felt bad for the Rhea girl, waiting in the Mac's hopefully. He was going to talk to Josephine the next time he saw her on the street. *Don't give out my phone number,* that was all he really planned to say.

THE WAYS OF THE WORLD

In the store, Reena waited in the aisle of candy. How much sweetness there was in the world, in this one aisle alone. Snickers, Mars Bars, Toblerone, Reese's Pieces, Coffee Crisp. Her mother forbade chocolate. It was impure, like nicotine and gin, all the sweet, bad poisons Reena craved. Only yesterday, she'd felt so lonely she'd wanted to die, but now she was still alive, surrounded by all this sweetness, waiting for Colin Jones.

Colin Jones had not yet arrived at the Mac's.

Her crush was so strong. Girls wrote the names of boys in notebooks two hundred times. They stared at posters of Leonardo DiCaprio and watched *Titanic* three hundred times. Was it in the genes, a sudden rush of hope? Please. Colin. Please.

Perhaps Syreeta and Marissa were in the store, waiting while their boyfriends bought cigarettes. The cashier would ask for ID, and Marissa would be giggling when Warren strolled out, his baggy pants starting to slip off his hips, the white hems dragging on the concrete. Warren would put his arm around Syreeta, and Dimitri would hold Marissa's left hand, and they'd head up to the tracks like this, entwined.

They would not have noticed Reena, for they did not

attend Shoreline with her, and she'd never been to the parties on the beaches or soccer fields.

Perhaps all of View Royal passed through the Mac's, as they would so often, buying cigarettes and candy and magazines, and the things you forget until the last minute and don't really want but still somehow need. They would get what they needed and return home.

Nobody noticed the girl wandering in the aisles, staring at her blue nails, afraid to look at the numerals on the red clock, a gift of Du Maurier Cigarette Company. She had gotten there so early, and besides, Colin was cool, and cool guys were usually late.

These comings and goings were so random and common that the town kept no record. A boy skates across a bridge, his arms outstretched. A mother buys milk for her family. Young couples in love hold hands and head for the train tracks.

In the Mac's, Reena raised her eyes as the door swung open, the bells made a faint sound on the glass. Hope kept her there, waiting, but Colin Jones, he never arrived.

• • •

Syreeta was wondering how to tell Warren of the denial. Really, it was no surprise. Her mother said, "Rita," when she asked her, and already then, she knew, the answer was no. There would be no argument, because Syreeta respected the decision.

"You know I like Warren," Syreeta's mother said, "but he just can't move in here."

"Why not?" Syreeta asked.

She did not ask, "Why not" because she was defiant, but only because she wanted to have a good reason to provide Warren. Tonight she would see him. He would say so hopefully, "Did you ask your mom about me moving in there?" And she would have to say no, and he would ask why.

Her mother wore an apron; the ties around the back dangled down over her plaid dress. Sometimes her mother looked like her twin, as though they were sisters, with the same length between their waist and the rest of the body. There was white flour on her mother's hands. She dusted sugar on the berries, then picked up a napkin, wiped the sugar and flour from her hands.

"There would be complications," her mother said, "and what if you got pregnant? It's just not a good idea."

"I don't know where he'll go," Syreeta said, but she did not argue.

Her mother put the pie in the oven. On the television, they were talking about Bill Clinton coming to Vancouver. Syreeta wasn't listening. She was just feeling really bad for Warren, just wondering where he would go now. If he left her, she thought, she would die. If he moved to California to be with his mean dad, or back to Nanaimo with his drunk mother, she would die. She would die. She would die. She rushed through her dinner. She wanted to call Diana, Marissa, Tara, and Felicity and ask them what they thought. It was unusual. Syreeta was the one everyone came to for help; her quiet and definite air of competence unusual in a girl so young, but this was her boyfriend, her first love, and they all loved him. All her friends loved him too, and nobody would want Warren to leave. They would die too. They all loved him so.

• • •

She is so young, Amy thought. She's someone who doesn't know the ways of the world.

They were walking along the beach though the sky was gray and sunless. Often she'd have her meetings with Reena on the beach, because they could talk more easily away from the counselor's office. Reena's hair was so long now, Amy thought, and she was wearing an Adidas jacket, which she said belonged to her boyfriend, Jack Batley.

Reena said Jack was a Crip, and because he'd given her the jacket she was a Crip too. Later, in her notes, Amy would write that Reena was "affiliating herself with the Crips because they were people who had respect." But on the beach, she just listened, thinking, *Reena's so young, she doesn't know the ways of the world.* Was that such a bad thing though? Some of the girls she saw knew too much about the ways of the world. They were so savvy and jaded and hard.

Days before, Amy had given Reena a diary with birds and the tree of life on the cover. "You need to have a voice," she'd said. Amy believed that girls should have a voice—it was a kind of feminist cliché, she supposed, the subject of all those books by Virginia Woolf and Carol Gilligan, and yet, she liked the idea of Reena writing in the journal. She'd been working as a counselor for only a year, and her own reports on

Reena seemed perfunctory and official. Words like *naive* and *cultural and religious struggles with family* did not quite capture the yearning quality, the goodness she observed.

"The Crips are hassling me," Reena said quietly.

Amy heard Reena say this, but she was noticing the waves. The winds were strong; the waves were rolling in; they should leave the beach, she thought, before the storm of cold wind and rain.

Reena leaned down, and she searched in the sand. Amy's boyfriend collected glass shards—the shards worn and smooth from the waves. Reena found some small blue pieces of glass, and smiling, she handed these to Amy.

"You're so thoughtful," Amy said, and she tried to think of what she could say about the Crips. Were the Crips even real? Weren't they some gang in LA? Instead, she asked Reena if she had written in her diary.

"You should write about everything that's going on with your family. It just helps sometimes to write your thoughts down."

Reena nodded, but she seemed distracted. White foam on the waves; white clouds in the sky. Amy suggested they leave the beach and go for a drive or a coffee. As they walked over the sand, Reena laughed because the wind was filling up Jack's coat, and her body seemed as if it was shrouded in a billowing sail.

Once they'd reached the parking lot, Reena reached into her pocket and drew out something shiny. Reena handed Amy the shimmery object, looked down at the concrete, shyly, as if her kindness might be met with indifference or mockery. "Because you've helped me so much," she said.

The ring was gold with three white stones set into a little cluster, like a small flower.

"I have one too," Reena said. "It's a friendship ring."

Amy slipped the ring on her third finger and hugged Reena, and Reena said the same thing again, which made her feel guilty and grateful at once. "Because you've helped me so much," she said, and for some reason, they both began to cry. The wind may have caused their tears, as sometimes the winds of View Royal could bring tears to your eyes.

• • •

Colin Jones did not set out to find Josephine in a vengeful, deliberate way, nor did he pursue the girl by chucking rocks at Nevada's window or even phoning Kelly Ellard's home. Once he saw Kelly's big brother drive by in his Monte Carlo, with the windows tinted and the silver trim, and he felt a vague pang of envy for the vehicle but neither motivation nor passion to yell, "Where's your sister and her little troublemaking friend?"

Later, he couldn't even remember where he saw her and when. Of course, the police wanted to know all those facts, and Colin, "typical stoner," was not a compendium of details. He knew only that around the first week in November, he saw Josephine.

"Why did you give that Rhea girl my number?" he asked.

Josephine stepped forward, and her face reddened, and her eyes blazed, and all the softness seemed to leave her skin. "That little bitch," she said. "I'm gonna kick her face in."

"She called me, like, every day," he explained. "Ten, maybe twenty times."

In the months he'd known her, when she'd corrupted Nevada, taken the cars of strangers, insulted Nevada, wrecked Tommy's party, dressed sleazy, and bothered him late in the evening, Josephine had never once apologized. Apology seemed a feat, like grace and kindness, that was never to be given by the girl. And yet now, she looked at him. Her eyes wide and genuine as her rage had been earlier, she said, "Colin, I'm really sorry. She stole my address book. She's been calling everybody. I'm really, *really* sorry."

He sighed. He suddenly felt indifferent to it all, and he just wanted to go home and listen to Metallica.

It was embarrassing and petty, a stolen address book and the secret crushes of girls.

He turned away, not before giving her a look of sincere disdain.

"Don't worry," Josephine said, and he didn't really think much of it, until later, of course.

"Don't worry," Josephine said. "You won't be hearing from her again."

THE CONVERSATION

I have a bad headache," Josephine said to her mother as she stood in her mother's doorway.

Elaine Bell stood in the doorway, unsure. ("Sometimes Josephine just came in through the window because she doesn't have a key.")

"I'm feeling sick," Josephine pleaded, willing herself to look pale and faint, though her complexion was perfect, aided by her large stolen cache of Maybelline. Her cheeks were always pink, and her skin was even and a color called summer sand. She did not look sick at all.

"I'm really tired," Josephine said, rubbing her eyes and yawning.

Her mother looked at her skeptically.

"I'm hungry," Josephine said. At last her mother relented and opened the door. Josephine sashayed into the kitchen, elevated by her thick black stolen soles. "They don't feed me properly at Seven Oaks."

"That's because you miss mealtimes," Josephine's mother said.

"I don't want to go to school," Josephine announced. "Can you call them and tell them I'm sick?"

She opened the cupboard, took down some cereal, and began to eat the cereal ravenously.

Perhaps under the spell of her daughter's seemingly

innate, slightly regal, skill at issuing commands, perhaps feeling guilty, perhaps not up for a confrontation at 9:30 on a Wednesday morning, Elaine Bell followed her daughter's order. ("I called Shoreline. I told them she wouldn't be there that day and that she had a headache.")

Josephine was soon lying on the sofa, talking loudly on the telephone.

The Conversation went on for quite some time. The Conversation would last almost two hours.

Josephine at first spoke of boys and clothes and parties. "The part when I started to pay attention," her mother would later recall, "was when she started to talk about how to kill this person."

Elaine Bell heard a name, Rea. ("It's an unusual name, so I was alert to it, I guess.")

And she heard Josephine say: "We should go in the forest somewhere and dig a big hole in the earth and make it so that it's, you know, deep enough like a grave, and then put things on top of it to cover it up, and then walk with Rea to the forest and have her fall in and then start burying her alive."

Elaine listened to her daughter discuss walking a girl to the forest, pushing her into a hidden grave, and burying her alive.

But it struck her that her daughter's tone was not a serious tone. Later she would recall the murder scheme was described as a "sort of what-if scenario."

We should go in the forest somewhere. Dig a big hole in the earth. Make it so that it's deep enough. Like a grave. Put things on top of it. To cover it up. Cover it up.

Then walk with Rea. To the forest. And have her fall in. Have her fall. In. And then. Then. Start. Start burying her alive.

Mrs. Bell was hearing only one side of the conversation, of course, so she was not hearing the plan of murder suggested by Josephine's friend, only her daughter's response.

Josephine laughed. She said, "Oh you! That's awful."

Various ways of killing Rea were discussed, and to some suggested by her friend, Josephine would say, "I couldn't do that." Josephine lay on the sofa, her heels over the curved end, reclining, a devious girl in repose. Her mind was full of so many possibilities. In the movies of the men she loved, she had seen so many ways for the nemesis to get whacked or iced. Bodies were stashed in trunks. There were execution-style killings, but Josephine and her friend, they did not have guns.

Elaine heard her daughter exclaim, "I couldn't do that," draw in her breath, and then declare: "I could do this!"

Another plan was devised, a plan that Josephine could do. Her daughter discussed her plan to kill Rea for another hour or so while lying on the couch, her blonde hair like a gold fan across the embroidered mauve pillow.

So this is what Elaine heard: her daughter discussing digging a hole in the earth, covering the hole, pushing a girl into the secret grave, and covering up the grave with leaves so it would remain undiscovered—a grave, deep and secret and closed.

"There was definitely hostility there," Elaine observed.

"It wasn't clear to me what Rea had done to make Josephine so angry, but it was clear that there was hostility toward her, for sure. She was a 'bitch' and deserving of some sort of punishment."

When Josephine hung up the phone, Elaine asked her only this: "Who were you talking to?"

"Kelly," Josephine said.

She then yawned and stood up, heading toward the mirror. Josephine applied some lipstick, and Elaine did not ask her daughter anymore about what she'd heard: Kelly and Josephine making plans to walk Rea to a grave and have her fall in.

JUST KINDA KIDDING AROUND

At Shoreline School, the foyer was by the trophy case and the pay phones. The foyer acted as a de facto platform, a selection process, a gated community. To be seen in the foyer, to sit in the foyer, this was similar to living in a mansion on the hill—exclusive, privileged, arrived. In the foyer, Josephine and Kelly discussed their plan to punish a girl.

Melanie was just sitting there when Kelly came over and sat down and started talking with Josephine. "They starting talking about this girl they didn't like," Melanie recalls.

"This girl," Kelly explained to Melanie. "We're going to beat her up. She's talking behind Josephine's back."

Teachers walked by wearing red poppies. Melanie looked at the red felt petals pinned above their hearts. Tomorrow would be Remembrance Day, a day they would have an assembly and remember the soldiers who died in the war. They would read "In Flanders Fields" in English class, the poem they read every year, even though none of them had ever been to war, and were too young to even know a veteran. They would stand and chant and try to look tough, because it was really corny, but sometimes a few girls would cry.

We are the Dead. Short days ago
We lived, felt dawn, saw sunset glow,
Loved and were loved, and now we lie

So Melanie wasn't really listening when they talked about how they were going to beat this girl up, because she was waving at Tessa. Tessa was one of the girls who always cried when she said the words of Remembrance Day: "If ye break faith with us who die. We shall not sleep though poppies grow." Melanie moved from the foyer. In the principal's office, Syreeta and Marissa were handing in their donation boxes. Marissa had put the box of poppies on the counter at New York Fries. Syreeta had placed a box at Brady's. The proceeds went to veterans. The girls gave Mrs. Olsen all the donated coins.

Melanie was wondering how she found herself in this heavy body, which did not match the way she felt, so nomadic and weightless, like she should be winged and tiny. Marissa had that look to her—like an angel, the boys said, with her sweet laugh and tiny hands. Melanie forgot all about the idle chatter of Josephine and Kelly, because on that day, she had bigger concerns, like why she was drifting about, never in the same group, always feeling so lonely.

• • •

On the Songhees Reserve, the girls knew vaguely that they were inheritors of stolen lands and that their tribe was once called the Kosampson. More important, they knew the hour that the video channel played hip-hop videos, and they could lie in front of the TV and hope for a view of the bragging and ruthless American men. Once the principal at Shoreline asked Margie and Chantal to give a talk on Multicultural Day about the potlatch or the sweat lodge. They laughed in her face. They didn't even know what she was talking about. Multicultural Day at Shoreline, and the principal asked them to come in and tell everyone about their "native heritage."

Chantal was over at Margie's on a Wednesday after school. Usually the friends would hang around and talk about guys and make some phone calls. Have dinner. Around 8:30 or so, while they were watching a half-naked American girl shimmy and "shake her booty" on *Rap City*, Josephine and Kelly called and asked Margie if she would help them beat up somebody.

"Yeah, sure, why not?" Margie said.

The plan itself was quite vague. The invitation to the beating had no date or place or time. "They said they were supposed to beat up some girl," Margie later told the police. "They didn't say when. They didn't say where. They didn't say what they were going to do."

Yeah, sure, why not.

Margie didn't really think Josephine was serious. "I thought she was just kinda kidding around. 'Cause usually when we say that we're going to beat someone up, it never really happens."

THE RETURN OF
THE DANGEROUS LADY

The staff at Seven Oaks are required to keep notes of the comings and goings of their troubled residents. Josephine, and later Dusty, would find this surveillance an unbearable pain in the ass. And yet as events unfolded, they would be forever grateful for these records, which would provide a kind of redemption and, in more pragmatic terms, an alibi.

"Friday. November 14th. 1997. Dusty Noble arrived at Seven Oaks Receiving and Assessment at 3:30 P.M.

"Staff observed that 'Dusty knows Josephine, and they buddy up immediately.'

"Between 3:30 and 7:20 P.M. staff overheard a resident relay a message to Dusty that Reena had called her and left a message. Josephine and Dusty left at 7:21 PM. They told staff they were 'going to a park to party.'"

AN INVITATION

When the telephone rang, Reena had not yet begun to write in her journal or play cards with Aman. She was still eating soup. ("I'm on a diet," she'd told her mom.)

Josephine sounded excited and asked Reena to go to a party.

Reena was uncertain. "I think I'm going to stay home tonight," she said.

Hearing Reena hesitate, Josephine handed the phone to Dusty, who was more persuasive and a better liar, though both girls were well practiced, perhaps even gifted, when it came to dishonesty.

"Come on, Reena, come and party. We're not mad at you anymore. Just come on."

"I heard you want to rock my ass," Reena said.

Perhaps she thought the two girls had both tried to shun her, and she had showed them that she wasn't so bad after all. She thought Dusty must have forgiven her for her dalliance with Jack Batley. She'd showed them. She'd proved. She could be just like them. She could kiss the same boys. She could be a troublemaker. She'd won their respect, it seemed, for they were *begging* her to go to this party.

"Yes, I'll meet you at the Wal-Mart and we'll go to the party."

Aman looked so sad, his little pout, holding the pack of cards. "We'll play tomorrow," she promised.

"I'll be home by 10:00," Reena promised, grabbing her knapsack, which still held her pajamas and some perfume and her new diary, emblazoned with the tree of life.

Suman thought of warning her, but warnings, there'd been so many, and her daughter was strong-willed, and hopeful too. There was so much hope in her eyes as she set out to meet the girls she hoped were her friends now. The black knapsack was on her back as she set out down the street, lighting a cigarette. Jack's jacket filled with wind, fluttered like a sail when the sky is against the cloth, and forward she moved, toward the Wal-Mart where she would meet the two girls who would bring her along to what she believed would be a Friday night party.

LIGHTS IN THE SKY

The Gorge is a misleading name, with the suggestion of an abyss or funereal crevice. The waterway has always been a place for idylls. In 1861, Lady Jane Franklin, widow of the Arctic explorer, sailed up the Gorge in the course of an around-the-world voyage with her niece Sophia. Miss Goodie McKenzie, their Canadian host, arranged for the ladies to be picked up by canoes and brought to the banks of the Gorge, where they picnicked under the boughs of the oak tree. Goodie's cousin, Alice, a girl who'd come from England in 1857, recalled in her memoirs how "the roar of tumbling waters from the Gorge at low tide made a lullaby for me."

On the night of November 14, two occurrences—one natural, the other man-made—enhanced the beauty of the waterway. There was a full moon on November 14, so large and full, the radiance illuminated what was normally hidden and so difficult to see. Another kind of light would break suddenly and wondrously through the dark above. According to the North American Aerospace Defense Command, this phenomenon occurred at precisely 9:12. At 9:12, the sky was silent, and yet it seemed as if fireworks were above, streaming across the sky, like wisps of fire, red and yellow, these lights, which left a glowing trail, shimmering as if in competition with the boldness of the moon.

At 9:12, a Russian rocket fell back to earth and exploded as it fell. The fuel tank and motor, all the mechanics of ascent, collapsed, and jettisoned, slowly, and could not orbit around the earth, and instead burned up as they hit the atmosphere. A scientist could better explain this demise. Debris in the sky turned to a light show and left no hazardous materials on the ground. There was merely an implosion and transformation to fire in the sky. And in this way, the night sky, already so clear and rainless and lit with moon, had never before been so strange and fiery.

On the Gorge that night, Patrick O'Connor was in a canoe with friends when he witnessed the sight. "We lucked out," Patrick O'Connor later recalled. That night, the Gorge seemed possessed of a magical beauty, as idyllic and wondrous as a place could be, and the men paddled. "We were in the right place at the right time," Patrick O'Connor would later say.

Others in Victoria were frightened by the fire in the sky. The phone rang rapidly, more so than usual, at the police station. Dispatchers received thirty-six emergency calls from people saying, "I heard a gunshot." "I saw something weird in the sky." "I think there's a fire outside." "There was this noise, this light, I don't know what it is, but something went up somewhere; something lit up and burned." The dispatcher, Derek Morrison, told the frightened citizens of his city not to worry. "It's a four-stage SL 12 rocket," he told one particularly interested but skeptical former military man. "That's right, sir, a Russian rocket. Nothing to worry about. Just a little spacecraft debris."

In the morning, the U.S. National Weather Service's Spokane, Washington, office would further reassure those frightened by the blaze above when they reported that the "space debris landed safely in the Pacific Ocean off the coast of Washington."

In Victoria, the morning paper would report on the vision with a headline telling the townspeople to relax. "Relax. It was the Russians, not the Martians."

On the field at Shoreline School, at 9:12, Tara and Dimitri and Warren and Marissa, Jen and Syreeta, Kelly and Josephine, Chelsea, and Tenille and Richie D. and many others gathered for a party, would also look up, at the moment, look up to see the full moon and the rare and bright burning in the sky. Forever after, they would remember this evening, and as the police divers used the words "carefully floated" to perhaps add some poetry to the discovery of a dead girl in the Gorge, the students of Shoreline would, when speaking to police or judges, inadvertently title the evening as if to soften the horror of all that unfolded after the rocket's fall. They would not say, "That was the night of the death," nor would they say, "The night she got killed." Instead, they would say, when speaking of that night, "That was the night of the Russian satellite."

THE NIGHT OF
THE RUSSIAN SATELLITE

Marissa's going to meet us down at Shoreline," Syreeta
said to Tara as the two girls locked up Brady's Fish and
Chips and waited outside for Syreeta's mother to arrive.

Brady's was spotless. Both girls were never lazy, nor
did they want to leave Diana's parents' restaurant in less
than perfect condition. It was a kind of respect. They
liked knowing they could walk away and return the next
morning, to take down the chairs and refill the ketchup
bottles and cash in, with all in order and no disarray.

"Party at Shoreline!" Tara said, imitating a tough boy,
drawling her words.

"Party!" Syreeta said, although she wasn't in much of
a mood. Sure, she liked to see her friends and walk
around the field, and that night seemed as if it would be
like all the others, with Warren's arm around her and
Diana making her laugh and Tara finding out some gossip she'd sworn not to tell about who all was hooking up
in the bushes, and getting a little light-headed and
swooning around on the moonlit grass. Yet Syreeta felt a
sharp pang. She did not know Josephine or Kelly's plan,
and had never heard of an unmarked grave, and yet on
that night, as they waited for her mother to arrive outside Brady's, she felt a sudden pain in her stomach.

Tara, pink cheeked and unharmed, was looking up at the sky.

Syreeta looked up too, and saw the moon, immense and complete.

• • •

Someone screamed. Everyone seemed to scream around her. All Syreeta's friends were looking up at the sky. The lights came quickly, burst out of the darkness, rapid and beautiful, red tumbling before turning to yellow, a bright red she'd never seen in the sky before. The red slashed through the blackness, like a tear of silk, followed by a pale gold flame that dangled and disappeared, leaving the sky black again.

Someone said it was a meteor shower. No, it was a satellite. It was from Russia. What was it? They didn't know, only that they all watched it together, here and then gone, and Syreeta was glad she had seen it, with all her friends around. Before she left that night, they'd all seen the lights in the sky.

Warren poured a little bit of vodka into a Mac's cup filled with Coke. He watched Willow's face as the thing fell through the sky. Willow was with her best friend, Maya, and she was sharing a mickey of vodka with Eve, the pretty girlfriend of Erik Cash. Everyone said Eve should be a model. She was tall and black and her cheekbones were so high. On the field there were only a few girls whom Warren did not know. He'd never seen Dusty before, and she seemed like a big and noisy presence. Kelly and Dusty were standing beside Josephine, and there was a fourth girl who Warren did not know—

the fourth girl was Reena Virk. There were so many girls on the field that night. All of the Crips were up at Brandon's house for his birthday party. Warren hadn't gone because he wanted to spend the night with Syreeta. He was getting tired of the Crips as well. He'd even asked to be jumped out—to take another beating in order to officially renounce his membership. *You'll either end up dead or in jail.* "You really want to leave the family, 'bro?" Erik had asked, and Warren had mumbled something about his girlfriend and being in love.

On the field, Warren looked at Maya and thought of the rumors he'd heard—that something really bad had happened to Maya, really bad, like worse than you could ever imagine. He thought of this mystery now, observing the way Willow stood so protectively beside Maya. Willow's kind face was rapturous, there, in the brief second, tilted upward, with her lips parted as if she was still stunned by the moon, lasting and full, while the pieces of the rocket burned up and looked like falling stars. She saw him sitting there, worrying, and she smiled at him, while the last light of what he thought was a spaceship fell somewhere to the earth in Seattle or Oregon. Looking at her sudden smile, he willed himself to forget it, stop worrying, forget about the fact that he was totally fucking unloved and unwanted. *Just forget that,* he told himself. *Forget that you don't have a home.*

• • •

Soon after the satellite fell from the sky, Syreeta knocked on the front door of Shoreline. She wanted to call her mother to come pick her up because she just wasn't feeling very well. The school was locked, so Syreeta set off in search of Warren so she could tell him she wanted to go home.

Soon after the falling lights left the sky, Laila, a girl with rings on each of her fingers, walked purposefully onto the field. Her hair was long and black and she was trained in martial arts, with a particular skill at kickboxing. She wore heavy black eyeliner, and this, and her regal bearing, had earned her the nickname of Cleopatra. "I'm here to fight a girl," Laila announced to no one in particular. "Her name starts with an R or an S."

Hearing this, Reena began to run.

Soon after the debris burned through the darkness, a boy named Nate hurled a rock at the window of Shoreline School.

Nate couldn't have known that the simple act of throwing a rock would change the night forever, and later, he could not even recall why he had thrown the rock. Just something in him—boredom, or being fourteen. He just picked it up and chucked it, and then the window broke and with it, the Friday night idyll of the kids on the field under the full moon.

The janitor inside the school called the police at 9:25 to report an act of vandalism by a large gathering of youth. Constable Basanti and his partner, Hodginson, arrived at the school, as they often did, for the youths of View Royal gathered there almost every Friday and Saturday evening. Arriving at the school, Constable Basanti saw, as he would later testify, "a large number of youths, maybe fifty or sixty." He and his partner told the kids to move along. Leave the premises. Go home.

"Have a safe night," Constable Hodginson said to some of the kids before they walked away.

Warren was not on the field when the police arrived, for he'd walked Syreeta to the bus stop.

"I'll walk you home," he offered.

"No, that's fine," she said, a choice she would later often reflect on.

He gave her money for the bus, and as he did so, he thought that the only time he really felt peace and comfort was when he was beside Syreeta. He would have to find a way to stay in View Royal, to stay with her always. She left him that evening, kissing him on the cheek. He gave her money for the bus because he did not want her walking home alone.

The girls Syreeta did not know—Dusty and Laila—and the girls she didn't really admire—Josephine and Kelly—had caught up with Reena. Syreeta was on the bus as the girls surrounded Reena on the street.

Reena was surrounded now, and all she wanted was to go home.

"We're not going to fight you," Dusty promised. "We want you to party with us."

Reena's face was pale, and she looked up at Laila.

"It's true," Laila promised. "I was talking about another girl, and she's not here."

But Reena was not convinced. Why had they all come running after her so suddenly? She turned and went into the pay phone, ignoring Dusty, who pressed her blunt face against the glass and kicked at the door.

"I'm coming home," Reena said to Aman. "Can you tell Mom? I'll be home soon."

The thought of her little brother bolstered her, and since he could tell she was crying and frightened, he encouraged her as best as he could.

"Come home," he said.

Dusty's face was still pressed against the glass, glaring. Laila, kickboxing champion, lifted a long strand of black hair from her face, lit a cigarette, and looked up at the sky.

Syreeta was not yet home. The bus moved through View Royal, past the Four Mile Pub and the firemen's hall.

Reena, in the safety of the phone booth, was afraid to emerge, and when she did, Dusty grabbed her arm roughly.

"I'm going home," Reena said. "Let me—"

"You're being a bitch," Dusty said.

"Why are you being such a bitch?" Josephine yelled.

"I'm not—"

"We don't want to beat you up," Josephine said. "Come on."

"Come on."

"Come on, Reena."

"Stay with us."

"Stay with us and party."

"I want to catch the bus," Reena said. "I have to go home."

Dusty was blocking her way; the girth of the girl was wide and obstinate. "Give me your bus pass," Dusty snarled.

"No," Reena said, unsure once more. There was nowhere to go.

Dusty said again, "Give me your bus pass, and I'll let you go home."

Reena fumbled in her knapsack, found the yellow laminated paper, and handed it to Dusty, who ripped it up.

Dusty and Josephine now moved to either side of Reena and linked her arms through their own. "They both walked on either side of Reena, arm in arm, like locked," Kelly would later testify, "like friends would walk."

Pieces of Reena's bus pass floated off the concrete.

Maya and Laila were sharing a joint when someone said, "There's cops around. We shouldn't smoke this here. Let's go under the bridge."

UNDER THE BRIDGE

This place was not a teen hangout, and they had never been there. A girl named Jen wasn't sure why she went under there, with Dimitri and Marissa and Tara and Warren. Later she tried to explain to police this movement, which occurred twenty minutes after the fall of the rocket. "We went under the bridge. We didn't know where to go 'cause we were asked to leave Shoreline. And I'm not sure why we went there. It was just some people started going under there."

Under the bridge, right under the bridge, there was a dark wall, covered in graffiti, and the area was like a dirty cave. Uneven, the land sloped down to the water's edge, pebbled and with well-trodden grass. There was a wooden stairwell leading down with a railing that looked slightly rusty and precarious. You could hear the cars rumbling as they clattered overhead, the drivers unaware of the cavern beneath.

Under the bridge, there was barely room for the fourteen girls and two boys. Marissa thought of sitting on the stairs, but the stairs seemed so grimy and damp. She stared down at the dark water where moonlight lay, broken by the wooden beams of the bridge. She did not like being under there, where there was little light and the ground was worn and rough, and the grass that remained was brown and flecked with shards of bottles, broken and small.

Marissa, who looked like a pixie and was not yet fourteen, and thus the youngest girl under the bridge, was taken by surprise when she heard Josephine suddenly scream. Josephine screamed: "Why are you trying to ruin my life?"

She yelled this at this girl Reena, who looked startled as well.

"I'm not—" Reena started to say, but then Josephine's voice rose up, and all the girls under the bridge heard her yell again at Reena. "You're trying to ruin my life!"

Reena protested. "No," she said. "I'm sorry. I—"

"Why are you talking bullshit?" Dusty said, or maybe it was Kelly, or maybe Laila. The voices were a blur of accusations and girls' screams.

"No—" Reena said again. There was a lit cigarette in Josephine's hand. She pushed the burning cigarette into Reena's forehead, searing the girl's skin. Reena cried out and swung back at Josephine, and as she did this, as she moved to hit Josephine, Kelly rushed forward, by Josephine, and reached out as well, hitting Reena with a closed fist.

Dusty moved closer to Reena, but Marissa backed away. She left the dark cave under the bridge and scrambled up the hill, and she joined the other frightened girls and the two boys, Warren and Dimitri, who had also run up the stairs. Marissa buried her face in her boyfriend's arm.

"Oh my God . . . ," Tara was saying beside her. "Oh my God."

Below them, a semicircle had formed, and this semicircle was surrounding the girl on the stairs, Reena. She had tried, and she tried again, to run through and past the girls who surrounded her.

"Don't let her leave," someone yelled as she moved, or tried to move, out of the circle and up the stairs. Stopped by the swarming circle, she was thrown, forced down on the railing, and the circle tightened around her, closer, the fists to her head, the slapping hands on her skin, the fists on her shoulder.

Watching the circle below, Tara turned to Jen, and said, "I can't watch this. It disgusts me."

Later Tara would tell the police, "They just kept beating on her and I can't . . . I don't even know what it was about."

While Marissa cried in his shoulder, Dimitri saw Warren running down there, down the stairs, and he saw Warren kick Reena. Kick her in the head. A girl. *Why is he doing that?* he wondered. He doesn't even know that girl. Dimitri left the frightened girls then, and he bounded down the hill, and he grabbed Warren away from the semicircle, which was beastlike and black, crouching, wailing, shrieking. "Chill out, Warren. It's not your fight." He wanted Warren away, wanted Warren calm and not part of this at all.

But Warren seemed possessed of a sudden adrenaline, drawn by the Furies, and he did not leave the circle. Willow kicked Reena's feet so Reena slid off the stairs and landed face down in the mud, and as she lay there, she pleaded with the furious girls around her, "Stop! Please! Stop!"

"I'm sorry," she said, covering her face from the blows and the roars, as she lay in the mud, beneath them all, felled by the force of the Furies.

Tara would later tell the police, "I remember when she was down there, she was sitting with each of her hands over her face and saying, 'Stop, stop. Stop.' She had her hands over her face. 'Stop it. Okay, that's enough. Stop it now.'"

It was Laila who became Reena's protector, suddenly. Laila leaned forward, raised her voice. "Next person to touch her," Laila said, "gets a shot from me."

"And nobody did it again," Dusty would explain later, "because Laila is a tough girl, and everybody is afraid of her."

The girls left Reena alone then, and Marissa looked down, and she saw Reena with her hands on her face, as if she was trying to clean her skin, and she was crying, so it might have been tears, Marissa thought. She was crying so it might have been tears, but it might have been blood.

Dusty walked by Reena scornfully.

"I'm sorry," Reena said. "I have to go home now."

Dusty kept on walking, and her fist was sore.

Willow left as well, walking up the stairs past Reena. "When I left," she would later say, "Reena was sitting down there, going, 'Stop, stop, stop,' and it was dark so I couldn't even see if she was bruised, but I could still hear her voice when I was going up the stairs."

They scattered, both the fighters and the fearful. The scattering caused a kind of confusion, a disparate unraveling of the group, and the frenzy that cohered them only five minutes before dissipated, and some of them were ashamed. In this scattering, there was, as it would later turn out, a true confusion as to the whereabouts of all involved.

But they all could agree that Reena walked up from under the bridge, and she passed them, ashamed too, not asking for help, only leaving them, broken, bleeding, heading over the bridge to return to her home and her family.

Marissa looked over onto the bridge, and saw that "Reena was staggering, a little. She looked light-headed. She looked a little dazed." Marissa wanted to go home as well, for the tough girls must think she was prissy and delicate, and she did not really care, only she did not want them to see her like this, still trembling and horrified. Marissa walked over to say good-night to her friends, who were waiting for their mothers in the parking lot. There was a garish light on the girls; they seemed swept with an orange that was lurid and false, and the real moon was fading. Someone had taken Reena's knapsack, and Maya was throwing the pajamas into the water, and another girl was ripping the pages out of Reena's diary, and someone threw the diary down into the dark water. Laila held Reena's bottle of Polo Sport, for while the diary and pajamas were unwanted, there was value in an object from Ralph Lauren. Tara was not there, later, when the bottle was finally destroyed as well. The bottle smashed and the perfume evaporated into the concrete, and the shards of glass remained.

As she walked home, Tara worried at the cruel acts that she had seen. She would have to call Syreeta now and tell her that Warren had kicked a girl in the head. Syreeta would not believe it, as Tara did not believe it, for it made really no sense at all, and it was wrong, she thought. Everything she'd seen was wrong, and she bit her cheek hard.

Tara returned home, considered calling Syreeta, but she decided she would tell her in the morning. It did not occur to Tara to tell her parents of the fight she had witnessed, because "that would only worry them, knowing their daughter was around people who could be cruel like that." Marissa too did not tell her parents when she returned home, fearing the story would worry and upset them, and why would she tell her parents of such a horrible thing? ("What am I going to say? 'Hey, I just saw a big fight!'") She lay in bed, thinking of Dimitri and how he'd protected her, and how she hated it—hated seeing those girls scream and kick and turn savage as they had never been.

• • •

Josephine and Dusty were signed in by the night supervisor at Seven Oaks. Her notes show their return at 11:03. Nothing unusual was reported in their appearance, and the girls were visually inspected for signs of intoxication or impairment. No such signs were observed.

Josephine lay in bed, and she thought, "Reena's probably gonna go home with a black eye and she'll wake up in the morning and she'll say, 'I'm not going to talk shit about Josephine Bell anymore.'"

• • •

On this same evening, around 11:30, Syreeta awoke, though hours earlier she had brushed her teeth, undressed, put on her pajamas, and drifted, suddenly, unexpectedly, to sleep. Sometimes the events of her day would coalesce in her mind, not for examination so much as for appreciation. She thought of the careful way she had closed up Brady's. Yes, she had locked the cash register and brought down all the blinds. Her white shirt, yes, she had checked in her closet to see if it was clean and pressed to wear tomorrow to the mall. She thought of Warren's face as she hopped on the bus and how he'd offered to walk her home—wanted her to be safe and accompanied on the dark roads. She wondered who the girl was on the field, whom she had never seen before, with the scared smile and the broad shoulders and who was the girl on the field with the Cleopatra eyes. All of this, she thought, and then she just felt odd. She slept, but she woke. She felt the oddness once more. She wanted to be out of her bed, as if her bed created the sensation she'd felt earlier, felt even before she was on the field with all her friends, watching the satellite fall through the sky.

"I put my pillow on the bedroom floor. I felt really funny."

The phone rang, and it was Warren. His voice was gentle and apologetic. Perhaps he said something about a fight, but she wasn't listening, and she said, "Warren, I'm sleeping. Call me tomorrow." She returned to the floor and clutched her knees. She felt as if she was being submerged, as if her breath was being pulled out of her, replaced by a rope with tiny blades. *What is this bad feeling,* she wondered, *when I have not hurt anyone and no one has hurt me?* The night went on, darkening and star filled, with the full moon above, and the police noticing they had not received the usual calls about teenagers partying, only calls of concern about "something in the sky." All over View Royal, her friends slept. Diana, and Felicity and Marissa and Tara, they slept in their rooms with the posters of Snoop Dogg and Michael Jordan and Leonardo DiCaprio, slept with their childhood dolls and their normal dreams, but Syreeta could not sleep and she lay on her bedroom floor, overtaken by what may, in fact, have been dread, instinct, or empathy, but which, she in her youth, at fourteen, could only describe as "a really bad feeling."

The Killers

"You don't catch a killer. He catches himself."

—Fyodor Dostoyevsky,
Crime and Punishment

PART TWO

The Killers

YOU CAN'T SEE ANYTHING

On Saturday morning, after the sun had risen over the Gorge, a man by the name of Gerald Morris set off to visit his son. Every weekend, Gerald, a dark-haired man of thirty, would get on his mountain bike and head down to Gorge Park. He biked slowly that day, appreciating the calm beauty of the waterway. Canada geese floated on the surface, soon rising to the rainless sky.

As he approached the hill where the quaint white schoolhouse stood, Gerald Morris lifted his body slightly to add pressure to the bicycle pedals, so he could make it up the slope. He rode over the fallen copper leaves, past the tall oak tree with branches outstretched and empty. And near the white schoolhouse, something caught his eye, and he braked, very suddenly.

He did not notice the blood right away.

He got off his bike and looked down at the grass where the objects lay. An Adidas jacket. A pair of girl's black shoes. The jacket and the shoes, he would later testify, "were pretty soaked from the morning dew. From the morning mist, they were pretty wet."

It was strange, the haphazard position of the shoes, for as he noticed, "They weren't together like somebody took them off in one spot. They looked like they'd just been dropped there." The shoes were black platform shoes. ("I don't know how you'd describe them, but they were a thick pair of shoes.") He thought again that it was strange the way "they were separated, maybe two feet apart from each other."

In the grass, also wet, was the Adidas jacket. He lifted the jacket from the grass, and as he did so, he saw it then—"a trickle of blood." On the inside of the jacket on the white fabric, Gerald Morris saw "four or five drops . . . it didn't look like much blood."

He picked up the shoes, and placed them together, side by side, on the steps of the old white schoolhouse.

He placed the jacket on the white picket fence.

Murder or violence did not occur to him as he touched the clothes of a girl. Instead, he thought of being young, of his former nights of abandon when he was a student at Shoreline and would go to this very place for revelry. ("I used to party in that park.") Lying on the hill, looking at the stars, the dizzy stars. . . . Gerald Morris did not think of beatings or lonely girls, only of parties and crowds, and he thus came to the conclusion that a teenager had lost their coat and thrown about her shoes in the midst of a good time. He himself had "lost a lot of jackets the same way" when he was young. And so, kindly, he placed the jacket on the fence, "figuring the teenager would come back and look for it."

As he biked away, he thought of wild youth and tossed shoes and those years when there were no worries of taxes and car payments and alimony. He thought to himself, "That must have been some party!"

• • •

Ernestine Anderson, a woman in her fifties, saw the Adidas jacket on the fence as she was driving to work at Thrifty's Foods.

"That's Robby's coat!" she screamed to her boyfriend, Tim. It was a strange coincidence, for as she explains, "The night before, Tim and I were at my friend's, and she told us that her grandson Robby had his black and white Adidas jacket stolen from school, and that had been his *third* jacket stolen."

"Let's get it!" Tim replied.

Ernestine, Erna to her friends, then turned her car around and drove back to the schoolhouse and the picket fence. "As bizarre as it may seem," she recalls, "the jacket was gone."

Staring at the fence, Tim and Erna turned amateur detectives. "There was that woman jogging by," Tim said. "I bet she took it."

"You think so?" Erna said, recalling the trim blonde jogger.

"Go, get her, Erna! Go!"

In pursuit now, Erna drove over the bridge while Tim looked out through her window, searching for the jogger. "There she is; she's on the trail." Erna parked the car hastily, and she and Tim went running down the hill to the jogging trail by the Gorge. Sure enough, the blonde jogger had the Adidas jacket tucked under her arm.

"I believe that jacket belongs to a friend of mine!" Erna said. Tim glared at the woman in her velour track-suit.

Confronted by the two, the woman did not put up

a fight. She merely hurled the jacket onto the wet ground, declared, "I was going to give it to the Salvation Army anyway," and then she continued to jog briskly.

Erna placed the jacket in the backseat of the car, and as she did so she noticed no blood. Erna and Tim had a good laugh about the jogger lady. ("I was going to give it to the Salvation Army!" Tim mimicked. "Yeah, *right*!") Neither Erna nor Tim knew of the earlier route of the coveted coat. They did not know it belonged once to a boy named Jack Batley, who slept in the child's playhouse on the back lawn of his mother's home near the Tillicum Mall. They could not have known the jacket never belonged to Robby, but to this boy—described as "rat faced"—but nonetheless loved so fiercely by Dusty and Reena. The jacket itself was common and unexceptional, and yet Dusty, seeing it on Reena last night, had punched harder, punched so hard she'd bruised her knuckles. The jacket reminded her of the brief love she'd known and lost so suddenly, as if Jack's love could be stolen like Josephine's notebook, stolen rather than merely never felt or true. Erna knew none of this, knew only that she had seized the jacket back from that jogger lady, and she and Tim drove with their new possession away from the schoolhouse.

At Robbin's Donuts, Erna purchased coffee, and she waited in line in front of two police officers, but she did not hear their conversation. "Quiet night, last night," Basanti remarked, and Hodginson thought it was unusual as well, because usually on a Friday night, in this part of town, they received what they called "youth complaints" up until around 2:00 A.M. Yes, the quiet night was unusual, Hodginson thought, and perhaps he remembered two pretty young girls who smiled at him as they headed away from the dense and vivid green field. "Have a safe night," he'd said to the two young girls. They'd smiled at him then, eyes shining, as if enlivened by the shimmering spectacle of a starship falling to their part of the world, or perhaps, just merely, as Syreeta said, naive and carefree.

Erna forgot about the coat in the backseat of her car, and she went about her day, selling Wonder Bread and eggs and frozen steaks. In the evening, she cooked herself a meal of pork chops and green beans and settled down to watch the nightly news.

The television news reported neither the fight under the bridge nor a diary thrown into the water. Erna only remembered her discovery, suddenly, and thought, "Robby will be so happy to have his coat returned." She went out to the car to get it, looking up at the sky, but of course, the strange lights the paper described ("a blaze of red and gold trailing through the sky") were no longer on display. The jacket was still very damp. Erna thought this was strange, for it had been in her car all day and was waterproof, so why was it still damp as she lifted it from the backseat in her car?

When she was in the laundry room, as she lifted the coat toward the machine, she saw blood. There was blood on the inside of the sleeves. There was blood on the white stripes. There was blood on the back of the coat. There was blood everywhere on the coat she had found hanging on the white picket fence by the old antique white schoolhouse.

"Whoever stole Robby's jacket must have got in some fisticuffs!"

She shook her head and washed the coat in cold water with a teaspoon of bleach. She washed away all the blood and then hung the jacket on a brown wood rack, where she would find it in the morning, clean and dry.

SOME KIND OF FANTASY

The girl was too excitable. That was one reason he didn't believe her.

She wore a small gold stud in her nose. He'd never met her before.

Alan, a Filipino boy, was walking away from the house where he lived with his grandmother. He was at the bus stop when this girl came out of nowhere, this girl he'd never met before.

She's kind of cute, he thought, with that gold stud in her nose and her brown hair and brown eyes. He wasn't all that confident, being only fifteen and shy, but since this girl, whom he didn't even know, just stopped him right on the corner of Eltham Road and Adderly Place, he thought he would try his luck. "I was trying to hit on her," he would later recall.

The girl's hair was damp, and the day's rain was on her shoulders as well. He didn't really notice the rain as he watched her mouth and her lips and the way she talked so fast as all girls talked—really fast—and yet she talked faster than any other girl he had talked to before. It was as if she wanted not only to talk, but to somehow be listened to so suddenly and immediately, as if the listener might soon be invisible, leaving her there with a story unheard. He caught phrases. Seriously. Something about being part Spanish. Or part Native. Something about her brother. He was trying to think of how to hit on her on that Saturday, but she just talked so fast. The stud in her nostril was gold and reminded him of a girl at his school who wore a ring in her nose, like a bull.

Her run-on sentence went like this:

"I got in a fight with a girl and I beat up a girl and she was beat up so bad she didn't even know who she was anymore. She was beat up some more. We beat her up some more. I offered to walk her home. She was beat up more. She was beat up really bad. And now she's dead."

"I'm sure whoever you beat up is not dead," Alan said.

Another fast sentence, so fast:

"No, she is dead because her head was under the water and all this red stuff floated up and it was bubbly and it came from her and it was around both of us like it was around me this red stuff and then she floated to the top. I saw her float. I saw it but there were other people there too, it wasn't just me, other people helped kill her."

A lot of lies, he thought. It was all a lot of lies. He caught the phrases. *Floated to the top. No, she is dead. I saw her float. Other people helped kill her.* But he couldn't really believe that. How could you believe it was true? "It just didn't seem real," Alan would say later, adding that he thought the girl's story of killing was just "some kind of fantasy."

So little attention had he given to her that he didn't even listen to her name. "Kelly, Jennifer, don't ask me.

Something. Ah. Sarah. I don't know. I didn't pay attention to her. I thought she was lying," he would later unhelpfully volunteer when telling the police about the brown-haired girl. "I don't remember that much about her, and I don't remember her name."

There was a little gold stud in the brown-haired girl's nose. She walked away from him down toward the long concrete valley of the Tillicum Mall. A lot of lies. All that stuff she'd said so quick, like rat-a-tat-tat, her rapid-fire biography: I'm part Spanish, she said. No, I'm part Native. I have a brother and he drives a really nice Monte Carlo.

• • •

Dusty and Josephine took the bus downtown, where they were less likely to be recognized. No one paid attention to them as they moved into an alley downtown, for they seemed possessed of neither beauty nor menace. Their actions were completely unobserved.

Nevertheless, they still moved furtively. In the slim and secret alley, they stood now near a rusted green Dumpster. Dusty kept watch while Josephine removed the black platform shoes from her Guess bag. She gripped the shoes, and her hands were so delicate and pale, and Reena's shoes were clumsy and heavy and dark. She clenched the shoes and then tossed them upward, one and then the other. The shoes fell into the Dumpster, covered in ashes, leaves, and debris.

SYREETA DOES SOME LAUNDRY

Warren heard the sound of falling water.

He stood outside the door. Syreeta poked her head out of the shower, and he gazed up at her clean skin and the still hidden shape of her naked body. Her long hair draped across her bare shoulders, and her shoulders shone from the water.

"I heard you kicked a girl in the head last night," she said, reproachfully.

He stared at the tiles, and she stepped out of the shower, ignoring him. She wrapped herself in a towel.

"Who told you that?"

"Tara."

"Tara should keep her mouth shut," he said.

"Well, why'd you do it?"

"I shouldn't have done it," he said, still looking at the floor.

From the room downstairs, she could hear the low rumble of the television and Marissa's familiar giggle.

"So why did you do it then?"

"I don't know," he said, and he looked very ashamed, but she still was angry, and turned her back to him, and walked away, into her bedroom.

She took a long time dressing. She wasn't quite sure why. She tried on her jeans, and then changed into her khaki pants, which were flared slightly. She parted her hair in the middle, pulled it into a ponytail.

When she went downstairs, she moved toward Marissa, who lay on the pale blue couch. Dimitri was sitting near the screen, cross-legged, enraptured by the American superstars throwing around a basketball.

"Are you feeling better?" Warren asked her, but she ignored him still, and looked toward Marissa. She was not sure why she did this, only that she did look at Marissa then, and she noticed how Marissa's face seemed so impossibly tiny, like a little treasure you would want to hold on to forever.

Several minutes went by before Warren dared to speak to her again, and when he spoke, it was only with a request for her to do some laundry.

He did not tell her that he was afraid to ask Grace to do his laundry. He had not yet found a place to live, but he knew he must leave by December, and he wanted to be a good guest and not bother her with chores. He did not tell Syreeta he had no money for the washing machines. Though his father said money was on the way, he had not yet received an envelope from California. It was pretty embarrassing to tell your girlfriend you didn't even have twelve quarters to your name, like he was a scrub, or a grub, or whatever, a guy with no money.

Though he did not tell her this, she knew instinctively the reasons behind his request, and so without asking for reasons, she lifted his laundry bag and headed downstairs to the washing machine. His Mossimo sweater was inside, along with his white jeans. He'd once asked her to bleach the sweater, weeks before. He did not like the cream color, he'd said, and she knew he liked white, and the sweater was not white. It was cream or beige or ivory.

Syreeta did not know how to use the washing machine, and her mother was not home.

She went back upstairs to ask Marissa for help, but Dimitri leaped off the couch, and he loped across the floor, swinging his left arm, as if in imitation of the rangy and determined basketball players. "I'll show you how," he said confidently.

In the basement, Dimitri turned the dials, and Syreeta dumped out the clothes. She felt sad for Warren suddenly. He only had these three pairs of white pants. He had neither mother nor father to provide him with new clothes, to clean his clothes, to just take care of him.

Because she was half-blind, she did not see the blood right away.

She was holding his pants in her hands, while Dimitri turned the dials and unscrewed the top of the bleach, and she saw suddenly the blood. Two drops of blood observed to be "the size of a quarter." She pushed the clean hair from her face and remembered the phone call the night before. What had he said? Something about a fight. He'd said something about how he was walking with Kelly Ellard and some Native guy yelled at Kelly, and he'd gotten in a fight with the guy. She remembered this, and just then, Dimitri dumped the bleach into the washing machine, and she let the pants fall into the water that was rising up to her hands. She looked down, for a brief second, and saw everything before her, in the pure, clean water, turning about so rapidly.

• • •

On Saturday, Reena's uncle Raj rose, took a long bath, and hoped his legs would be steady as he climbed over the porcelain border. He planned to take Reena shopping because she'd said yesterday that she wanted to buy a Winnie the Pooh teddy bear as a gift for a little girl she babysat.

"Reena never came home last night," Suman said, when he arrived at Reena's home.

Suman seemed more frightened than angry, and she held on to a notebook she'd found in Reena's bedroom. The notebook belonged to Josephine and was full of phone numbers. Suman thought she would try to call some of the people in the notebook and see if they knew where Reena was. "I'm worried," Suman said. "She called here around 10:30 and spoke to Aman. She was just at the Mac's and she said she was on her way home."

"The Mac's by the bridge?"

Suman nodded. Raj knew of Reena's wanderings, and yet she *always* called him. He was the one she called. When she was at Kiwanis, she called him for a ride. When she had to meet her counselor, she called him, and he thought it strange she had not called to tell him she wouldn't be shopping after all. This wasn't like her.

By the bridge, he drove. He felt a little foolish, parking his car by the telephone booth, and wandering into the garishly lit convenience store. Kids bought Slurpees. Kids bought Cokes.

"Come and pick me up around 11:00," she'd said. "I want to buy a Winnie the Pooh teddy bear."

He returned to his car and thought of her beside him only days ago. He thought and hoped he would return to his house and find Reena cuddling up with her grandmother, drinking some tea and saying she'd just spent the night at a friend's and overslept.

The simplicity of the Missing Person's report is a fraud of sorts, a betrayal. The few lines have almost no relation to the tragedy of their meaning. And yet there they were. Filed by a dispatcher at 1:50 on November 15, a Saturday.

Reena Virk. Date of Birth: 83.03.10.
Due to return home at 2200 hours, 14 November, 1997.
Address: 1358 Irma Place.

So began and ended General Report 97-27127 headed with four words: *Missing Juvenile Female Report*.

REMEMBRANCE DAY

On Monday morning, the young girls of Shoreline met in the foyer.

"What happened under the bridge on Friday night?" Brandy asked Willow.

"What happened to that girl?" Ashley said.

"Be quiet," Willow said. "Don't mention anything." She stood up suddenly, fixing the girls with a look, a little fierce, but mostly worried, and she walked away quickly as if pursued.

"Let's ask Syreeta," Ashley suggested.

"She wasn't even there that night," Brandy said.

"She wasn't with Warren?"

"No. She went home early."

"But she's always with Warren. Did they have a fight?"

"She had cramps or something."

Out in the smoke pit, with only a minute before the bell rang, Brandy and Ashley sat on the low gray wall. Boys on bicycles swerved over the long green soccer field and attempted tricks. The boys rose with their front wheel lifting off the wet grass; they reversed direction with a sudden and seemingly precarious contortion. Kiara looked to the clouds to see if they'd yet begun to float or fade. It seemed like they'd spent the month in fog. Two crows rose up in the sky, and maybe they were from the bird sanctuary, Kiara thought. She didn't understand why the crows always flew together, in pairs—these quartets of dark, beating wings. Poppies from Remembrance Day lay in the crevice of the concrete; some of the flowers were now burned and ashen. *We are the dead,* Brandy and Ashley had recited solemnly on the veterans' holiday. *Short days ago, we lived, felt dawn, saw sunset glow, loved and were loved.*

A boy sat alone in the smoke pit. He was often alone, though he smoked and wore a Nike sweatshirt and wore his hat just like Erik Cash. He was very small, with the face of an unfortunate urchin, and his body was far too delicate.

This boy, Terry, wished he was taller and meaner and could be adored by girls like Ashley and Brandy. They were so sweet, so cute, so pretty, so hot. Ashley's skin must feel like cotton. Terry talked to her once. She was reading a book in homeroom, and he went right up to her, yanking on his baggy pants, and he told her his favorite book was *Fingerprints* by R. L. Stine.

"Have you read that?" he asked her. "That is some scary shit!"

Often, when in his bedroom, watching *The Simpsons,* his favorite show, Terry would think that he looked like Bart Simpson, with his spiky hair and thin arms. He would be in his bedroom that night, alone, watching a movie on his "entertainment center" and he would think about what happened under the bridge because everybody was talking about it, and how everybody was saying to keep it secret, and so as far as he knew, nobody had said anything to a teacher. Everyone was saying keep it quiet. Later, Terry would recall that of the night under the bridge, he knew, but did not tell, because everyone was saying, "Just keep it on the down low."

THE RUSSIAN SISTERS

Nadja arrived at Seven Oaks on Tuesday, November 15. Nadja, whose family life was often described as "unfortunate," was nonetheless possessed of a certain nobility. Social workers who met Nadja were struck by the young girl, for she seemed unlike their other charges. Her family life may have been horrible, but Nadja was neither wounded nor fragile, and she worried more for the fate of her little sister, Anya, than for her own predicament, which was, more or less, orphaned. Anya and Nadja both had long, black hair and high foreheads and sharp noses and green eyes. Nadja had grown four inches in the past year, and she'd found herself towering over her little sister. She wore clothes from the Salvation Army. Flat black shoes and plaid shirts and men's cardigans. Sometimes she wore an old navy blue pleated skirt she'd found at the St. Vincent de Paul. She thought it must have been part of a rich girl's private school uniform. Nadja's last name was Barusha, and sometimes people told her it sounded like a car. "A *fast* car," Anya would say. Sometimes Nadja flipped off cops for no reason at all. She didn't like cops, and she didn't trust anybody. Her new roommate was Josephine.

This girl is full of herself, Nadja thought, seeing the

photos on the wall, the photos of Josephine. The fashion magazines, the photos of models taped to the mirror. Nivea cream and Chanel perfume and a Guess handbag were all dumped on the empty bed, her bed, so Nadja picked up the clutter and chucked it on the floor. She wanted to sleep. She'd had a rough day, getting "assessed" by these people at Seven Oaks. She hated talking about herself.

She wanted to call Anya and tell her she was okay now, in this place called Seven Oaks, but Anya would be asleep in her new foster home. Anya's new family were retired shopowners who lived in the tiny suburb of Oak Bay. "I've got a skylight here!" Anya exclaimed. Nadja missed Anya terribly.

She climbed into bed. Several hours later, Josephine arrived and turned on the light, and Nadja introduced herself. Josephine stared boldly at Nadja: another assessment of sorts. She observed the green eyes of Nadja, her long neck, her slightly crooked nose. Nadja said very little and then turned away, lying on her side, looking out at the trees, wishing to forget the things she remembered sometimes when she slept.

"Have you ever heard of me? I'm Josephine Bell."

"Yeah, sure," Nadja said, though she had never heard of Josephine.

"I'll tell you something, but you can't tell anyone," Josephine said suddenly.

"Yeah, I won't."

Who is this girl? Nadja wondered. I've just met her and she starts telling me all this.

"I hate Reena. I *hate* her. She lied to me all the time.

She made up all these stories. I got pissed off. She hated me because I'm so beautiful."

Nadja turned toward Josephine and saw only the pale curve of the girl's cheek. Their room was very dark, and the light was of the moon through the forests. Was Josephine so beautiful, she wondered, and she listened some more.

"We beat her up, and then this friend of mine," Josephine continued, "she called me in the morning, and she said, 'Reena's dead.' And I was like, 'How is she dead?' And my friend said, 'We continued it and we threw her in the water and blood was coming out of her mouth.' My friend told me that she drowned Reena and Reena tried to get out of the water."

Nadja turned away from Josephine, turned so her body lay closer to the forests and the moon. Nonetheless, Josephine went on with her story, indiscreetly and carelessly. She did not even know Nadja and must have assumed the girl was like the others in View Royal, who had listened to her story and been both skeptical and unconcerned. Nadja, in her worn white T-shirt, with her slightly slanting green eyes and rare Russian surname, was in fact very much unlike the others in View Royal, and, thus, Josephine would have been wiser to not boast so callously.

THE FEROCIOUS FELINE

Josephine and Kelly asked Principal Olsen if the school had a newspaper.

"Well, we usually do. What do you need a newspaper for?" Principal Olsen replied.

"One of our friends is missing, and we want to see if there's anything in the paper about it," Josephine said, breezily.

"Yeah, we want to check it out," Kelly said, chewing on a strand of hair.

"She was with us on Friday night at the Mac's," Josephine volunteered.

Kelly nodded, her eyes never leaving Josephine's face.

"Well, that's just terrible that she's missing," Mrs. Olsen said. "What do you think could have happened to her?"

"She runs away all the time," Josephine suggested. "Maybe she tried to kill herself."

"I saw her walk up the highway," Kelly interjected. "So she probably got picked up by a bunch of guys. That's what guys like to do. They probably took her away with them and that's why she's not around."

"Well, I think she jumped off the bridge into the Gorge!" Josephine announced, excitedly.

"I really hope your friend is found," Mrs. Olsen said,

before reminding Josephine that she should really demonstrate her commitment to education by attending class that afternoon.

Mrs. Olsen would later write, "As a principal and former counselor, I have both training and many years of experience in observing both verbal and nonverbal communication. I was left with the clear impression that both Josephine and Kelly were mixing together fact and fiction." Moreover, she found that "neither girl expressed any emotion or concern about the missing girl. There was a distinct lack of effect." The whole conversation with her two students, Principal Olsen notified police, was "very disconcerting."

• • •

Kelly and Josephine perused the *Times-Colonist* for news of a missing girl. ("I think that was the first newspaper I ever bought," Josephine said later. "I usually just buy magazines.")

Their hearts may have skipped when they saw the headline of the newspaper dated November 16: TEENAGE MURDER REMAINS UNSOLVED. But the article reported on the case of two Oak Bay teenagers who had gone to Seattle for the weekend and been discovered shot and killed in a town in the middle of Washington. The killers had never been caught; the killers committed their murder ten years ago.

As for local news, the weather forecaster predicted for Wednesday, showers; for Thursday, showers; for Friday, heavy mist. Under the drawings of clouds and raindrops, a line of text read, "Rain, rain, go away, but it won't."

Masked bandits had smashed into a home and made off with two thousand dollars. Gingerbread house recipes were on page C5. Councillors refused to okay a high-rise.

As for crime and attacks, the only news concerned a woman who had been badly bruised by a "ferocious feline." The unfortunate woman had been taking her silky terrier, Rufus, for a walk when a cat in an alley lunged at her. "I've never seen anything like it," the woman, now with one hundred and twenty-nine bites, explained. "It was behind a Volkswagen and it took a six-foot leap out at me, with God as my witness."

Kelly and Josephine might have come across the pan of *Mame,* put on by the Victoria Operatic Society. The play about a high-spirited woman living in New York in the 1920s was "marred by melodramatic acting," and an actress who "gives the part her all, but can't yet carry the brash self-assurance the role demands."

The girls expected the headlines: BODY FOUND IN GORGE, or even, MISSING GIRL, 14. But the absence of such news of Reena confused them as the absence of her body in the black waters would soon confuse the men of the Dive Unit.

"So where's Reena?" Josephine asked, reaching for the comics and the classified ads.

"I don't know," she'd later say was Kelly's sardonic reply. "She's probably floating around somewhere."

MRS. SMITH OFFERS ADVICE

With barrettes in her brown hair and the sleeves of her sweatshirt pulled down over her hands, Kelly sat before her guidance counselor.

Mrs. Smith looked at the notes from Kelly's teachers:

Kelly challenges me constantly.
She is angry.
Confrontational.

"Kelly," Mrs. Smith said, gently, "what are these issues with your teachers about?"

"I'm a slow learner," Kelly said. "I need to learn at my own pace. And teachers make me keep up. And they make me do the work. And I get angry. And I explode."

Mrs. Smith nodded. Mrs. Smith was a soft and comfortable woman who wore very large glasses, and her hair was gray, and though she was beloved by many students at Shoreline, she had, on this Tuesday morning, heard not a word about the missing girl, the beaten girl, the drowned girl.

Mrs. Smith was meeting Kelly to discuss the referral process, which was a polite term for removal. Later, Kelly's parents said it was Kelly who wished to leave Shoreline because she didn't like all the bad kids, but

Mrs. Smith's notes from the counseling session of Tuesday, November 18, state that Kelly was being referred to another school due to her confrontational manner and the fact that she was constantly "disrespectful," "disobedient," and "disruptive."

Mrs. Smith needed to prepare a form for Kelly's transfer to the new school, and, as required, she asked Kelly if she had a probation officer.

"No," the girl responded, "but I might."

"Well, what's this about, Kelly?"

"People think I beat up somebody."

"Why do people think that?"

"Well, they think I was with a group of people who beat this girl up at the back of the Tillicum Mall. I wasn't anywhere near it."

"So you don't need to worry then."

"Yeah, but the girl who got beat up, her parents are phoning around and they say they heard a rumor that *I* beat her up and that *I'd* thrown her body into the Gorge."

"Well, boy!" Mrs. Smith replied.

"But I didn't do that, Mrs. Smith."

"How would her parents know about you in the first place?"

"I don't know," Kelly said, and she began to spin around in the chair.

Mrs. Smith looked at the girl spinning about. She observed her to be "fidgety" yet "calm and collected." Mrs. Smith told Kelly the girl's parents were probably very concerned about their missing daughter and probably called people they thought might know something about her whereabouts. Kelly stopped spinning in the chair then, and Mrs. Smith returned to the business of their meeting.

"Kelly," she said, gently, hopefully, warmly. "I'd like you to see a counselor at S. J. Willis."

"Why?" Kelly asked.

"Well, Kelly, you've always refused counseling, but Kelly, there are some issues you need to explore. There are some issues in terms of how you can work at not exploding in class and being angry and confrontational. Kelly, something needs to happen. We need to make sure—I need to make sure that when you go out the door here, you're going to get some help, because my feeling is that nothing's changed, Kelly. You're still that angry little kid you were in grade 8."

"Yeah, I know," Kelly said to Mrs. Smith. "I know I have this anger, Mrs. Smith. I know it." Gazing at her feet, she spun in the chair slightly, a half-turn. "I like to punch people."

"I know you do," Mrs. Smith said. "Your suspension record clearly shows that."

"Punching bags just don't do it for me. They just don't cut it."

"No, Kelly, punching bags don't seem to work for you."

"Yeah, I like to hit people. I like to punch them." At this, she began to make a smacking sound, punching her own palm, demonstrating the punching that she liked to do.

"You need to address that. Otherwise you're going to carry this around to your old age. And things are not going to get better for you. It's time, Kelly. You're making a fresh start at another school. It's time to make a fresh start in your personal life too. You know, I would really like for you to make an appointment with a counselor at S. J. Willis. I'd really like for you to take that next step and have a counselor approach you the minute you get in the door."

"Okay," Kelly said.

"Will you promise me that you will see a counselor the minute you get in the door?"

"Yes," Kelly promised.

"Good. That's a good thing."

And later in her file, Mrs. Smith, who believed in the teachings of Jesus Christ and Oprah Winfrey, would write: "Kelly is well aware of her anger. We discussed it quite openly."

STICK WITH DA CREW

Laila lifted the straw to her lips; she sipped on the Coke, and then removing the straw and brushing back her long hair with her fingers, each adorned with a different golden ring, she whispered to her friend. "Teha, if I tell you something, you can't say anything. I trust you."

"I promise you," Teha said. "I won't say anything."

"Well, last Friday, something really bad happened."

"What?"

"Okay. Before I tell you, do you know a girl named Reena? She used to go to Colquitz. She's in grade 9. She's East Indian."

"I've seen her walking in the halls a few times, but I don't know her that well."

Laila gazed around the food court. The girls were sitting near the A&W, where they often went after school. Next to the A&W, there was New York Fries, and next to New York Fries, there was Wok About. On the wall, there was a poster of the ridiculous bear, almost obese, dressed in his orange sweater, with the A&W logo, and he grinned.

"Well, anyway," Laila said, still whispering and leaning slightly forward now, after turning around and making sure the other girls eating french fries were farther away. She said, "Well, anyway, we were out with her on

Friday night down by the Gorge, near Shoreline, and she was talking some shit, saying she was a Crip and all this other stuff. So we all started walking down to the water to smoke up, and the next thing I know there's everyone beating the fuck out of her. There was like five people on her, kicking her ass. She had blood all over her face, and she wasn't moving, so I started freaking out, and saying, 'If anyone fucking touches her one more time, they are getting a shot to the head!' Because she wasn't moving! We were all so scared, so we jet. Me and my friend went back the next day to see if she was all right or was lying there because we didn't know what happened to her, and when we went back, her clothes were lying all over the beach. I think she got raped. I'm so scared, though, because two days ago, her mom called me and asked me if I knew where Reena was, and I said no. Reena's mom said she hadn't come home for five days."

Laila looked solemn, and for a moment she looked scared.

"I think she's dead, Teha. I don't know what to do or what to think, but fuck, imagine if she's dead! That's so fucked up! If you know anyone talking about it at school, tell them it's not true. I just know any day she's gonna show up."

"Oh my God, Laila. That's fucked up. Who started beating her up in the first place?"

"I don't know. I was smoking a j and I turned around and people were beating the fuck out of her."

"That's fucked up. How could somebody do that to someone?"

"Fuck! I tried to stop it!"

Laila tossed her french fries and Coke into the garbage. She braced herself as if waiting for Teha's reprimand.

Teha licked the last of her root beer off the plastic lid.

"You better hope to God she's all right, 'cause if not, you are going down with everyone else," she warned Laila.

"I know. If one of us goes down, we all go down. We stick with da crew, no matter what."

"I know what you mean," Teha said, because she had heard the expression somewhere before and it sounded familiar, like a line from a dream or a song or a movie. *If one of us goes down, we all go down. We stick with da crew no matter what.*

AFTER SCHOOL

Syreeta was surprised to see Warren in the smoke pit, talking with Kelly and Josephine. Why is Warren spending so much time with Kelly suddenly, she wondered, for Kelly was not his type at all, and he had never been friendly with her in the past. Now he was getting in fights to defend her, and now he was standing there, beside her, and for a second, Syreeta considered walking away. As he saw her approaching, Warren turned to Kelly, who was speaking, and he said to her, "Shhh!"

Kelly smiled then at Syreeta, in a manner that was neither friendly nor apologetic, only rather insinuating and amused.

"There's nothing you can say to Warren that you can't say to me," Syreeta said.

"Oh, I think there is," Kelly retorted, with a mocking and knowing grin.

"Why are you keeping stuff from me?" Syreeta asked Warren, but before he could answer, she turned suddenly and raised her voice and said to him, "Keep on talking. I'm leaving."

"We're done talking," Warren said, and he went to take her arm, but she had already turned her back to him and made her choice to leave the school, as she had left the school on the night of the Russian satellite. The pain wasn't back in her stomach. Rather, she was flushed with a feeling in between shame and anger. Warren ran after Syreeta as she turned and walked away from the smoke pit and onto the field where the grass seemed tinged with gray, and soon it would be December and there would be no snow on their island, only the sad and constant fog, like a cloud fell from the sky and landed on the grass and robbed the color from the ground.

Syreeta had a particular ability to be both languorous and defiant, and sometimes even the way her hair fell over her full lips could seem like a reprimand.

Kelly wasn't Warren's type at all. She just wasn't. Her mother might have told her a lady doesn't worry and a lady doesn't bother with jealousy. Still, it was rude of him to whisper to Josephine and Kelly, and then let them know that she was not to hear, that she was to be left out. Ever since she'd left Shoreline that evening of the Russian satellite, with the strange and fierce pain under her heart, she'd sensed something had occurred in the darkness of the night. Could Warren have betrayed her? Had he kissed Kelly? It seemed impossible to imagine. But then why had he kicked a girl in the head? The blood on his pants . . . why would he kick a girl he did not know and had no reason to harm? It all made no sense to her. Warren, as she would later say, "was the gentlest guy I ever knew."

Now he was running behind her, yelling her name, and she felt both stiff and very cold, and yet unsure as well, and then he caught up with her, and he was beside her saying he was sorry, and he was holding her hand.

Though she held his hand, she stayed silent, to punish him, and she did not speak to him or ask him why he was sharing secrets with a girl like Kelly. Walking in silence, they passed some boys with baggy pants and gold chains who were younger than Warren, but dressed a little like him, with baseball caps backward and the revealed waistband of their Calvin Klein underwear. Warren gave the boys this look, as if he was a leader protecting his territory.

"Oh, you're real cool, aren't you?" Syreeta said.

"I don't like grubby kids like that," he explained. She rolled her eyes, and her silent disdain did not cease when they walked past the mallards on the long driveway, and past her friend Alicia who was riding a bicycle that seemed red and silvery. Alicia waved back to Syreeta, and the geese scattered away from the wheels and ran down to the reeds.

All the houses were the same in the complex, and Chris Fox's house was the same, and inside there was a black leather couch and a TV. *This house is a house,* Syreeta thought to herself. *It is not a home.* Grace Fox was always at work. Syreeta wondered why Grace was kicking Warren out. It wasn't like her boyfriend would be sleeping in Chris's bedroom. Warren could have still stayed there. Maybe she'd change her mind. Maybe Dimitri's parents would let Warren stay there, though this seemed unlikely because Marissa said that Dimitri's dad was an old "military guy" and super-strict and didn't even like Dimitri hanging out with kids from View Royal.

She walked away from Warren and called her mother. "Can Warren come for dinner?" she said, because even though she was angry at Warren, she knew she would forgive him, and besides, he hadn't really done anything wrong, and she did not want him to be alone in this house without a meal for dinner.

In Warren's temporary and soon to be no more bedroom, she lay on his bed while he went into the closet to change out of his gym clothes. Spice 1 was singing, the song violent and catchy, and the words had a thudding and rising rhythm, and the rap song was the only sound, for she was still not speaking. After a few moments, Warren asked her if she really wanted to know what he was talking about with Kelly and Josephine.

"If you don't want to tell me, I don't want to know," she said.

"I'm asking you," he said, and he left the closet and walked closer to her.

"It doesn't matter to me," she said.

The chorus of the song had not yet begun when Warren got down on his knees beside Syreeta. She thought he seemed as if he was about to pray.

The cross was on his neck, but he did not touch the cross. Rather, he took her hands and held on to them, and their hands were clasped and intertwined. He closed his eyes, and he whispered even though Grace Fox was not home. He said, "It's not true what I told you about the Native guy."

"You don't need to tell me," she said, but he did.

"Haven't you wondered why that Reena girl hasn't been around?" he said.

"Well, she got beat up, so she probably doesn't want to be around," Syreeta replied.

"No, I mean, hasn't been around anywhere."

"I didn't know she hasn't been around anywhere," Syreeta said.

Then he was holding her hands even tighter and whispering even softer. She listened to the lyrics of the rap song. *187 me say the murder the murder he wrote.*

The song soon ended, with the rap star saying something about how he was "a soldier" with a "song out of the streets" and Syreeta rose off the bed. Warren's eyes seemed very large to her then, impossibly large, and he asked her not to tell anybody, please. She let her dark hair cover her eye, the eye from which she could not see. She told herself he was just trying to act tough, and he was telling stories, like Spice 1, just being the way boys wanted to be.

Warren turned off the stereo and left a note for Grace, telling her he would be at Syreeta's for dinner. The geese and pheasants must have been in the reeds, for they were not on the concrete. Syreeta saw Alicia's new bike locked to a long and thin tree, with orange leaves fallen on the leather seat. The sign near her home still said Daffodil Point. Everything was still the same. She still walked through her door, and she and Warren took off their shoes so they wouldn't get mud on her mother's clean floor. The Chagall print was still by the door, the pale pink man with the violin, floating into the pastel sky. Her mother was wearing her navy Pacific Coast Savings sweatshirt, and her dark hair was shining and the three of them watched *Friends* and ate lasagna and talked about the article in the paper that said the thing falling through the sky was really a Russian satellite.

YOUR YOUNG OAKS

In the posh, traditional neighborhood, home to lawyers, heiresses, and passionate gardeners, the arborist, Mr. Christopher Hyde-Lay, spoke to the Victoria Horticultural Society about his favorite tree—the **Garry oak**. He would be listened to respectfully because of his passionate delivery and perhaps because his name let listeners know that he shared their British ancestry.

Mr. Hyde-Lay began his lectures on the Garry oak with a modest statement: "The Garry oak is one of the most distinctive and certainly one of the stateliest trees growing in the Oak Bay landscape. We're really fortunate. It's such a rare and beautiful tree, and it adds so much character to the community.

"The Garry oak grows to massive proportions in the deep, rich, loamy soils found in many parts of Oak Bay. It can grow as tall as seventy feet. But, as you know, it's always under urban pressure." He paused and his listeners nodded, sharing his fear of construction on their beloved gardens.

"Now, I thought I would tell you a little about growing your own Garry oak. The first thing I would say to you is be careful. Be careful where you plant your acorn because the tree will be enormous, and it could live for four generations. The best time to collect acorns for planting is October and November. There are, of course, a few predators that enjoy consuming the Garry oak acorns—the filbert weevil and the filbert worm find the acorns particularly delicious."

After the laughter from the elderly crowd, Mr. Hyde-Lay discussed the merits of a bathtub test for the young acorn, and the types of garden soil to be chosen, and the best way to plant the tiny acorn in the dark and ready ground.

He then warned of the dangers of transience and darkness.

"Garry oak trees develop with a deep tap root and can be very difficult to transplant if left in temporary locations for too long, so keep this in mind if you plan to move your young oaks. The deep tap root gives the young Garry oak a very good degree of tolerance for time without water, but when choosing a planting site, it should be noted that the Garry oak seedlings will begin to decline if their light requirements are not met."

Mr. Hyde-Lay then reached for his woven basket, and he moved to the tables covered in floral cloths. He dispensed acorns, perfect acorns, without bruise or flaw, and the members of the Horticultural Society seemed grateful for the unexpected gift.

"In closing, remember that once your young oak begins to grow, it may be necessary to protect them from browsing animals. Fend off those lawnmowers and weed-eaters too. As a rule of thumb, to guarantee the survival rate of your native oaks, allow the most natural conditions to prevail."

• • •

"Josephine gives me this little piece of paper," Nadja told her little sister, "and she's like, 'You want proof? Well, this is your proof. That's Reena's mother's number. Call it up. Ask her if Reena is home.' So I called, and I had to lie. I had to pretend I knew Reena. I asked if she was there, and her mom said, 'No, I haven't seen her since Friday.' She just sounded so sad, Anya, and she said she was really worried. I could tell she was."

"Oh my God," Anya said. "We're going to the cops right now."

Nadja lit a cigarette, and she looked at the trees.

"We're walking there right now," Anya said, with the dramatic surety of a thirteen-year-old girl. "I know where it is. It's right near here, and that sucks that the cops are right near me, but that's the way it is. Come on. Let's go. There's one cop there who's a nice guy."

Nadja nodded, and the two girls began to walk away from Anya's foster home. The drivers in their Jaguars and Mercedes may not have recognized the two sisters, for they were strangers in the cloistered neighborhood, and Anya had been living with the benevolent strangers for only a few weeks now. Oak Bay was many miles from View Royal, and the two girls did not need to worry about being spotted by Josephine or her minions, and yet before they reached the police station, they both hesitated.

The Russian sisters were not fond of cops, and both girls had lived in ways that Josephine and Dusty may have dreamed about in their fantasies of being tough and outlaw. The two sisters were, as their many probation officers and social workers could attest, "street smart," and yet this did not mean that they were lacking either bravery or morality.

The girls were so close to the station. The station was on Hampshire Road, and the sisters were now on St. Ann's. A yellow traffic sign emblazoned with a black duck normally might have amused them—only in Oak Bay would there be a "brake for ducks" sign—but today their mood was grave. Thin wisps of cloud drifted over the evergreens.

The girls hesitated.

Dusty had threatened to "fuck up" anyone who told on her, and yet this was not the reason they stopped and remained near the willow tree.

Nadja reached in her black leather purse for a cigarette. "Let's have a smoke," she said, "and then we can decide."

• • •

Suman called the Saanich police station once more. "I was so frustrated," she recalls. "I'd phoned there a few times since the Saturday. I told the man on the phone that Reena was with Dusty and Josephine. The police just said, 'Hey, kids go missing.' They just treated her disappearance like it was one more kid who'd gone AWOL. I told myself, maybe she's partying, but I still had this horrible feeling because Reena *would* phone."

Suman took it upon herself to call Seven Oaks, and she spoke to both Dusty and Josephine. "Have you seen Reena? I know she went to meet you on Friday night."

"I saw her at Wal-Mart," Dusty said, "but I left and she didn't come with me."

"Well, let me talk to Josephine," Suman said, wearily.

"Reena didn't come home last night, Josephine. I know you said you haven't seen her since Friday, but I'm worried about her so can you please tell me if you've heard from her?" Suman tried to steady her voice as she spoke to the blonde girl. She'd met the girl once on Halloween. Josephine had come to her house on this night and Suman had observed the girl as a dark force. "She is blonde, but she's dark," Suman explained to her husband. The darkness, she felt, was in Josephine's spirit, in her heart, in her eyes.

Now, Josephine seemed indifferent to her concern over her missing daughter.

"Harsh," she said, brusquely. "I'll let you know if I hear from her."

Now, as the Russian sisters hesitated by the Oak Bay police station, Suman went into her daughter's room and sat on the bed by her daughter's teddy bears. She held a cup of tea with cumin and fennel and yet she could not warm herself or settle the unease. "I just knew she was dead," Suman recalls, "but I didn't want to say it out loud. I knew she was lying somewhere dead, but I thought she must have been in an accident. I never thought she was murdered. Murder never entered my mind."

• • •

Nadja lit the cigarette and said to Anya, "I don't know if we should do this."

Anya nodded. Though she was only thirteen, she was quite wise, and neither reckless nor naive. She thought for a while, and then she announced, with great conviction: "I think we *have to* do this."

"What if it's not true?" Nadja asked, and she leaned against the tree, her shining hair much more vivid than the dull and aged bark.

"It's true," Anya said. "It's true."

"But you don't know that," Nadja argued. "Josephine could be talking bullshit. You know how people bullshit me all the time. I could say to you, 'My mother's dead. My boyfriend's dead. I killed them.' It doesn't mean it's true."

"But you talked to Reena's mother, right? And you said she sounded so sad." Season's Greetings, a sign said on the grand old fire hall. Nadja looked, too, at the firemen's decorations—the merry tinsel bells. "Christmas is coming up," Anya continued, "and Reena's mom won't see her daughter. I can't let this go by me. I'm sorry." Anya shook her head and looked at her big sister, fiercely, pleadingly. "I can't. . . ."

"Okay," Nadja said, and she brushed the dust of bark from her hair, and stubbed out her cigarette. The two sisters walked to the blue door of the police station. Together, the two sisters walked inside.

Not much had changed at the Oak Bay Police Department since 1906. In those days, the only crime in the village occurred during the carnival or the horse races, when pickpockets (out-of-towners) roused constables to search the streets. Otherwise, the village was peaceful and sirens seemed not to exist.

On the day the sisters appeared, a dispatcher was on

the phone. "You've got a cat stuck in your car?" she said to the elderly gentleman. "Okay, sir, just calm down. . . ."

Nadja sat on the leather bench, impressed by the fact that there were *carpets* here. She had never seen carpets in a cop station before. Brochures on the wall behind her advertised missing children, like a young boy who had been missing for as long as Nadja could remember, a boy named Michael Dunahee. Photos of children aged by computer technology were pinned on the wall. FIND THIS CHILD, the sign said, MISSING SINCE 1989. Nadja looked away toward the pamphlets on drug addiction, VICTIM'S RIGHTS. CELEBRATE CULTURAL DIVERSITY, another pamphlet said, above the photo of a white-haired woman in a crimson sari. "We have much to gain from each other," the pamphlet said. "Celebrate cultural diversity. It's who you are."

Anya was up by the glass window of the front desk, yelling at the lady. Anya often yelled for no real reason other than she liked to be heard.

She said she wanted to speak to Don Gardner. "What's it regarding?" the lady asked.

"It's confidential," Anya replied.

Sergeant Don Gardner could tell you, proudly, "Oak Bay has one of the lowest crime rates in the entire province." Why is that? "There's no real slums. It's affluent. It's a high-end community, so most of the crime we're dealing with is rowdy teenagers."

In fact, the most recent homicide in Oak Bay occurred in 1971, meaning there had not been a murder in the village for twenty-six years. Sergeant Gardner could hazily recall a few details of this one murder on his watch—a gay lover, a gay couple, some kind of dispute.

So, here were these two girls before him now. He took them into an interview room. He recognized Anya right away. She was hard to forget for she had the charisma, the energy, of a volatile actress. Once, a friend of his had been driving his car down the sedate Hampshire Road when he'd caught sight of Anya washing her foster father's car. Even the way she held the hose, the rather joyous, slightly erratic manner in which she pranced about, created an unusual spectacle on the street of the elderly.

"I'd dealt with Anya before and I guess she thought she could trust me or I treated her fairly," Don Gardner recalls.

Rapidly, Anya told him that a girl named Josephine from another foster home, not her foster home, but another one where Nadja lived, this girl, Josephine, she said she went with this girl Reena Virk to the Gorge Bridge, and she went up to Reena, and she put her cigarette out on her forehead, and then they all started to beat her up and jump on her, and they broke her arms and her jaw and her nose, and then she was rolled into the water."

"Rolled into the water?"

"They killed her," Nadja said, suddenly, and with great contempt. "They killed her in the Gorge!"

"When did this happen?"

"Josephine said it happened on Friday night about 10:00."

Don Gardner looked at his notes, written in short-hand. Seven Oaks. Cigarette. All beat her up. Jaw. Nose. Broken. Water . . . Gorge. . . .

Don Gardner, knowing of Anya's theatrical ways, thought silently, Maybe a lot of this is embellished. But the sisters seemed so genuinely upset, that he wrote up a report and drove himself over to the Saanich police department, the station nearest to the Gorge.

• • •

Murders were more common at the Saanich police station, though still rare—two or three homicides a year, most usually occurring, the police will tell you, "when someone's high or in a bad marriage." Murders by young girls were rarer still, and thus there was some cynicism about the story of the Barusha sisters. "It sounded pretty farfetched," a Saanich investigator said.

Investigators looked into the records for last Friday evening. Friday 14, the night of the Russian satellite. A janitor called to report a broken window at Shoreline School around 9:25. Sergeants Hodginson and Basanti went to the school at 9:45 and broke up the crowd of youths. Later that evening, the dispatcher on duty received several calls of concern about the "thing in the sky." People were worried a fire in the distance might be spreading their way; people believed there might have been a plane erupting in the sky. But there were no reports of this fight, so vicious and savage. Certainly no one in the homes, well lit and respectable, with water-front views called in to report seeing a fight or a beating, down by the Gorge.

Constable Green called up Shannon Lance, a detective in the Youth Unit and he asked her to take a look into this story reported by two sisters.

"It was a bizarre story, but you never know, sometimes the most bizarre thing can become reality."

Five minutes later, Scott Green's phone rang, and Shannon Lance told him she'd looked into the missing persons files. "Scott," she said, "Reena Virk *is* missing. I'm looking at the report right here. 97-27127. Her mother, Suman Virk, has called Missing Persons several times since Friday. It says on the report that on 11-14, Reena went to meet two friends, Josephine Bell and Dusty Noble, at the Wal-Mart. She phoned her young brother from the Mac's at Craigflower and Admirals and said she was on her way home. That was at 10:30. That was the last time her family heard from her."

"She never came home?"

"No. She said she was on her way, but she never arrived home."

"When Shannon Lance received the Missing Persons report, that's when we started to feel something untoward could have happened to her," Scott Green recalls. In this way, Reena's file was moved from Missing Persons, and labelled as: Possible Homicide.

THE STORY

Early on Thursday morning, around 8:30, Constable Shannon Lance of the Saanich Police Department drove up the long and steep road that led to the group home named Seven Oaks. She was unarmed and in plainclothes when she spoke to the supervisor of Seven Oaks. The supervisor was not surprised by the appearance of a police officer, for the girls in Seven Oaks were without families, and often they were without manners or spirituality, and thus often they were in some kind of trouble. They stole cars; they overdosed; they consorted with criminal types. The detective was brought into the home, and Dusty was introduced to Shannon Lance.

"Do you know why I'm here?" she said.

"Is it about Reena?" Dusty replied.

"As a matter of fact, it is about Reena."

"Well," Dusty said, earnestly and easily, "the last time I saw her was on Friday night. Josephine called her to see if she wanted to come to a party with us, and we all agreed to meet up at the Wal-Mart. But when we met her, she didn't want to go to the party with us after all. She said she would see us later. She left with some guys. Me and Josephine went to the party at Portage Park, but we never saw Reena there. We called her on Saturday, and her mom told us she was missing. That's what happened," Dusty said.

Constable Shannon Lance observed how soft Dusty's voice was and how easily she told of Reena's whereabouts. Dusty's voice did not seem to belong with her heavy body and her shiny black leather coat with a thick belt wrapped around the waist.

Dusty herself ran right up to Josephine's room soon after speaking to the detective.

"Oh my God, Josephine," she said, "the cops are here. They're downstairs. They want to talk to you."

"We're going to jail," Josephine said. "You know, Dusty, we might go to jail!"

"Jail's not so bad," Dusty said. "I've been there before. It's kind of fun." But she started to pace, and both girls, as Josephine would later recall, were "harsh freaked out."

Dusty said, "I told them we met Reena at the Wal-Mart, and she didn't want to party with us, and she left with some guys."

Josephine nodded and smiled approvingly at her sidekick. She lifted her lipstick but did not have time to apply the gloss, for a Seven Oaks worker knocked on the door and told her that her presence was required immediately in the office. "Right now, Josephine," she said. "Go downstairs."

"Do you know why I'm here?" Shannon Lance said to her.

"Is it anything about Reena?" Josephine asked, and then as Shannon Lance would later note, she "quickly rattled off similar information to Dusty."

"We went to the Wal-Mart and met Reena, and she said she didn't want to go to the party with us, and she left with some guys. Her mom told us she's missing, but we didn't see her after the Wal-Mart." Josephine smiled at the detective, and then said, arrogantly, slightly bemused, "Is that what you wanted to hear?"

"I could not corroborate or disprove the story," Shannon Lance later wrote in her report.

Another girl may have been frightened by the arrival of the detective, frightened that she would be punished for being a rat and a traitor, but Nadja was not. Nadja observed the arrival of a police car, and five minutes later, saw an unhandcuffed Dusty run outdoors, as if she "was flying out of the house."

Nadja walked outside, straight over to Dusty.

"Why are the cops here?" she demanded of Dusty.

"That thing about Reena," Dusty said, and her voice trembled, and she seemed near tears. "The cop is here to investigate that."

"Dusty, is this just a stupid story? I'm gonna kick your ass if you've been bullshitting me."

"It's true. It's true," Dusty said. "She's dead." She said it several times then, as one chants a pledge. "She's dead. She's dead. She's dead." And then she began to pace and smoke and cry, and she turned away so Nadja would not see her tears.

Nadja would later describe Dusty as being "off the walls."

"Holy shit," Dusty said. "I'm so scared." She lurched forward slightly and clasped her hands to her face.

"So why are you going around telling everybody if you didn't want to be ratted on?" Nadja asked her.

"Because I trust the people I told."

"Yeah, well, when it comes to something like murder, there's going to be somebody who can't keep it to themselves."

Dusty looked up at her then, and she was very wide-eyed and timid.

"This is really hard for me," she said. "I can't believe this all happened. I just punched her a few times. I didn't mean for this . . . I left—"

Suddenly she stopped and seemed to steady herself, and she rubbed the tears from her cheeks. Josephine was crossing the lane, wearing a certain look of triumph, and on her cheeks there was a rosy blush.

"Dusty," she said, "the cop totally believed my story!"

Dusty seemed to cheer up and she smiled at Josephine, turning away from Nadja. "The cop, she believed me too."

"What did you guys tell her?" Nadja asked.

"We said we saw Reena at the Wal-Mart and then she left with some guys and we went to Shoreline but she never showed up."

"Nice story," Nadja scoffed. "You think they're going to believe that?"

"Oh, she totally believed it," Josephine said. "She was saying, 'Okay, okay.'"

Josephine's wrists were unhandcuffed as well, without bruises, impossibly slim and white.

"Well, I've lied to cops before, and they said okay, and the next day, they arrested me," Nadja told her.

"Really?" Josephine asked.

"Yeah, cops lie," Nadja said, as if speaking to one who was very naive.

"I know they lie," Josephine said, and Dusty began to cry once more.

"They're going to wipe your mop," Nadja said, somewhat wistfully.

MEXICO

Josephine, as she often did, now sat in Kelly's bedroom, away from the drum kits and the bookshelf, by the mirror. "I could do my makeup for three hours," she would later recall. It was a kind of art, the art of her vanity. She would marvel at the curve of her lips and the blue of her eyes. Mascara, she could place it on her eyelashes without the slightest smudge.

"I can't believe the cops came to you," Kelly said. "How the hell did they get your name?"

"Well, they came to *my* house, so *I'm* the one in real trouble."

"Do you think Dusty ratted us out?"

"No way. Dusty's totally paranoid. She won't even talk on the phone because she thinks our phones are tapped. She always told me jail was fun, but now she's just crying, 'I don't want to go to jail! I don't want to go to jail!' Plus I talked to Laila, and she said she told Dusty to not say anything."

"Look," Josephine said suddenly, and with great enthusiasm, "if the heat comes down, we'll go to Mexico!"

Kelly, who was sitting on her bed surrounded by laundry and schoolbooks, smiled suddenly at the suggestion of escape.

"We can learn Spanish!" she said, and perhaps envisioned herself as suntanned and fluent in the warm climes of Tijuana. "Yeah," she said, "if the heat comes down, we'll go to Mexico."

"Dusty did say jail's not so bad," Josephine said. "She said it's actually kind of fun. It would be kind of cool to go to jail, and then when you got out, you could say to your friends, 'Hey, yeah, what's up, I just got out of jail.'" Josephine seemed to consider this idea, suddenly, and seriously. After all, what could prove more to her minions that she was truly hard core than having served some time in lockdown?

"I'll kill myself if I go to jail," Kelly said. "I'm going to Mexico." The idea had enthralled her, and so Josephine decided to indulge the fantasy, though later she would admit the girls were not so organized in their plan of escape. ("We didn't figure anything out. We didn't even think about getting fake passports.")

The girls said it several times, so it sounded like a song: *If the heat comes down, we'll go to Mexico.*

"I'm your best friend, Josephine," Kelly said. "I'll always be there for you."

"Kel," Josephine promised, "I'll do anything for you."

THE OTHER SIDE

When Nadja woke, she saw Josephine sitting before the mirror.

To Josephine, she said: "Why don't we go down to the Gorge, and you can show me what happened and where the body is."

"Sure," Josephine replied, bending forward to rub Nivea cream into her soft knees.

Nadja thought to herself, *If the cops can't figure out this shit, then me and Anya will.*

The two girls took a bus first to Oak Bay Junior High School to get Anya.

Anya, in her classroom, heard her sister yelling her name. Here comes Nadja! she thought, and she asked her teacher if she could go see her sister in the hall for a second.

"Jo's going to take us to the scene," Nadja told her, "and show us what happened. Get your stuff. Let's go."

In this way, Anya found herself asking for permission to be excused from class. Almost feverishly, she said, "Don't tell anybody, Mrs. Aitken, but me and my sister are trying to find out what happened with this murder down in View Royal."

"Well, I guess that's more important than school," Mrs. Aitken said.

"I think so," Anya replied, and she grabbed her cigarettes and schoolbooks and ran out to the field where Nadja and Josephine were laughing at the rugby players in their huddle, their stupid jock jerseys so full of sweat and dirt.

The girls rode on the bus, rode away from the green and floral streets of Oak Bay to the suburb just off a lonely highway. Nadja observed the location carefully. A Mac's store at the intersection behind a gas station, the Comfort Inn, a bridge with green handrails.

The girls went under the bridge. They entered the cavelike space. Nadja looked toward the dark water, saw the wooden beams that held up the bridge. Seagulls flew above, but there were no police officers in the dark waters looking for the body. None. Nobody at all. She cursed the cops silently and wondered, *Why did they not listen to me?*

Anya's acting skills on this day were extraordinary, and Nadja bit her lip to keep from smiling proudly.

"I can't believe you killed her," Anya said. "That is so cool!"

"This is the log," Josephine said, "where Reena sat, and she was sitting right here when I pushed my smoke into her face."

"Harsh!" Anya said. "I can't believe you did that! That is so cool!"

Encouraged, Josephine went into greater detail. "Her skull was crushed," she said. "We kicked her, and she was just lying right here, and we broke her teeth and kicked her in the stomach. She was screaming, so we knocked her out."

"I'm so proud of you!" Anya screamed. "You killed her! The bitch is dead!" She jumped up and acted impressed.

Nadja shivered suddenly, and the sky was so gray, and it had started to rain.

She moved closer to Josephine and said coolly, "Who were the other girls?"

"All Shoreline people, and Dusty," Josephine said.

Nadja covered her nose and felt queasy suddenly. There was such a terrible smell. "It just *reeked* under there," she would later recall. Still, she persevered.

"So," she said, walking toward the water's edge, where the grass gave way to the rough sand, "you pushed her in here?"

"No," Josephine said, and she raised her hand and pointed across the bridge, toward the shore below the old white schoolhouse. "She was pushed in over there."

Nadja looked over to the land by the schoolhouse. The distance was a significant one, and surely Reena couldn't have been carried so far, for Josephine had said she was fat, and if Reena was beaten up so bad that her skull was crushed, surely she couldn't have walked on her own across the bridge.

"How the fuck did you get her over there?"

"I have no idea. I wasn't there for that part."

Anya now looked as well to the dark pool of water below the schoolhouse, and like her sister, she wondered how Reena could have made it to the other side of the bridge. "How in the world did she get over there? Did she fly or something?"

"I told you. I wasn't there for the second part."

"I'm trying to believe you here," Nadja said, impatiently, "but this is not making sense."

"Well, let's go over there. I'll show you."

The rain was falling still, and Nadja was wearing her short navy pleated skirt, and she did not want to go over there. It smelled so bad, the most terrible smell, and she was shivering. She began to walk away without saying a word, and the two girls followed.

She walked up the stairs where Reena too had walked and fallen and been dragged and walked again. Nadja turned back just to see the place once more, to inscribe the site into her memory. The water was very dark and murky, and the waves were slight but still rising. Nadja wished to see a man with a black wet suit and an oxygen tank, a man who was searching for a missing girl who may have been on the bottom, alone and wounded, but no man rose from the depths of the Gorge.

• • •

Anya spoke to Scott Green first, a polite and amiable young officer from a family of crimefighters—his father in the Victoria Police Department, his great-grandfather in the Sioux City Police Department, a relative of his mother's in the FBI. He was only thirty-three, and yet his hair was starting to recede at his temples. Anya stared at the hair on his forehead, and she thought it looked kind of funny, the way the front dipped down and then receded. "Your hair kind of looks like the McDonald's M," she told him.

"Thanks a lot," he said, but he laughed. "So you had Josephine take you to the scene. Can you tell me where it was?"

"It's by this bridge. We went under the bridge with her, and she showed us this log. That's where Reena was sitting. Josephine told us she went up to Reena and put a cigarette right out on her forehead, just *burned* a hole in her, and then everybody surrounded Reena and started beating up on her. They just beat the living crap out of her. Josephine told me she was screaming." Anya shook her head. She was talking to herself more than to the police officer now. "I'd like to see how Josephine would go through pain like that. Just imagine that you were that person getting beaten up and thrown in the water, with your arms broken. That is so. . . ." She paled then, and it seemed as if she'd been hurt herself, as if she was wounded too.

"Did she say who beat Reena up? Did she give you any names?"

"Well, there was Josephine and another girl who lives with Josephine. She's a big chick. I forget her name. She's got blackish hair. She thinks she's a Miss Tough Girl. Whatever. She thinks she can beat up anybody. Josephine told me Reena was screaming! So they knocked her out by kicking her in the head, and then they took her to the other side."

"The other side?"

"Yeah. I don't believe that part. How could they get her to the other side when she was unconscious? How could they bring her all the way over the bridge and then down to the other side? They would have to do that because there's no way Reena could have walked that far. We asked her, and she just said, 'I have no clue.'"

"But you do believe Reena's dead?" Scott Green asked, thinking, *This is one* bizarre *story.*

"Yeah, I do! She's been planning this for a while. She wanted to kill Reena because Reena lied about some guys, and because Reena was jealous of her beauty, or something. Her beauty? Come on! Give it up! Jealous of her beauty? She's kind of ugly. Sorry, anyway, she told me they killed her on Friday night around 11:00. I don't even get the point of killing someone. What's the point of doing that? What's the point of beating somebody up? Josephine is so proud of it. She goes around telling everybody. Well, someone could go right behind her back and just go to the police. I mean, that's what me and Nadja did."

Scott Green nodded, and the girl ("a typical teenager," he would later say) continued.

"And the other thing I don't get is: what was Reena thinking? Wouldn't she think, 'Hey, something's up. There's all these girls who don't like me and they want me to go under a bridge.'" Anya reached for a cigarette and lit the match on the zipper of her black boot. "I'd figure it out right there. I wouldn't even go under the bridge. You know why? Because I, like, watched this movie once, and this one girl brought this other girl to a dark place and beat the living crap out of her and killed her. But the girl, the killer, she left one of her earrings behind. She lost it, accidentally I guess, and the cops found it when they were investigating, and they traced it back to the girl, the killer. So when we were down there today, I was like, 'Josephine, did you leave any earrings? Did you leave anything they could find if they investigate?' She goes, 'Nope. I was being very smart. Took all my jewelry off. Went there, beat her up. I made sure I had no blood on me. I made sure that she had no blood of mine.'"

Sergeant Scott Green interrupted Anya then as soon as she reached down to put out her cigarette on the precinct floor.

"Anya, how would *you* suggest we solve this case?" he asked, and if there was a slight condescension, she was used to this in the voice of older men.

"I would suggest that me or Nadja talk to Josephine's friend on the phone and get her to admit it. You guys could record her on the phone talking about killing Reena. And if you guys had a tape recorder, I could record Josephine on the phone. You'd see how stupid she is. She is a really stupid girl. I could get her to admit everything. She would just tell me exactly what she did. She thinks no one will find out what she did. Well, *duh*. There's Reena's family. She thinks nobody will find the body. Well, come on . . . you guys should *investigate*, you know. Try and look for something, like blood, down at the place where it all happened."

"Sure."

"And do you know those people who go underwater to find a body? I think that should happen because she could be down at the bottom. And after everything is sorted out, I think Josephine should be arrested. She planned this, and it happened. And Reena's been missing since Friday, and when Nadja called her mother, she said she sounded so miserable and sad. Christmas is coming up. This is going to be the hardest thing for her parents. I think I have the right to tell you guys this. I do have the right."

"Of course you do."

"Just imagine the pain she was in, and Josephine's so proud of herself," Anya said, but she noticed the constable seemed like he wasn't listening to her anymore and perhaps was even smiling. She had offered to tape the killer, but he did not take her up on this suggestion.

She looked at the officer once more, before leaving the room.

"Your hair is really weird," she said, and she smiled at him while he walked her to the door.

Nadja was more forthright with Scott Green and she did not even notice the strange pattern of his hair. "I saw the cops yesterday at Seven Oaks, and I almost had a heart attack. I was like, 'Oh my God. What are they doing here?' I asked you guys specifically to keep this confidential."

"We will. We've only told the supervisor at Seven Oaks because we had to get permission to speak to Dusty and Josephine."

"Well, you can't trust people. I certainly don't. Anyway, Josephine took me to the bridge this morning, and she showed me the place where it happened. It's on the other side. They finished beating her up and threw her in the water. I don't know how they got her to the other side. I think she mentioned something about low tide, so maybe they dragged her over there if the tide was really low. I asked Josephine how she got her over there, but she said she wasn't there. All I know is Josephine set it up. She's planned this for a long time. She didn't do it, but she was the one who caused it. She did most of the beating, and Kelly killed her."

"Why did she want Reena dead?"

"She told me the first day we met. I was going to bed, and she just starts telling me. She said Reena lied to her all the time and made up stories, and Josephine got pissed off. She said Reena was jealous of her and hated her for her beauty. She told me she knew how she wanted it to go, in her mind. She wanted Reena killed. And then Kelly phoned her up on Saturday morning and said, 'She's dead.' Kelly drowned her in the water."

"And you believe her?"

"At first I thought she was bullshitting me, but now, I do sort of believe it. But it does bother me, the part about her getting to the other side. If Reena was heavy, how could they carry her? I find that weird. I don't get that part. But you guys said Reena is really missing, and she hasn't been found. Josephine gave me Reena's mom's number, and her mom said Reena hasn't been home since Friday and she's missing and she's worried. So just in case it's true, I thought I should tell you guys. Maybe it's a fluke. I don't know. Maybe those girls found out a girl named Reena is missing and they decided to make up this story. I just don't know if it's true, but I want to know if it's true! I haven't had much sleep since Josephine keeps bragging to me about this fucking murder shit. My sister thinks it's true. I just don't know, but if it is true, I guess I'm going to pack myself up and get out of that house. I'm not going to share a room with those two psychopaths."

"Yes, that could be hard on the sleep. Now, do—"

"Josephine's pretty stupid, you know. I keep asking her all these questions, and she's not even getting suspicious. Dusty's really worried though. She's miserable. Oh, I know something else!"

"Go ahead."

"She said they ditched Reena's shoes downtown in the garbage. And she said Reena's jacket is missing. They went back on Saturday, and they looked for Reena, and they looked for her clothes, and they couldn't find this Adidas jacket. She said there was blood on the jacket. Somehow, somewhere. And another thing, I'm scared for my little sister. I don't want her being taken back to school in a cop car. Can you get her a taxi?"

"Yes, we'll have a taxi take you back."

Nadja sighed. The thought of anything cruel or violent happening to Anya troubled her, and she suddenly wanted to leave the station. "That Mr. Officer, I spoke to before I met you, he was being a real shithead to me. Sometimes you cops are nice, but he was *really* mean to me."

"We'll make sure that the officer who takes you back is nice."

Nadja sighed once more. She did not ask for anything in return for her bravery, and no medal of honor was offered on this particular day. She thought again of the waters and the darkness. She raised her voice suddenly, and she stared at the detective so directly that he looked away.

"I told you this on Wednesday," she said. "I've been wondering why haven't you guys searched the water."

"Well, we need more help to find out if this did in fact happen."

She raised her voice even louder now. "I want to know for a fact if this happened or not!"

"So do we," he said, meekly, agreeably.

"I'm getting told this is true. I'm giving all this information to you. I don't even know if it is true. All I know is this girl Reena is missing." She screamed then, at the silent room, and the silent man. She screamed: "How many Reenas are there in this goddamn world?"

SOMETHING'S HAPPENED HERE

Two young girls have come forward and told us they've heard about a girl who was killed. It's our belief that it is a suspicious circumstance. We don't have a list of suspects, though it seems that they're all young girls living in the vicinity of View Royal. The girl, the alleged victim, is named Reena Virk. She has been missing for a week."

A week? Sergeant John Bond thought to himself. A week, and we're just talking about this now? John Bond, a charismatic detective with a shaved head and abundant energy, had been called in to attend the Joint Forces meeting. Bond was considered one of the best detectives in View Royal, for, as one admirer says, "He just gets people to confess everything. They feel like he's their big brother. He's the kind of guy you just want to bare your soul to."

"Maybe she's walking the stroll on Government Street," he said.

"No. There's no indication that she's been involved in the sex trade."

"Well, has she ever run away before?"

"Yes. She was at Kiwanis for a few days. But she's always been accounted for."

Okay. Every night for the past fourteen years, she's

accounted for, and now she's not accounted for—for seven days, John Bond thought to himself. Something's happened here. He glanced at the file on the table marked "Barusha: Suspicious Circumstances."

"Any boyfriend in the picture?" Sergeant Ross "Roscoe" Poulton asked. He was a healthy-looking man, with a neatly trimmed mustache and piercing blue eyes. Like Bond, he'd been a cop since the age of eighteen, and yet due to the peaceful nature of the island, both men had dealt with fewer than a dozen homicides.

"No boyfriend," Shannon Lance said, and she handed the two detectives the photo provided by the Virk family. It was Reena's last yearbook photo, and in it, her lips were almost black. The photo was not particularly flattering and yet anyone could see the clear hope in her closed, broad smile.

"There was possibly some type of encounter under the Craigflower Bridge," the detectives were told.

A list of names—in police lingo "the players"—was written on a blackboard. Josephine, Dusty, Kelly, Laila.

"Some of these girls are supposed to be from Shoreline School, Krista," an officer said to the young constable who worked in the Street Crime Unit in View Royal. "Do you know any of the girls who might be involved?"

Krista thought of the young girls she often encountered when she broke up parties on Shoreline field. The only Kelly she knew was Kelly Ellard, the daughter of her husband's good friend Lawrence Ellard. She'd known Kelly for years, even gone camping with her.

In a small town coincidence, Krista had been at Kelly's house last Saturday, the night after Reena Virk had gone missing, sitting in the kitchen, eating chili. Her husband and Kelly's father drank beer and talked about their slow pitch softball team.

She remembered now how Kelly had come downstairs, saying she was going out to "look for a missing girl." Seeing Krista, the cop, at the kitchen table, Kelly's face went white. "My husband said, 'What's Kelly's problem? She looks like she saw a ghost.'"

"A light bulb went on," Krista recalls of that moment in the Joint Forces meeting. "I thought to myself, 'This is going to get ugly.'"

"I knew Kelly better than any investigator on the file, and I thought, 'She's the type who could get away with this.' I wanted to walk away."

Out loud, she said, "The only Kelly I know is Kelly Ellard."

Another detective spoke up. "We got the records from Shoreline and Kelly Ellard is the only Kelly in the school."

"What do you think we should do?" the detectives asked Krista, for she seemed to be the one with the most knowledge of the teenage players.

"I have a kind of bond with this girl Maya. She's a good friend of Kelly's, and if Kelly was involved in something at Shoreline, chances are Maya would have been there."

"Why don't you talk to Kelly if you know her?" a detective asked.

"Kelly's the type who will just tell you to fuck off."

*

Back in his office sitting under the photographs of vintage planes, John Bond decided this: the Gorge should be searched by helicopter immediately. Even if it was a useless exercise, it, at the very least, would show the girl's parents there was an effort to find their daughter. Unfortunately, all the helicopters were in use. The APEC conference, a meeting of world leaders, was to be held in Vancouver, and the helicopters were required to protect the security of President Clinton and the prime ministers of Canada and Japan.

Because all the police helicopters were unavailable, he called his friend Glen Dychuk at 1:50 in the afternoon. Glen worked for the Coast Guard and told Sergeant Bond he could take him up in the Messerschmitt first thing in the morning.

Sergeant John Bond went under the bridge.

"I bumped into some guys from the Identification Unit. They were already looking for anything suspicious." The detectives from Ident would report:

"The area under the bridge consists mostly of dirt and gravel with infrequent vegetation. It was noted that there was a myriad of broken glass, cigarette butts, and pop bottle caps indicating frequent use of the area, likely by teenagers. No evidence supporting any untoward activity was obvious to the writer. There were no clear foot impressions observed in the soil. The route from the underside of the bridge going up the stairs to the east of the bridge was examined for any forensic evidence with negative results. The writer searched underneath the bridge on the north side of the waterway. This search was negative in looking for any evidence of a struggle."

Recanvass is the term they use. Return to the area of the suspicious circumstances, return to the area where the victim was last seen. The same time, the same place, the same day. "You might come across a paperboy or a milkman," Sergeant Bond explains. "You find people who have the same pattern of movement."

The detectives set out for Shoreline Junior Secondary.

Often he went undercover in these bars: the Carlton, the Tudor, the Esquimalt Inn. John Bond could grow a mustache, wear a leather jacket, but these were not the reasons he fit in. Quite simply, he just didn't seem like a cop. Once he bumped into a convict he'd gone undercover on, living in the same cell, getting the guy to talk about his prostitution ring. Bond had bumped into him in the courthouse just before he was set to testify. He was even wearing a tie, and still the convict had no idea. "What are you doing here?" he asked Bond. "You get busted again?"

But now he wasn't going into a prison or a biker bar. He was going into the world of the youth of View Royal. He was, he knew, likely to be out of place.

At 6:15, John Bond and Krista Hobday headed for the home of Maya Longet.

"Maya acts tough," Krista warned, "but she's never lied to me. She wants to be liked by other kids, but you can just see underneath it all she's a sweet person."

She asked Bond if he knew of Maya's past, and he nodded grimly. Maya's father had been brutally murdered ten years before, and six-year-old Maya had been in the house while her father was stomped on and knifed. A drifter named Bob Case and Maya's mother had been arrested but never convicted. Maya had been adopted by her father's sister, Belle Longet.

The two officers parked in Maya's driveway. "If anyone knows what's going on, it will be Maya Longet," Krista said as they walked toward the door.

At Maya's house, Kelly Ellard was in the kitchen. So were Willow and Eve, two other girls who'd been under the bridge. The girls were preparing for a Friday night dinner, and after dinner they planned to go down to Shoreline, just like they always did, just like everything was the same and ordinary.

To Maya's aunt, John Bond said: "Belle, there's some talk about a teenage girl missing. We're just trying to get it all together, and we think Maya might know something about it. Can we take her to the station and ask her some questions?"

"Sure," she said, and she wiped her damp hands on her denim apron. "Of course you can. That's no problem at all."

"Who's she with?"

"Willow, Eve, Kelly. . . ."

"I'd like to bring in one of those girls," he said.

"Sure, take Kelly," Belle replied, with a slight laugh. She found Kelly rude and unpleasant, and she had heard that Kelly once slapped her own mother for no reason at all.

"I think we'll take Eve," Sergeant John Bond said.

"That's fine," Eve said, but there was "a nervous laugh" from the girl.

Kelly ran out the door as soon as the police left.

"I just didn't clue in," Belle would later admit. "I had no idea what was going on."

When the phone rang, Belle's home was empty of teenagers, and she expected and hoped John Bond would say she could come and pick Maya up. She hoped he would say Maya's been very helpful; the missing girl, she's been found. But he said, his voice in the manner of apology, "Well, it looks like Maya's a little more involved. You need to come down here."

Involved in what, she wondered, as she gathered her keys and went out to her car. Gray clouds moved over the white shadow of moon as she drove over the bridge. She thought, as she drove, about the murder of her brother long ago. She thought about the doctors saying, "It will probably hit Maya when she's sixteen. That's what usually happens with buried trauma." Whenever Belle tried to talk to Maya about the murder, "She'd just get this look in her eyes, like she'd gone to some secret place," Belle recalls. "She just shut down, but I did that too after my brother died. It was the only way I could survive." Sometimes she'd wander into the basement and find her secret envelope of photos and the newspaper articles. One day, Maya would want to see these:

Woman, 28, Accused of Murder
Police Find Victim's Daughter
Pair Faces Murder Charge

Almost a decade later, some cruel force seemed to be pulling her back into the places of tragedy.

"The Saanich station was where I went when my brother was murdered," Belle recalls, "so it was very, very hard for me to go back there." Still, she went inside, past the trophy cases filled with antique rifles and handcuffs.

• • •

In the interview room, John Bond and Krista Hobday asked the sad-faced girl what she knew about a missing girl named Reena.

"I know a Reena at my school," Maya said. "She's got blonde hair. She's skinny with a weird last name."

"Do you know an East Indian girl named Reena?" Bond asked, and then showed her a photo of Reena Virk.

"I've never seen her."

"So where were you last Friday night?"

"I was in Gordon Head all night, at the teen center."

"Look," Bond said, raising his voice, "our purpose here is to try to find this girl so we can notify her mom."

"I haven't seen her," Maya insisted. ("Maya had this 'kiss-my-ass' look on her face," Krista recalls, "and John's giving it all he's got.")

"Do you want to deal with me now, or do you want to go to court? Let's hear the truth. This isn't about somebody stealing a candy bar. It's murder!"

"She gave it up in bits and pieces," Krista recalls. "She told us she was under the bridge. She admitted to hitting Reena. That's when we chartered her and warned her." Bond then went to look for Belle while Krista prepared to take Maya's sworn statement.

"What's going on?" Belle said to John Bond, when he came out of the interview room, his face more worn and worried than when he'd shown up at her house.

"Belle, we've read her her rights. She was more involved. . . ." Something about a missing girl, she heard, something about Maya's friends, and then she followed the detective into the cramped and airless room and saw Maya on the sofa. There was a slightly sullen look on her face, the kind of look she would throw at her mother when asked to do a particularly tedious chore, and she chewed on her lip. The small gesture of defiance bothered Belle, and she spoke to her daughter sternly: "Maya, if someone's child is missing, you're going to tell them everything you know. I don't care if your friends are involved or not. This is someone's life, someone's child."

She said the word *child* with a force that seemed to rouse Maya, and she nodded; she agreed. "She told them everything she knew," Belle says. "She told them all she knew."

"She laid it all out very clearly," John Bond recalls. She told of the fight under the bridge.

But Maya had seen something else that night.

"Willow's mom picked me and Willow up from the Mac's just after 11:00, I guess it would have been, 'cause that's Willow's curfew. We got in the truck and I was by the window and Willow was in between. We drove over the bridge, toward the schoolhouse. And we saw two people on the bridge, like walking back, away from the schoolhouse. We waved, but they didn't see us."

"Who was it?" John Bond asked.

Maya told him, and he wrote down the names.

Though she did not know this, Maya had just given the police their first real "break" in the case.

"I shut down the interview," Sergeant Bond remembers. "I went out and found Downie. I told him straight up, 'We've got a homicide here.' I gave him my notes. I said, 'Here are the names of all the players.'"

Eight names, eight players, eight teenagers.

"We just carried on working through the night." Calls were made to the undercovers with the names of the players. There were already detectives at the school, and now they were given permission to do more than investigate. Arrest all of them for murder, Bob Downie said. In this way, the teenagers on the field were now as Reena had been a week before. On the field, unaware of the forces about to descend on them on a Friday night.

ON THE FIELD, THE FIELD
THEY WERE ONCE ON

On that Friday evening as the detectives received their orders to arrest, Syreeta cashed out at Brady's Fish and Chips. She touched the money, arranged the brightly colored bills in stacks, wrapping them with yellow rubber bands. Tara cleaned the bottles of vinegar; she gathered the shakers of salt and pepper, then picked the paper napkins off the chairs.

There was a new mechanical aspect to their movements. They did not laugh about lecherous customers; all the joy of the week before was absent and yet not eradicated. It seemed to Syreeta as if their former happiness was being held somewhere, suspended, and she hoped the happiness would soon fall over them once more, elate them, so they could enjoy life as they had when they were carefree.

"Are you going to the party?" Tara asked her, and Syreeta nodded. Yes, she would be picked up by her mother and go to Shoreline and meet up with Warren, Marissa, and Dimitri.

After locking the door, the two friends stood in the parking lot. They leaned against the window of the sari shop. Lilac and amber cloth stood in rolls, thin fabric with threads of gold. There was no satellite in the sky, and the moon was not full, but together for some reason, both Syreeta and Tara looked up at the sky. For some reason, Tara took Syreeta's hand, and both friends kept their eyes toward the sky not yet full of stars, and then Syreeta's mother was driving up and they were getting into the car and they were going to the field, where they thought there would be a party.

The nights with all your friends held certain promises. A girl would have her first kiss. A boy would get high for the first time and with his red eyes he would laugh at the sky and say it looked like a lake. Syreeta rarely got high, and she had no desire to hallucinate, but when a boy would talk to her about the strange mirages, she'd listen patiently. Sometimes it seemed tempting to have the world shimmer and split and shift. Still, even sober, she'd felt shivers of joy on this field. She'd stared at the tall, almost elegant, trees and her friends, knowing they'd all literally grown up on this field, grown larger, as all her friends had moved from childhood and lost their childish bodies. She herself had grown three inches this last year, and she was taller than Warren now, taller than she had been the night of their first kiss.

But now, there were cars at Shoreline, cars she did not recognize. Adults were on the field, and she had never seen so many adults on the field on a Friday night. These adults held notebooks; they looked dorky and uptight to Syreeta, and she thought, *Who are these adults here on this field where they have never been before?*

In his unmarked car, Sergeant Poulton watched

Syreeta and Tara approach, their purses dangling on their shoulders, their heads bowed. He'd been watching the school for a while, and this was surveillance of a strange sort. The Canadian flag blew in the wind. The kids moved onto the field and embraced, and boys rode by on their bicycles and boys with skateboards under their elbow sauntered by, and one even knocked on his window and grinned. He sat in his car just watching the kids hanging out at the school, and he had to remind himself that these were all suspects in a homicide case. Those two pretty girls who passed him only moments before might be names on the list of those he was now to arrest.

"It was a cold and miserable night and it had an air of surrealism about it," Sergeant Poulton would later say of this stakeout at Shoreline. "There was a suppressed air of nervousness among the kids."

Sergeant Poulton got out of his car. He headed for Syreeta and Tara. He walked onto the field, and he could feel his gun, strapped to his waist, colder than it often felt when he felt it there, against his skin.

Syreeta moved across the field, unaware of the man following her. The green field seemed full of intruders. The intruders were adults, and they were moving through the field—a sacred place for kisses and secrets and longings and *just kinda kidding around*. The strangers, the adults, held notebooks in their hands, and they were writing down the names of all her dearest friends. Warren was not yet on the green field, which was not yet covered in dew.

She realized then, the adults, with their broad shoulders and bellies and bald spots, these were undercovers.

Syreeta saw them take Tara away, and she thought to herself, *Why are they taking Tara when she did not do anything?*

As she moved toward Marissa, she heard the adults ask:

"What is your full and legal name?"

"Where were you last Friday night?"

"Have you ever met a girl named Reena Virk?"

"Have you seen Kelly Ellard?"

She saw Marissa crying, and she heard an officer say, "Marissa, we have information you were under the bridge last Friday. We'll need you to come with us."

She turned then, past Geoff and Paul. Geoff, with all the attitude, saying, "I ain't got nothing to tell you, man. Yo, I never been under that bridge." She heard Paul say, "Why you axing me? I'm not a rat. I didn't see anything." She heard the boys, and they were keeping it on the down low.

The field she walked through was now a ruined assembly, an intrusion of something more than adults, but of that adult word as well: *consequences.* She heard the pregnant police officer yelling: "We're talking about a missing girl here!"

She thought then of the words Warren whispered in his bedroom.

Haven't you wondered why that girl hasn't been around?
No, I didn't know she hadn't been around.

She recalled with a start the promise she'd made.

Don't tell anyone.

I won't.

She had not even moved across the field when the man came right up to her. His hair was neatly combed. She could not see his gun. She could smell his aftershave.

He said, "We're looking into a missing girl. We need to know your name."

She gave him her name, and she thought he peered at her then, with abrupt recognition, but he let her keep walking, and she walked off the field, hoping she could find Warren.

Warren, he was not on the field but wandering around near the train tracks. He knew the police were at Shoreline. He'd heard it from Geoff and Paul, but yet he did not consider running. He thought to himself, *Where can I go? I ain't got no money. I'm just a stupid drunk kid. Emotionally wrecked. Fucked up large.*

He wanted only to find Syreeta.

He was not the tough rap star in the music video, powerful and brazen, armed with Glocks or an Uzi, though his pants were baggy and he wore a blue bandanna. He was not a Crip with a crew, and he was only dizzy and very hungry. He thought of Syreeta's sarcastic rebuke. *Oh, that's cool. You kicked a girl in the head. You're real cool.* He thought of Syreeta and hoped he would find her on the field before he was taken away. He wanted not to warn her but to tell her he loved her. Near the Mac's, he saw a dark-haired young girl under the lights where gas was sold. Syreeta, he thought, and he walked quicker now.

But in front of the Mac's store, Syreeta's friend Felicity was by herself, shivering.

"What's going on, Warren?" she cried. "Why are the cops all over the field?"

He didn't answer Felicity.

"I probably won't see you again," he told her. "I'll probably be going to jail soon."

He asked if he could borrow some money and Felicity gave him a few dollars and he bought a Vanilla French Latte from the machine inside the bright store.

Sober up, he told himself. *Stupid drunk kid. Emotionally wrecked. Fucked up large.*

Felicity had told him Syreeta was at Shoreline, and so he hurried toward the school, knowing that the undercovers would likely be there as well, but it didn't matter to him. He walked very quickly, with his head down so low he thought he might fall into the gasoline spilled on the pavement.

Before he was on the field, Warren stepped onto the parking lot where gravel gave way to concrete. The names of all his teachers were painted on the small yellow markers, and a few feet in the distance, he could see the green field with the pieces of grass seeming separate and silver-tipped from the light of the moon.

Syreeta was just getting into the back seat of Diana's dad's car, just fastening her seat belt, when she saw Warren through the window. Warren did not see Syreeta.

He saw instead the gold Taurus moving toward him,

and he knew then that the gold Taurus would take him away.

A man, lean and looking like his father's twin, this man who looked so much like his dad, left the gold Taurus and said his name. "Warren Glowatski?" Bruce Brown inquired, and Warren nodded, and he lifted his hand as if to be polite, as if they were being introduced. Bruce Brown shook his hand, and then told him he was under arrest for the murder of Reena Virk.

Handcuffed, he bent slightly to move into the Taurus, and just then he saw Syreeta through the cop car window. She too was behind glass. They looked at one another through the small windows in the cars of adults. Her mouth was open, as if she had started to scream, and there were tears on her face. He thought, *She shouldn't be seeing this. She shouldn't be seeing this at all.* He ducked into the car, and he looked down at the rug of his captor's car.

"What's Warren getting arrested for?" Diana's dad said. "Vandalism or something?"

"I have to get out," Syreeta screamed. "Stop driving!"

Mr. Davis stopped the car. He seemed to consider the vagaries of letting Syreeta escape. The policeman would probably not appreciate a somewhat hysterical girl throwing herself on the vehicle. He braked, but turned to tell Syreeta to stay in the car.

"Why are they taking Warren away?" Diana said. "He didn't do anything!"

Syreeta's seat belt was already unfastened. She saw Warren raise his head and look at her through the glass. She began to get out of the car.

But as she opened the door, Diana's dad stepped out of the front seat of his car, and he put his hands on her shoulders.

"Syreeta," he ordered, "you get back in the car!"

"Please," she yelled. "Just let me say good-bye!"

Mr. Davis kept his hands on her shoulders. "Get back in the car!" he ordered once more, and he blocked her escape. Besides, they had already taken Warren away from her. *Just let me say good-bye,* she yelled, even though he was already gone.

UNDER ARREST

By 11:00, the police station was, as one lawyer would later recall, "a total gong show."

"It was chaotic," Sergeant Poulton admits. The interview rooms and cells were full of teenagers. Mothers were vomiting in the bathroom. Lawyers began to arrive.

This is pandemonium, Sergeant Poulton thought. *The station is teeming with kids.*

Officers tried to keep the teenagers apart so they could not "contaminate their stories." Pagers were going off, and girls were screaming.

In the waiting room, the mothers were like a chorus. The mothers, together, they wailed.

Belle sat with the mothers of her daughter's friends, women whom she had known for years. She had been with them at bake sales and barbecues and nights at the kids' dances when together, they were chaperones. Now, their daughters were detained for *murder.* In the uneasy moment, she found herself silent while the other mothers wailed and sobbed and hugged. She was not part of this chorus, for she could not cry, not yet. "Jill was devastated, and shocked," she recalls. "And Rosemary was hysterical, totally hysterical. It was all very emotional and there was a lot of fear. We were all pretty afraid.

'What's going to happen?' I remember being really worried about that girl who was missing because at that time there really wasn't any proof that she was dead. We were all in one room. We didn't know what was going on. Finally, John Bond came in and he told me that they couldn't decide whether to move the girls to jail or to keep them in the cells at the station.

"I think I went into a robot state. I'd been there before with my brother. I think that's where I went. I have to do that. Have to do that or I'll fall apart.

"When I looked at Jill and Rosemary, oh, I just felt like we were in a dream. *This cannot be happening.*"

• • •

The lead detectives were assigned to different suspects, and as he'd later recall with a slight laugh, John Bond and Bruce Brown "took" Warren. "We just thought it was a job for him and me," he recalls.

Sergeant Poulton, said by John Bond to be "a class act, a very intelligent guy," entered the interview room where Kelly lay on a sofa. "Kelly, you're here under arrest for murder," Sergeant Poulton said to this very young girl with a stud in her nose and sleepy brown eyes.

"You haven't yet been charged. We're trying to get a hold of your mother. I've read you your rights. Now. . . ."

She interrupted him, and her concerns were not those of a murderer but those of a teenage girl. "Where are my friends? When can I see them?"

Before he could answer, she spoke up once more, her voice more indignant than terrified.

"When can I go? I don't know anything about what's going on."

She slept for a while then, lay down on the couch, and slept in the children's interrogation room, on a couch beside a box of building blocks and teddy bears.

Susan, Kelly's mother, a slight woman with soft gray eyes and a soft voice and a soft sweater, arrived near midnight. Her husband, the soccer champion, waited outside, pacing, thinking, "How can this be happening?" His stepdaughter, who never missed her curfew, arrested for murder. How could this be?

"Mom," Kelly cried when she saw her mother. "I was just with my friends and I got taken in. I didn't do anything. I don't know what is going on."

Sue sat beside her daughter, slowly, as if dazed and unsure. ("Nothing like this has ever happened to anyone I know," she would later say.) Protectively, she seemed almost to enfold her daughter; she stroked Kelly's hair; she held her hand; she looked at her daughter with worry and tenderness.

"We're just trying to get to the bottom of what happened to a girl named Reena Virk," Sergeant Poulton explained to the shocked mother.

"Reena? I thought her name was Trina," Kelly said, and she yawned.

"Where were you last Friday night?"

Yawn. She placed her hand over her mouth, yawned again. "I told you. I went to the Mac's, and then I went to the Comfort Inn and then I went home."

"Well," he said, "we've heard quite a different story.

We have a number of witnesses who have given us information that—"

"All those people are fools!" Kelly screamed. "They're
just trying to save their asses." She turned away from the
detective decisively and raised her head so she seemed
taller than her mother, and certainly, she seemed the
stronger and more assertive of the pair.

"Mom, I want to go home now," she announced.

Her mother stayed silent, continuing to stroke her
daughter's hair.

"Why were you telling people you beat up Reena that
Friday?" Sergeant Poulton inquired.

"I did not tell anyone that. Rumors fly around. This
is high school. It's gossip, gossip, gossip!"

"How can I make you understand?" Sergeant Poulton
said, after hearing of gossip and rumors, frustrated by the
vagueness of her answers and her petulant tone. "This is
murder! Of a fourteen-year-old girl! A mother has lost
her child! You're looking at a murder rap here. Get a
grip!"

"I have nothing against her," Kelly insisted. "I don't
even know her. Listen to me! I'm very pissed off right
now! So quit asking me stuff! Leave me alone!"

Poulton moved toward the door. He'd been working
for fifteen hours straight, chasing down girls in flared
pants and hooded sweatshirts. And now he was facing
the logic of this fifteen-year-old alleged killer. *It was
gossip. It's gossip, gossip, gossip.*

"I'll be right back," he said sighing, and he left the
room, left mother and daughter alone.

"Why is this happening to me?" Kelly wailed.

"It's happening to everyone," her mother replied. "They're all crying now."

"I hate this asshole," Kelly said, "He's intimidating me."

There was a video camera on the wall taping her, and Kelly's mother pointed this fact out to her daughter. Nonplussed, Kelly stared at the camera.

"I hate cops!" she screamed. "I hate the system!" She raised her middle finger to the camera. She scowled. She persevered with her outrage at her own misfortune: "I'm going to beat up everybody who said this about me," Kelly roared. "I am going to kill them. I'm not going to school anymore."

Susan Pakos put her head in her hands.

"Mom," Kelly commanded. "I'm scared! Can't you take me out of here?"

"I can't just take you out of here, Kelly."

"You own me! You're my mother. Get me probation!"

"I knew something was going on on Wednesday," Sue said, as though to herself, since Kelly was not listening. Full of fury, Kelly stood up and stormed over to the box of stuffed animals sometimes used to help children describe and remember sexual abuse. Kelly kicked a teddy bear across the room.

"Pick that up," Kelly's mom said wanly, and when Kelly ignored her, she herself got on her knees and picked the teddy bear up because her daughter had kicked it halfway across the floor.

Sergeant Poulton moved to interrogation room 3 and looked inside to see both Brown and Bond interviewing a boy. That's Warren, he thought, surprised, for he had imagined the lone boy in the case would be a burly kid, a deadened thug, and there he was, spritelike, with his hair bleached and curly, and he was even smaller than Kelly. He thought Warren was smaller than Kelly, although later he would find they shared a strange physicality, as if they were twins. Both were 5'4, and both weighed exactly 115 pounds.

Dreading the return to the screaming and hostile girl, he lingered for a moment by the door, and he thought he'd find out what Bond and Brown had gotten out of the Warren kid. He peered through the window once more, and it surprised him again that the boy was so small.

"It was tense," James Bulmer would later recall of the atmosphere, "and I was just trying to figure out what was going on. I knew they'd all been arrested for murder, but the details were unclear. I asked if there was a body, and I was told, 'We haven't found one yet.'"

James Bulmer was a duty counsel lawyer, who the court system provides to represent those who cannot afford or find a lawyer at the time of their arrest. He'd been in the cells so many times, but had never seen anything like the scene at the station that evening. In the cells, he noticed the heating system was not functioning normally. "The cells were absolutely stifling hot," James Bulmer would later recall. The cells were in the basement, so he felt as if he was walking into some accidental inferno.

He spoke to Maya and Willow and Eve. He filled out forms. He tried to find out what was going on. He told the girls they'd have to go before a justice of the peace and be formally charged. Since it was the weekend, the justice of the peace would come down to the station and they'd go before a proper judge on Monday.

He did his duty, but found himself bewildered by the sight of these murder suspects.

"It sure as hell didn't compute to someone who has two daughters to arrive and find, basically, my daughters in custody. You expect to see adults when you walk into those cells. They were just kids. They all had different personalities. Some were emotional. Some were scared. For others, it didn't seem to have sunk in yet. But they all looked to me like children."

MAJOR CRIMES

When he received the call, Stan Lowe was sleeping, and so as not to disturb his wife, he rose from his bed, wrapping himself in a plaid bathrobe, and headed out to his garage. Christine, his wife, was also a prosecutor, and she would not have been surprised by an 11:30 phone call or by his thoughtful desire to shield her from the intrusion of criminality. Her husband was thoughtful. She had always known this, perhaps from the first moment she saw him in a Vancouver classroom where they were studying civil litigation. Their first date lasted four days, and three weeks later, they had moved in together. He was always thoughtful, still now, twenty years later, when they both had risen to the top tier of the profession: the MCPU—Major Crimes Prosecution Unit. On that night when Stan Lowe rose from his bed, there was a paperback copy of *Seven Steps to Spiritual Success* beside his bed, next to a black and white photo of his mother, Lee Shoon-Hwa, a woman whom he affectionately referred to as "the matriarch."

He couldn't see anything outside, and he walked blindly over the lawn. We're Sleepy Hollow, he often said of the suburb where he lived, far away, a refuge from the worlds of his work: crack houses, biker bars, bordellos, morgues. Sleepy Hollow, with the only sound that evening the slow whirl of a sprinkler, the rise and fall of soft water. Victoria averaged three murders a year, his sleep was most often undisturbed, but "when someone dies, they call me."

Light flooded the garage suddenly. He sat in a slightly rusted lawn chair. Around him, there were golf clubs, training wheels, surfboards, a well-used set of skis. The bathrobe did not suit him, for he was a tall, elegant man, with a bearing and intellect well-suited to the formal black gown Canadian prosecutors wear.

Now he was in his garage, in a bathrobe, shivering. This was Stan Lowe's inauspicious introduction to a case that would soon linger in his own life in ways he could not have foreseen.

"It's not confirmed, but I think we have a murder. We've arrested a number of teens," Sergeant Bob Downie, the File Manager, told him. "All the stories, they're starting to show a consistency." He briefly summarized for Stan the story of the assault under the bridge and the subsequent murder. "We're running out of cells," he said, "and we've got Bond, Brown, and Poulton with the main suspects, but we haven't got a confession of murder."

Stan recalls, "I knew they were convinced they had the right people. I knew by the caliber of police officers involved they had reason to be convinced. But it was pretty early on; there wasn't a body."

"I looked for alternatives," he recalls. "I said, 'Is there a boyfriend in the picture?' 'Could she have gone to a friend's?'"

"We've looked into that," Downie said. "We're pretty sure she's in the Gorge. Bond's arranged for a Coast Guard helicopter to go up in the morning, and the Dive Unit's going in to search as soon as there's sunlight."

"I've got a real hesitancy laying charges at this point," Stan Lowe said. He hung up after giving a simple order: "Find me the body."

PART III

An Unusual Investigation

"It's an unusual investigation. We have rumors but no evidence that a crime has been committed. We're having to work backwards here."

—Police spokesperson
Sergeant Chris Horsley

SATURDAY MORNING

President Clinton smiled in the scarlet room of the Pan Pacific Hotel; he smiled before a room of reporters and told them how glad he was to be in Vancouver. "My family and I had a wonderful vacation here back in 1990, before I was president—back when I had a family life that was normal." He paused and the crowded room of reporters laughed at his suave self-deprecation. "We loved Vancouver," he said, smiling even more. "This is a great place for the APEC summit."

President Clinton, along with eighteen other world leaders, was in Vancouver for the annual Asia Pacific Economic Co-operation Summit, a high-profile gathering to discuss trade and economics.

There was much to be discussed. As Clinton announced on this morning in the hotel conference room, Canada's Prime Minister, Jean Chrétien, and himself were committed to "find a meaningful solution to the problem of climate change, democracy in Haiti, and criminals who are using cross-border telemarketing schemes to prey upon both Canadians and Americans." There was also the issue of Pacific salmon. "This issue has gone on too long," Clinton said passionately. "It's caused too much friction between our people."

As well, the world leaders would spend the weekend discussing the economic crisis in Asia: the exodus of dollars that began last summer in Thailand, Indonesia, and Malaysia, spread to Korea, and was now threatening Japan. South Korea had asked the International Monetary Fund for a bailout package totaling $20 billion. Japan's fourth largest brokerage firm, Yamiachi Securities, was near collapse.

While world leaders discussed the economic fate of Malaysia in scarlet boardrooms, the sky in View Royal was thick and gray on Saturday. The story was still unproved, yet spoken of now in the interview rooms in the strange slang and rhythms of young girls in flared pants and ponytails. By morning, with the order of "Find me a body" echoing in their ears, the men boarded a helicopter and set over the captive waterway. The men pulled on their black suits and went underwater, attached to a rope, into the darkest underground.

The girls remained in the cells, stifling and airless. They called out each other's names. "Dusty," someone yelled. "Maya!" another screamed.

At Diana's, Syreeta was too distraught to sleep. At 6:30, she had called her mother and asked her to come pick her up from the home where she had first kissed Warren, on the porch, after telling him that she was getting braces.

Diana had tried to comfort her. "It's just a disgusting story," she said. "I'm sure Warren didn't do anything.

Maybe the girl who's missing, maybe she decided that she had nothing to live for and she drowned herself. And maybe the police heard Kelly's disgusting story, and they decided to arrest a bunch of people but they'll find out Kelly was just lying and they'll find out what maybe happened to that girl, and Warren's not going to be in any trouble."

Syreeta did not speak to Diana of the things she had heard, the things she had not believed when Warren was on his knees, holding her hands in the bedroom. She did not tell her mother either when her mother arrived to pick her up and take her back to her own bedroom.

It was not yet afternoon when two police officers knocked on the door of the Hartley home. When the police arrived, Syreeta could see them through the stairwell and on seeing the two men, she began to cry and ran into her bedroom.

And she was crying still when she sat in the interview room. She wore a blue shirt with a camouflage pattern and denim overalls. The cops asked her if she could give a statement and she cried some more.

"Okay," Constable Cameron said gently. He was a large man with an innocuous and classic babyface— full cheeks and pink skin. "If you want, we'll try and get a statement, and if your emotions make that impossible, we'll stop. I think you'll probably get through this, and I think it's probably going to help you in the end. Syreeta, what I want you to do is start with Friday. Can you tell me what happened from dinnertime to the time you went to bed? Can you do that for me?"

The young girl spoke through her tears. She said: "I went to Shoreline and everyone was there. That was the night that the Russian thing was going through the sky. We were all watching that. And then I started feeling sick. I started feeling really sick, so I was going to find Warren and see if I could get into the school. I was going to ask my mom to pick me up. But the doors were locked, so I couldn't get in. Someone yelled out, 'Bitch fight,' and everyone started running up to the bus stop except me and Marissa. We stayed behind. We just slowly walked up there, and when we got there, there was Laila and everyone was talking and they're like, I don't know, laughing or something. And then Warren asked me what was wrong, and I told him. I said, 'I don't feel good.' He asked if I wanted him to walk me home. I just said no. He said, 'Why don't you catch the bus? I'll give you a dollar. I don't want you walking home.' So I got on the bus and I left, and I got home at about nine o'clock. He called me at about quarter after eleven. I answered the phone; I told him I was sleeping, so that's all that happened to me on Friday night."

"And did you see him Saturday morning?"

"Saturday afternoon he came over."

"Could you describe what happened when he came over?"

"Well, I was talking to my friend Tara earlier in the morning on the phone, and she told me that the fight had happened. She told me that Warren kicked a girl in the head. And I asked him. I said, 'How come you didn't tell me you kicked a girl in the head?'

"He said, 'I didn't want you to know because I shouldn't have done it.'

"And I was like, 'Yeah, well you still did, so why did you?'

"He said, 'I don't know.'

"And that's all he told me about that. It's hard to remember what happened then. . . .'"

"Did you do some laundry for him?" the cop asked, and Syreeta wondered to herself how they knew this. Maybe Warren confessed everything.

"I washed his gym clothes, and I washed a pair of white jeans because he told me he got in a fight with some Native guy because him and Kelly were walking down the road, and the guy said, 'Hey you and your hoochie,' and then he went and got in a fight with a guy. That's what he told me happened."

Syreeta paused.

"Okay. Could you describe those jeans to me?"

"They're just white baggy jeans. There was lots of mud all down here, and he folds them up so there's mud in the creases, and there was maybe two splatters of mud on the leg, but that's all there was."

"What about the blood?"

Syreeta hesitated. "I saw some blood, but the blood was two splatters. There wasn't much."

"Two splatters—"

"Not much at all."

"Did you wash a sweater for him?"

"I bleached his sweater for him. His sweater didn't have any blood on it."

"Okay. Now as the week's gone on, there's lots of conversation about what happened on Friday evening. Lots of speculation. Lots of rumors at school. Did Warren talk to you again about this?"

"Yeah," Syreeta said, with the slow air of someone slowly understanding a mystery. ("I was just putting it all together as I talked to the cops," she would later recall. "I was trying to make sense of everything that hadn't been making sense to me.")

"One day after school, he was going to come over to my house. He was talking to Josephine and Kelly, and I went over to him and he was telling everybody, 'Shhhh. . . .' And I got mad at him. I was like, 'Are you trying to hide stuff from me?' And he said, 'No.' I'm like, 'Whatever. You can keep on talking. I'm going.'

"He said, 'No. We're finished talking.'

"We had to go back to his house first. I was lying on his bed while he got changed and ready to go out. He asked me, he said, 'Do you really want to know what happened?'

"I said, 'If it's a big deal, and you don't want to tell me what happened, you don't have to.'

"He said, 'I'm asking you. Do you want to know?'

"I said, 'It doesn't really matter to me.'

"And he just, there was a song on the CD that he was listening to and it said 187. 187 in gang talk is murder, or whatever, I'm not sure. And then he said exactly that.

"I said, 'What are you talking about?'

"He said, 'That girl named Reena.' He said, 'Well, there you go.' And that was the end of the conversation. I didn't ask him anymore. I didn't want to know anymore, and that's all he told me."

"Did you have any conversation after that about it?"

"No."

"Could you try and be as specific as you can about when he was talking about 187? Did he say anything about how it happened or where it happened?"

"That's all he told me. I didn't—I didn't—I didn't believe him. I didn't believe him. I was like, 'Oh yeah.' I didn't think he had done it at that point. I thought he was just saying that it happened."

"And now, what do you think?"

"I don't know what to think," she said, and she began to sob.

"Have you spoken to Kelly at all about this?"

"No."

"Are you and Kelly friends?"

"Acquaintances."

"Are Kelly and Warren good friends?"

"They talk in school, and we all hang out with the same people, but I wouldn't say they're good friends."

"Okay. Let's go back to when he was at your house and you confronted him about kicking a girl in the face. What exactly did he say? Just take a moment and think about it. If you have to, close your eyes to concentrate and clear your head and think about it. We're not in any hurry."

"At first he asked me who told me, and I told him Tara. He said Tara needs to keep her mouth shut. I said,

'Too bad. Just tell me why you did it.' He said, 'I don't know why I did it. Everyone was doing it. I was just there. It just happened.'

"I said, 'Oh, that's really cool. You kicked a girl in the face.'

"He told me not to worry about it. That's what he always does when I try to get something out of him. He told me not to worry about it. That's all he told me."

"Okay. Let's start at the beginning of the conversation about 187. We'll get you to relax again, and just try and think about the conversation you had with him at his house. Was anything extra said other than what you've already told us? Try and add more detail. Give us as much detail about that conversation as you can. Can you do that for me?"

"We got to his house and I was lying on his bed, and he was getting changed out of his gym clothes. I went and called my mom to see if he could come over, and when I came back to the bedroom, he said, 'Do you really want to know what me and Kelly were talking about?'

"I said, 'No. If you don't want to tell me, I don't want to know.' And then he said, 'Exactly that. 187.' And we sat there. He said that he didn't want me to know because he didn't know what I'd think of it. He didn't want me to worry about it. I don't know exactly what he said."

"Did he say that he had done this 187?"

"No. He told me that him and Kelly or something happens. Something happened and Kelly was standing there and Kelly was . . . Kelly was doing something to her, and then, he told me that she got . . . I can't remember what he told me."

"We're going to get you to relax because again, you've come up with more stuff. It sounds like it's all right there. You start at the beginning of what he told you, and you grab a bit in the middle and then you skip to the end. I think if you really concentrate you'll be able to fill the whole thing in. And another thing, I notice you keep using the word *something.*

"I think if you really think about it, you'll remember exactly what that *something* is. I think that something is something very terrible, and so you don't want to say it out loud. We all know what happened is terrible. Your mom knows what happened. My partner knows what happened. I know what happened. It was a terrible thing that happened, but we're going to have to talk about it. If you could just get it all out, as opposed to just leaving it as 'something.' I think that you're just trying to—it's not real until you say it, but it is real. Okay? And it did happen. And nothing is going to change that it happened. If we could just get you to talk about that conversation again, and when you start to feel yourself say *something,* maybe just stop yourself and think about what that something is. Can you do that for us?"

"I'll try."

"Can you start with the conversation at his house?"

"I've got to think about it for a minute."

"Take as much time as you need."

"He didn't really explain much to me. I didn't want to know. He just kind of said that they'd gone down after and I don't know what happened, but then they dragged her into the Gorge. He said that Kelly held her head under for five minutes first, and then they threw her in."

Syreeta began to cry now, although she had been crying quietly throughout the interview. She put her hands to her eyes.

"Does that help, telling us about it? I can see that you've really got quite a burden here. You've been keeping this all inside for a week. I know there's still more inside of you, and if we could get you to try again. I know it's hard. He's your boyfriend, and it's hard to talk about what happened, but could you try for us?"

"I'm trying to think. He kept asking me if I wanted to know. I just said no, and then eventually the song said 187, and he said exactly that. I don't remember how he told me. He said that it wasn't true that he'd beat up a Native guy. They went down after, and something happened. I can't be exact. I don't want to pin it on anybody."

"We just want you to tell us what he told you."

"I think he told me that him and Kelly killed the girl. I really didn't want to know, but then he told me Kelly had, I don't know, kicked her, stepped on her head a couple of times, and then she stuck her head under water for five minutes, and they dragged her into the Gorge."

"Okay. That's more detail again. I know this is really hard, Syreeta. I do. I know you're not having any fun. This is the worst day you've had in a long time. This is the worst week of your life, I'm sure. And I'm not here to torture you or anything. I just want to get as much detail as I can get. You did really good that time. It flowed, it made sense, and it was in a logical order. Do you think if you just relax for a minute here, you could do it again and fill in all the gaps for us? Is that okay? Is that something you can do if we give you a minute here?"

Still crying, Syreeta said, "I can try."

"You're doing really well. You're great. We really appreciate what you're doing for us here. The truth is important. It has to come out. So just take a minute and relax, and when you're ready to start again, you can."

"I don't know what else there is."

"What did he tell you about him and Kelly going back down there?"

"He didn't give me much detail. He said that they went back down there, and Kelly was kicking and stomping on her head, and then she held her head under water for five minutes, and then they dragged her in the water. He said when they dragged her in the water, her pants came off."

"Did he say he was dragging her into the water with Kelly?"

"I don't know."

"You said earlier that 'they' dragged her in. Is that what he told you?"

"I was in shock. I didn't believe it, but I was in shock, so I wasn't really paying close attention to the detailed words like that. I didn't want to ask him questions about it. I didn't even want to bring it up."

"Okay. Reena's in the Gorge, and now you have Kelly

and Warren on the shore. Where do they go from there?"

"He never got to that point. I assume he went home because he called me at quarter after eleven."

"In your mind, do you see both him and Kelly dragging her into the water or just him?"

"I see him and Kelly. I don't think Kelly could drag her by herself."

"And in the same way, do you see Kelly stomping on her head? Or do you see him and Kelly doing it together?"

"When I picture it, I see only Kelly. Then I see them both drag her in. But that could be how I want to picture it."

"Well, that's a good point. I know he's your boyfriend. I know that entails some feelings and whatnot, and sometimes that can cloud the issue. So think about what he told you, and not of him as your boyfriend. Maybe you've forgotten something because of your feelings for him. Think about it again. Was he stomping on her too?"

"I think he told me that it was just Kelly who jumped on her head, but that could be because I got mad at him when I heard he kicked her in the head. I'm not sure about dragging her in. I think that was both of them."

"Can you think of anything else that you've been told by Warren that we should know? We don't want you to have to take any extra baggage back home with you. You've been dealt enough this week. He has asked you to keep this secret. He has burdened you with the knowledge of the murder of a young girl. And we want you to be able to leave here with a clear conscience that you've done everything in your power to right this wrong.

"And we're sure you haven't had a good week. You said you had an upset stomach. I'm thinking that's probably not from the flu. It's probably from carrying this around with you. That would be enough to cause anybody to feel nausea for a long time. I think you'll find that you'll feel a lot better tomorrow after being here if you can get everything out in the open. I think you'll have a much better day than you've had all last week. Do you want to sit for a minute and think if there's anything you missed?"

"I'm pretty sure there isn't."

"You're *pretty* sure, or you're *really* positive?"

"I'm really sure."

"You haven't subconsciously or purposely forgotten anything because of the relationship you've had with him? We can understand if that's happened. But we just don't want you to be stuck with this forever. Forever is a long time. You're a young girl. You're going to have a hard time forgetting this as it is and getting on, and it will only be harder if you're carrying some guilt along with you. We don't think you deserve to have any guilt at all. That's why you're in this nice interview room, sitting on this nice couch, instead of in some dingy room that's too hot. Okay? Because we don't think you need any guilt. We think that you're a nice person. You didn't have anything to do with this. You don't need to feel guilty about this. Okay? So is there anything that you've left out?"

"No."

"You're sure?"

"Yes."

"Okay. How do you feel now that you've told us all about this? Do you feel better or worse?"

"I don't know," Syreeta said, softly.

"You're probably pretty numb, aren't you, sweetie?" Syreeta's mom said, and she saw her daughter's face was full of tears. What Syreeta said next startled every adult in the room.

"I just want to see Warren," Syreeta wailed, with her voice like Juliet's.

• • •

"I was just chillin' with my friends," Dimitri told the detectives.

"We went down to Shoreline around 7:30. Everyone was just hanging out there 'cause that's what we usually do. Someone broke a window, and two police officers came and told us to leave. A group of us started to walk down toward the Mac's. Everyone started to go to underneath the bridge.

"Everyone was just sitting there and talking and then, all of a sudden, people were saying, 'Grab her! Grab her!' I saw what was going on. There was this girl. She was trying to get away from these other girls. I didn't know what was going on.

"Down by the bridge, they just started punching her. There was a whole bunch of other girls—they didn't have anything to do with this. They were all like, 'Oh my God. Oh my God.' I took them all up the hill and told them to just stay there so they didn't have to be involved. I told my girlfriend to stay where she was. My buddy Warren, he was down there. He was just looking and seeing what was going on. I went down and grabbed him. I said, 'Don't worry about it, man. Don't get involved. It's not your fight.' They just kept beating on her. I don't even know what it was about. I'm pretty sure most of the girls didn't even have anything to do with it. They rolled her into the Gorge. Well, not into the Gorge, but onto a muddy patch. They took her smokes and her bag and went to the Comfort Inn. I heard they grabbed her Polo Sport and then chucked her bag into the Gorge, and then just left, just split up. Everyone just split up and went their own way. I left at that point. I took my girlfriend. I don't know where Warren went after. He left. I didn't know where he went."

"Did you see this girl again after the beating?" a detective asked Dimitri.

"I did see her get up and start walking away. Over the bridge."

• • •

In the cells, the girls stood in blue paper gowns, for their clothes had been taken away. Ink remained, darkening their fingerprints. They pressed their faces to the small glass panes, desperate to catch sight of their friends. They had been arrested for murder, and yet they had killed no one. "Willow," Maya screamed, and she began to sob as she heard no answer from her childhood friend.

Mothers woke to their morning coffee; they fed their other, unarrested, children. Mothers read their newspapers and saw no story about the murder or a missing girl. Perhaps she had been found after all. Their daughters would be released. Their daughters would leave the cells and return to their bedrooms, messy with piles of jeans and jackets, fragrant with perfume, full of photographs and diaries and homework. *Please let the girl be found alive,* they prayed.

Lawyers arrived at the Saanich police department. The lawyers were all men, the men chosen to represent the girls. "The Shoreline Six," the girls who had been under the bridge would soon be called, as though they were renegade terrorists, a band of outlaws, rather than underage schoolgirls.

The lawyers advised the girls they would today go before the justice of the peace and most likely be remanded to custody until a formal arraignment before a judge on Monday. "Does that mean I'm going to jail?" Eve asked, and she pleaded with her lawyer—that she had never been in trouble and she surely had not killed a girl whose name she did not even know. The lawyers conferred among themselves. What were the cops up to? Arresting these girls for murder when they didn't even have a body! The lawyers returned to their Saturday activities. Laila's lawyer jammed with his band, playing Pearl Jam covers and songs by the Pixies. Dusty's lawyer polished his Harley; Kelly's lawyer planned his summer trip to the south of France.

Warren was "scared shitless." He'd been the only one sent to the Youth Custody Centre, and on Saturday morning, Bruce Brown came to get him and bring him back to the station for another interrogation. Warren asked if he could call Syreeta. But he was not allowed to call her, and so he called his father in California.

"Dad, I had nothing to do with this."

"You sure put yourself in a fine fix now."

"Yeah, I was at the wrong place at the wrong time. I guess my family's going to disown me now. Everyone is going to disown me."

"No, they are not going to disown you."

"I never hit a woman. I wouldn't do it."

"I believe you," his father said. "Let me talk to that Sergeant Brown."

Sergeant Brown asked Warren's father for the number of Warren's mother.

"She's an alcoholic," Warren's father said. "I have no idea where she is. If Warren had reason to hit anyone, it would have been his mother. He had no use for her. He just can't stand her. If there's anyone he should have hit, it was her, and he just walked away every time. He put up with her for years and years. He's never had any problems with the law. He's a good kid. He's always gone to school. The only problem he ever had is with his mother, and everybody in the world had trouble with her."

Warren's father then asked Sergeant Brown a question. "Is Warren being pinpointed for this?"

"No, we've got about eight other individuals in custody. They're going in front of the judge on Monday. We're going to detain them all until we get the proper truth out of them. I'll keep in contact with you and inform you what happens next."

Warren asked his father, "Can you come here?"

His father thought Warren sounded "very scared."

"I just got my green card, Warren, and I'm not going to have the proper travel documents for about four months."

"That's okay," Warren said. "Don't worry about it. Don't worry about me."

Warren was unaware of the words John Bond was now reading. Secretaries had been typing and transcribing nonstop, and as he read the girlfriend's interview ("that cute little girl from the fish and chip shop"), John Bond felt confirmed in his belief that Warren so far had been less than forthcoming.

"I know the script now," he told Bruce Brown. "Let's get him in here."

• • •

Sergeant Poulton drove up the long hill to Seven Oaks and found Josephine at last. She was in the bathroom, drying her hair.

Enthralled by her own reflection, she seemed at first not to notice the man standing there.

"Josephine," he said. "You're under arrest."

"What for?" she said, blithely, looking at him through her eyelashes.

"For the murder of Reena Virk."

She smiled at him and raised the hairdryer back near her clean blonde hair. He watched her, amazed. She turned to him then, and after she lowered the dryer, she bent forward, letting her blonde hair fall. She ran her fingers through her hair and then tossed her head back dramatically.

"Do I look like a murderer?" she said. She gave him a look of careless disdain. "Josephine Bell does not murder."

"Well, we can talk about it at the station."

"Who else did the cops pick up?"

"You're under arrest," Sergeant Poulton said. "We can talk at the station."

"Fine," she snapped, and she grabbed her Guess bag, and put into it her Nivea cream, her bus pass, her cigarettes, her Maybelline Great Lash mascara, and her Polo Sport perfume.

As they left Seven Oaks, she informed Sergeant Poulton of her wish. "Get me John Gotti's lawyer," she demanded.

"I don't think he's available," Sergeant Poulton replied.

• • •

She cried once more when she was told she could not see Warren.

"I don't think that's going to be possible," Syreeta was told.

"How long will it be before I can see him?"

"Well," the officer said, quite taken aback by the request, "we don't know that right know. This is as serious as it gets. This is murder." He realized his tone was too stern for the girl, who was so young, with her braces and ponytail. Her mother too seemed wholly stunned. "We really do appreciate your cooperation," he said to Syreeta's mother as he walked Syreeta and her to the door. "We really do know how horrible this is. We have spent these last few days dealing with kids, with teenagers."

*

Major Crimes prosecutor Stan Lowe arrived at the Saanich Police Department on Saturday morning. He surveyed the photos of the eight suspects. Warren looked absolutely petrified—his eyes immense, his lips parted as if mouthing a silent apology. Kelly was smirking, the stud still in her nose. Laila's eyebrows were very thin and arched highly above her slightly defiant gaze. ("She's a different cat," Sergeant Poulton told him. "All these girls talk really fast, but Laila talks so fast that when you finish a conversation with her, you have no idea what she was talking about. She's a kickboxer. She's like the West Side enforcer. If you're gonna fight, she's the one you call. But probably of all of them, she's the least culpable because she tried to stop the fight.") He saw Maya's photo and recognized her last name. ("I really like Maya," Poulton said. "She's the only one who told us everything.") Dusty's nostrils were flared and she looked rather menacing. ("Dusty's the most upset," Poulton thought. "She's the only one of them who really knew Reena.") Of all the girls, Josephine appeared the least menacing. She looked like she could be advertising Neutrogena soap; she looked like one of those twirling ballerinas on a jewelry box. Her smile was a bit odd. Who smiles in their mug shot? She was smiling, proudly and mockingly.

"They're quite a group of girls," Poulton mused. "Definitely tougher and more worldly than they look. They're all into rap, gangster music. They all want to be Puff Daddy."

This thought was interrupted by a tap on his shoulder

from the chief of police. The members of the Dive Unit had located a pair of underwear and jeans in the waters of the Gorge, not underneath the bridge, but farther away, a few miles out from the old white and historic Craigflower schoolhouse.

Sergeant Krista Hobday confronted Dusty with an adult version of the scene under the bridge.

"You're all under the bridge. You have Laila, Kelly, Maya, Eve, Josephine, Willow, and Warren. Maya has light red hair and really pretty green eyes. Warren has kinky blondish hair that comes out like a clown's on top of his head. Josephine butts a cigarette out on Reena's forehead. You're basically ticked off because Reena's been telling stories."

Dusty nodded, and tears fell to her closed lips.

"The fight is on. Some people under the bridge do nothing. They stand back. They don't punch her. They don't hit her. They don't help her. But you and the others kick her, punch her, pull her to the ground. Kelly grabs her by the hair, looks her straight in the eye, and punches her in the face, over and over and over again. Reena's nose is bleeding. Her eyes are being swollen shut. At this point, her ribs are probably cracked from the kicks. She is crying: 'Please stop! Leave me alone! Stop!' Laila finally says, 'Enough. Leave her alone. She's taken a bad enough beating.' Everybody complies. Everybody leaves. Reena's laying in the muck. Helpless, bleeding, broken, *because she told a story.*"

Dusty nodded, and as she opened her lips, her words turned to sobs.

"At any point, did you think to call an ambulance for this girl?" the detective asked. (All the detectives, among themselves, alone, and together, had found this one aspect of the night particularly terrible. "If one of those kids had called 911, we wouldn't be here," Sergeant John Bond said. "They wouldn't have had to give their name. It wouldn't have even cost them a quarter.")

"No," Dusty admitted. "Because I didn't think she was hurt that bad. She was walking. She was fine. I thought she could make it home. I didn't know they were going to follow her. She was walking. She was fine," Dusty repeated, softly, to herself.

"Dusty, where's Reena?"

"I don't know. I heard someone saw her downtown."

"Do you think after the shit-kicking Reena took that she would be downtown?"

"I don't know," Dusty said. "She was walking. She was fine."

"Do you know of any threats made against Reena?"

Dusty, somewhat startled by the vociferous outrage of the woman before her, finally elaborated:

"Yeah, a long time ago, when we were all in Kiwanis, Josephine said she wanted to beat up Reena. And then, after this happened, I heard that Kelly and Josephine had this all planned out. They had it planned for months."

"And what was their plan?" Sergeant Hobday asked, aghast that the script was only getting worse.

"To bury her alive."

• • •

Josephine sat in the detective's leather chair, toying with the black phone cord.

She thought she'd let the cop call her mother, and then when the cops weren't looking, she'd hang up and try to call Kelly.

She brushed her hair off her face and dialed her mother's number. Her blue nail polish was chipped.

"Hi, Mom!"

"Hello."

"I didn't do it!" Josephine said.

"You didn't do *what?*" she asked Josephine.

"We just beat her up."

"Beat *who* up?"

"But I went home, and I was home by curfew so I wasn't involved in the rest of it."

"*What* rest of it?"

"They dumped her body in the Gorge and she died."

Elaine, in shock, did not reply.

"I know who did it. I'm not gonna tell. What do you think, I'm stupid? My lawyer says I don't have to say anything, so I'm not going to say anything." She looked over at the officer and smiled, tauntingly.

"Well, what about remorse?" her mother asked. "What are you feeling?"

Josephine didn't answer.

"Do you understand what this means to the girl's family?" her mother asked her. "Do you understand what this will mean to our family? *Do you understand what's happened?*"

But Josephine did not seem to understand. She hung up on her mother and tried to dial Kelly, but she was noticed and the telephone was taken away from her.

"Who else is in here?" she demanded to know. "Where's my lawyer?" She was asked again if she would like to give a statement, and she declined, looking at the police detective with scorn. Did he not know that mobsters never ratted? "Do I look like I have a tail?" she asked him. He did not know of her adherence to a mafioso code of ethics, nor did he know of her fierce loyalty to Kelly, a loyalty that Josephine believed truly was mutual. Kelly, she had always believed, would do *anything* for her.

• • •

"Where's Reena right now?" Sergeant Krista Hobday asked Kelly.

"I don't know."

"In your heart. Close your eyes and think with your heart. Where do you believe Reena is right now?"

"It's hard to say. There's so much wacko stuff that goes on. She could have been abducted, or raped by an old man or something. She could have been drunk and passed out and hit her head, 'cause she was pretty drunk. Anything could have happened to her. I truly don't know. Now the cops are saying that apparently she got drowned. That was the rumor that was going around. If I didn't do it, then this person who started the rumor obviously did it."

"And who would that be?"

Kelly sighed, and then without flinching or hesitating, she said, "Josephine."

"Josephine's supposed to be your best friend. Josephine's doing this to you? She's sewering you?"

Warren Glowatski
(Photo courtesy of
the collection of the author)

Syreeta Hartley
(Photo courtesy of Syreeta Hartley)

Reena Virk (far right) and her family
(Photo courtesy of the Virk family)

Crime scene tape at the Craigflower Bridge
(Photo by Diana Nethercott)

Warren Glowatski's arrest photo
(Photo courtesy of the collection of the author)

above:
Prosecutor Don Morrison
(Photo by Diana Nethercott)

right:
Drawing found in the locker of Kelly Ellard
(Photo courtesy of the collection of the author)

right:
Students consoling
each other on the
Craigflower Bridge
(Photo by Diana Nethercott)

below:
Members of the
Dive Team search
under the bridge
(Photo by Diana Nethercott)

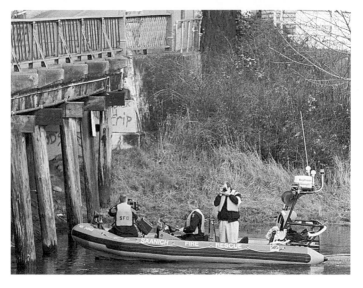

above:
Syreeta Hartley
enters court
(Photo by Diana Nethercott)

right:
Prosecutor
Stan Lowe
(Photo by Diana Nethercott)

Kelly Ellard enters court
(Photo by Ian Lindsay/Vancouver Sun)

Kelly Ellard on the day of her release
(Feb. 4, 2003)
(Photo by CH-TV)

Prosecutor Catherine Murray
(Photo by Ian Smith/Vancouver Sun)

Courtroom sketch of Catherine Murray and
Kelly Ellard. Background: Judge Selwyn Romilly
(Photo by Felicity Don)

Childhood portrait of
Reena Virk
(Photo courtesy of the Virk family)

Syreeta Hartley with her
mother Wendy
(Photo courtesy of
the collection of the author)

Warren Glowatski with the author Rebecca Godfrey
at Mission Institute in 2002
(Photo courtesy of the collection of the author)

"I have no doubt in my mind that it could have been Josephine," Kelly said, blithely. "She always says sick stuff—just weird, demented stuff. She wanted to *bury* someone. I think it must have been Josephine if she says demented stuff and she had lots of stuff against Reena."

"Then why isn't everybody saying it was Josephine?"

"People are probably saying it's Josephine."

"Nobody's saying it's Josephine. How's that for a tidbit? *Absolutely nobody.*"

"You don't know how much of a shock this is to me," Kelly said, seemingly bewildered by her fate.

"Kelly, all I want from you is the truth. Were you fighting under the bridge?"

"Reena pushed Josephine. So I just kind of punched her, I said, 'Don't touch my friend.' I said: 'Go home. Don't ever talk to any of my friends like that. We don't want you around here.' She was starting crap with *everybody*. I'm like, 'Go home.' She started to walk away, and everyone started beating her up. I don't know why, but I think it's 'cause Josephine was going around telling everybody that she wanted Reena to be beaten up."

"Kelly, your story just doesn't wash."

"That's 'cause they have a different story. I'm a different person."

"They all have the same story."

"What's their story?" Kelly demanded. "I'm curious to know."

"Their story is the truth."

"I could tell you their story is a lie if I heard it."

"I want the truth from you, because I've already got the truth from a number of people."

"Well, I'm not going to tell you that I did it if I didn't. Why would I do something like that?"

"I don't want to know *why*."

"Why would I put *my life* in jeopardy?"

"How about, 'Why would I ever hurt somebody like that?'"

"Exactly," Kelly agreed. "You've got brain problems if you're going to do that. Nobody deserves to die. Nobody."

"Not Reena."

"Obviously not. I don't even know if she's dead. How should I know?"

"Everybody else thinks she's floating in the Gorge." Krista leaned forward and tried to present Kelly with the logical path of rage. "Kelly, it's understandable, it's comprehensible that an argument turns into an altercation. A physical altercation turns into a shit kicking. A shit kicking turns into a murder. That's the natural procedure of violence. It goes from verbal to physical to violent to death."

"But I didn't do it! I'm telling you. The only reason I got brought in is Josephine wanted us to take credit for beating her up. Josephine thinks it's considered cool if you hurt people, and it's not. It makes you seem like a thug. Ladies don't do that kind of stuff."

"*People* don't do that kind of stuff. People don't *murder* a fourteen-year-old girl because she spread a few stories. *My God!*"

"Exactly! Why would I? I had no reason to. It was Josephine who had a reason, not me."

"Why would Josephine have a reason to beat the shit

out of somebody? Just 'cause she said some stories?"

"Josephine's got problems. She says weird stuff all the time. She always said she wanted to, like, kill Reena. She said how cool it would be if you, like, chopped her up. I was like, 'Josephine, you're sick.' I thought she was just kidding. Who knows?"

"So, Reena, according to you, has been abducted by an old man and raped?"

"I was just using the old man and rape as an example. And, obviously, if rumors are flying around, something happened."

"Do you actually think we'd go out and arrest people for murder based on a rumor?"

"Obviously, you do. You don't have a surveillance camera of me doing it."

"And if we did have a surveillance camera at the end of that bridge, what would it show?"

"It would show people kicking the crap out of her."

"And what if there was a surveillance camera down by the schoolhouse? What would that show?"

"I seriously can't tell you."

A GIRL IN THE REEDS

Constable Chris Horsley recalls the Saturday he boarded the Coast Guard helicopter to search for the body of Reena Virk. "It was a gray day. It was perfect for the search. There was no light shining on the water from the sun."

Together with Constable Ron Huck and the pilot, Gerry, he ascended in the red Messerschmitt, a German helicopter. "We took off and flew right up the Gorge. Ron was looking out the left, and I was looking out the right, starboard."

The men were not looking through glass, for they had the doors wide open, so they could see more directly.

The water, as he recalls, was "dark, dark, dark."

Honestly, the men didn't expect to find anything on that Saturday. They were aware it was a "rumor-based file."

"We were thinking, 'Is this legit?' Both Ron and myself didn't think we were gonna see anything. But we said, 'Let's do it.'"

The helicopter passed beyond the police divers purposely. "We didn't want to be a noisy bother. The downdraft of the helicopter would disturb the water, so we went low, but not so low that we were creating waves.

We slowly made our way up the Gorge. We'd just gone over the bridge to the north, about four hundred yards. That's when I saw her. It was surreal."

Chris Horsley saw a girl only slightly covered with the dark water, her hair floating behind her, and "with the way the light is," he could see her clearly.

"I've got her!" he said to his partner. "Three o'clock."

Into his lapel mike, he said on his police radio, "We've got something. Divers make your way to the position." With the noise of the engine, and the open doors, "We couldn't hear anything. We weren't sure if the divers even heard us."

The men hovered in one spot, above their terrible discovery. They waited for the divers to come into the waters underneath.

"Geez, can you believe it?" Chris Horsley said to Ron Huck. Both men were surprised that they'd found the girl, discovered her in the dark water so quickly.

• • •

The men of the Dive Unit were silent now. The men of the Dive Unit often speak of their discoveries of fallen bodies or stolen property as "odd rewards." In this case, though the girl had been found, the sight of her brought no sense of resolution or achievement. How far she had floated from the white schoolhouse. She was miles away from the murky waters where they had spent the morning, slowly searching. Most bodies sink to the bottom, but the girl had risen, as if lifted by a stranger's hands, as if kept away from the silt that might have dirtied her bare skin. Lifted her from the animals that might have torn at her flesh. The men, noting details for their report, observed the girl was untouched by animals that lived in the Gorge. But her face was bruised. Black welts under her eyes, a red mark between her eyes. There were bruises on her thighs, and bruises on her back, and blood in her nostrils, and on her hands the skin had started to slip away.

The water was so very still in the bay of recovery. On the silvery gray surface, copper leaves lingered, fresh from their fall.

Quietly, the men moved the body into a black bag, and a knife tore through the bag, letting out a slow hiss of water, so the bag would be lighter, without the weight of water. In the dark hair of the girl, the men thought they might have seen a glimmer of something gold.

All around View Royal, the machinery of discovery was observed. The red helicopter hovering over the Gorge. The men in black suits emerging from their descent. The sirens and the media satellite trucks disturbing the usual placid Saturday afternoon. Surely everyone noticed the yellow crime scene tape now spread like a banner across the clean white boards of the Victorian era schoolhouse. Would the townspeople take notice now of the life of the girl they might have passed by in the convenience store, unaware of her yearning for an absent boy named Colin Jones? Would the young people who'd heard stories now believe the stories were not "some kind of fantasy"? There was yellow crime scene tape on the bridge that the townspeople crossed daily on their way to work and homes, a place illuminated and built for safe passage. The discovery would soon be theirs to try to understand: a girl floating, in their midst, a young girl whom they might have harmed or might have saved.

Certainly one woman in Gorge Park on that Saturday afternoon was not indifferent to the activity, and her perceptions soon turned to a kind of tragic telepathy.

She stood on the green banks where her niece had once been photographed in a navy sailor suit in front of a cluster of white lilies. A photographer from the local paper, the *Times-Colonist,* aimed his lens toward the crime scene. The woman, named Amarijit, she stood in her lilac sari, her left hand holding her son's soccer ball. A memory, an image, flickered in her mind, like the light that shimmered suddenly under the dark waters. She saw Reena, her niece, laughing as she used to laugh, when she spoke of how she wanted to have "a ton of babies." The last time she'd seen her niece, she'd noticed the word on the young girl's hand. The word was written in black marker, and her niece was fourteen, and giddy. "It's a secret," Reena had said when Amarijit asked her why she'd written the word on her hand. *Crip.* Reena blushed then, so in contrast with the word from Los Angeles, the word of faraway violence and thuggery.

Amarijit knew the photographer because her husband was the circulation manager at the *Times-Colonist.* As she approached him, a coldness fell through her suddenly, and she realized she was clutching the soccer ball to her heart. "Ian," she said, "what's going on?"

"They found an East Indian girl in the water."

Even before she had heard this, she had known the

girl in the water was Reena. Grabbing her son, she rushed home, past the cameramen and gathering crowd. She phoned her husband, without the heart to tell him of the "East Indian girl in the water."

Instead, she begged him to call Suman.

"Why?" he asked, hearing the panic in her voice.

Still clutching her son's soccer ball, Amarijit tried to still the panic in her voice, her heart. "Just call her," she pleaded. "Just see if Reena's okay."

THE GUY IN THIS CASE

I should tell you right now: Reena's body has been found and she's dead," Bruce Brown said to Warren. "You're nodding your head . . . like, you know that."

"I know," Warren said, very softly, staring at the table as if it could absorb him forever.

"I feel bad any time someone's dead, especially a fourteen-year-old girl. It eats at me," Bond said. "Last night, I couldn't sleep because I felt sad for the girl. And I thought, there's only one thing that I can do now. I can talk to her mom and dad and say, 'This is what happened to your daughter.' So when they go the funeral, they'll understand, at least. They'll understand what happened to their daughter."

"You've had some time to think about this," Bruce Brown said. "You've had time to talk to your dad. You've had time to talk to Grace. You've had time to talk to a lawyer. I want to know right now if you want to tell us what happened. This would be for the record so there would be no confusion about what Warren Glowatski saw and did."

"I want my lawyer sitting beside me," Warren said.

"You want your lawyer sitting beside you?" Bruce Brown said. "Right now, we have a whole pile of people out there giving us information about what you did."

"I'll deal with you straight up on this, whether you have a lawyer in this room or not," Bond said. He often was so successful at interrogations because, as he explains, "I let the suspect know that their situation is not going to get any better. If they think they're having a shitty time now, I let them know it's only going to get worse."

Bond shifted in his chair, scratched his shorn scalp, stared down at the frail boy with the gold curls. "The bottom line is this: the girl who was killed is a big woman. The girl that's lined up for it—Kelly—is an average-sized woman. People put the two of you on the other side of the bridge with a big woman, and what they're gonna say is—this big girl, at fourteen, gets taken down. Now if that big girl and Kelly went toe to toe, it would probably be an even fight. When two people of equal size fight, very rarely does someone end up dead."

"I know what I saw that night."

"Oh I know," Bond said, "but we've got the body now. They're going to be doing forensic tests. You've heard about DNA? When they start checking and comparing, if they can show that you dragged her in the water, this is the time you want to be dealing with that."

"I know."

"The other problem you've got, Warren, is that her panties are missing. So people are going to start thinking that maybe you sexually assaulted her or raped her."

"I'm not—"

"Listen to me, Warren," Bruce Brown commanded. "Kelly wouldn't have done that because she's a girl.

You're the *guy* that's there. So people are going to start saying, 'Well, geez, maybe he went over there to rape her.' You knocked her unconscious. *You* raped her when she was unconscious, or even dead, for that matter. There's just the mere appearance of what it looks like— there's a guy and a girl there and a dead girl. Her pants and panties are missing. What are people going to say, Warren? What are people going to say?"

"Girls don't steal other girls' underpants," John Bond added.

"And we now have people saying they saw you kick her on the other side of the bridge. They saw you participate in the assault. It's no big leap of faith to suggest that you also assaulted her on the other side. You have serious trouble. You have a *serious* problem."

"I didn't even get close to her."

"People saw you kick her," Brown asserted.

"You kicked her," Bond confirmed.

"I told you . . . ," Warren muttered, before John Bond loomed toward him, a stocky, commonsensical man, with his voice full of warning.

"Hey," Bond said. "You want me to say it to you real nice and close?" He was close enough now that Warren could see the faint lines in the pouches under his eyes. "- You're going down. You're going down big time. We were the nice guys yesterday. Hey, we didn't really have the script figured out yesterday morning. A few hours of sleep, a bite to eat. I know the script now. You've got big, big problems. You have got to tell your side of the story damn quick."

"Because you know what happens?" Bond continued,

leaning back in his chair. "As a kid, you ever gone to a birthday party where there's lots of kids and not too much cake? If you get through the door a little late, there's no cake for you. It's like that here. Everyone's getting in to tell their story nice and quick. You're sitting on the fence. You haven't been too quick. By the time you wanna get your story out, it may be just too late for you. Hey, there's people that have you kicking her on the other side of the bridge."

"You got blood on your clothes," Brown reminded him. "You say, 'Oh, I got this blood on my clothes 'cause I just happened to be standing so close that it splattered on me.'"

Bond then pulled out a hidden dagger. He brought up something that might unsettle Warren more than being called a rapist or going down big time, and this something he brought up now was very powerful. Call it a boy's first love. "Your girlfriend, your cute little girlfriend that works at the fish and chip shop, you think she's gonna lie to twelve people on a jury, eight or nine lawyers, CHEK-6 television, the newspapers? She's gonna say, 'Yeah. He came home with blood all over his clothes.'"

"There wasn't blood all over my clothes," Warren said wanly.

"You've got a problem. Your girlfriend is gonna say she washed your white pants. Hey, do you think this is a magic show? How did I know that you were wearing white pants? How did I know that you were kicking her?"

"I told you guys that last night," Warren said.

"Everyone's telling us. You're saying it. They're saying it. Yeah, you're a kicker. Welcome to the party. You kicked. You're going to jail big time."

"I know what I saw," Warren said.

"What do you mean 'what I saw'?" Bruce Brown said, stiffening. Every sentence of the two partners fell forward like a particularly strong and lashing blow.

And still Warren hadn't broken. Yet. "I said everything last night."

"Well, you don't seem to get the picture here. We've got a whole pile of witnesses who are going to say Warren was part of the fight. Warren went to the other side of the bridge, and then she ends up dead. Reena's a hundred and fifty or sixty pounds. You've got little Kelly who's a hundred and ten pounds. Do you think anybody is gonna—"

"I can't even bench-press eighty pounds," Warren said.

"I don't give a shit how much you can bench-press!" Bruce Brown screamed. "I can't even bench-press seventy pounds. I don't even care. All I'm saying is you've got a bunch of people in court listening to you saying you never kicked her. However, the physical evidence will show that you have her blood on your pants. Two, three, four people will say they saw you kick her. Then you're gonna say, 'I just went to the other side and watched Kelly. I didn't do anything.' But because you lied about facts we can prove, do you think the jury is going to believe you didn't have anything to do with the murder? I don't think so. Her pants and panties are missing. She's either been raped—"

"As if I'm going to sexually assault her. I've got a girl-friend."

"I don't really care," Brown sneered. "How many pictures of girls do you have in your wallet? You've got twenty of them. What does that say to me? That says to me maybe you like a lot of girls. So you're not just a true-blue, one-girl man, are you?"

"I am."

"Yeah? I don't think so."

"You know," Bond said, leaning back now, folding his arms across his chest, still with alert eyes on the boy, "maybe they'll bring in one of your friends who says, 'Warren talks a bit kinky. He's a bit dirty.' They'll bring in teachers who say, 'Yeah, this guy has a bit of an attitude. A bit of a temper.' And then you'll say, 'Oh my God. I didn't think they'd be saying anything about that.'

"You think a jury is gonna believe you just sat there ten feet away while a murder happened? And all you're saying is, 'Let's go. Let's go. Let's go.' You didn't really care about Reena. All you cared about was getting your own skin out of there."

"Lots of people didn't get out of there. I don't even want to be where I am right now."

"Well, you are," Brown said. "So don't try to wish yourself away from it, Warren. You can't. You're here. Deal with it. And deal with it like a man."

"Lots of people are phoning up here now," Bond said, practicing the technique of trickery. "And they're saying, 'I saw two people dragging her into the water.'

Deal with that. Hey. With your hair! I kind of like the style, but it's distinctive."

"It is distinctive," Warren said.

"They're not going to be getting you and Kelly mixed up. Hey, you're distinctive. You're going down. So this is the time to say, 'Yeah. I did some shit here.'"

"I might have kicked her on the initial side, okay?"

"I *know* you kicked her. It's not a case of might have. I know. So tell me something I don't know."

"I never did nothing on the other side of that bridge," Warren insisted.

Bond then informed Warren about the significance of DNA.

"When we talk about DNA, this stuff is precise shit," he said. "You didn't pull her in? You didn't brush up against her? You didn't pick up her shoes? You didn't pick up her clothes or backpack?"

"I didn't touch anything of hers."

"You didn't pick up her pants? You didn't fold her clothes? You didn't touch any single thing of hers when you were over there?"

"Honest. I swear to God."

"Yeah," Brown sneered. "You were saying that last night, holding your crucifix and saying, 'I never kicked her. I like girls. I would never hurt them. I've been brought up to respect women. That's the last thing I would ever do.' And here you are, Warren, right in the middle of a homicide."

"Hey," John Bond said, offering Warren another reality to contemplate. "When you have twelve people on a jury, they may convict Kelly, but I know one thing: they're gonna be looking for a guy. Women on the jury want to see guys found guilty, and I think you happen to be the guy in this case. And if there's nothing we can do for you, well, hey. I've been in the business twenty-plus years. So has my partner. Hey, big stuff. We see a lot of people go down. They get convicted. You've got some problems."

"I know that," Warren said, hearing about a jury looking for "the guy in this case."

"You better deal with it."

"On the other side, I had nothing to do with that. I didn't even touch her."

"So why would you go over the bridge?"

"'Cause Kelly asked me because she wanted to go talk to her."

"And what did she say? She didn't say, 'Oh, I want to go talk to her.'"

"She said, 'I want to go talk to her,'" Warren insisted, and he began to cry.

"'I want to go and fucking *deal* with her' is what she said."

Brown said, "That sort of sounds like a plan to me. Everyone else had left. It's just the two of you, and Kelly says, 'Hey, Warren. I'm gonna go over there and do a number on her. I need some backup.' Now, if that's what she said and you didn't actually participate in the assault, that's one thing. But if you both said, 'Let's go over and fucking kick her ass.'"

"Kelly said, 'I want to find out what really happened with her getting beat up,'" Warren said, weakly.

"She knew what was going on. She was part of the beating. She wasn't at all confused about what the beating was all about."

"I should have left as soon as she hit her once," Warren said.

"You should have done a lot of things by then."

"I should have left even that night. I shouldn't even be here right now."

"But you are. Don't keep wishing it away, buddy."

"This isn't a bad dream," Bond said. "You're not gonna snap out of it. You think it's a dream? Here, go ahead and touch me. I'm here. I'm not something that you can't see. I'm not going anywhere. Hey, you went over the bridge. That's the bottom line. That's what happened. Go ahead. Tell me about the part where she's told to take her shoes off. 'Get your shoes off, bitch.' Tell me about that part."

"I already told you guys about that part."

"I want to hear it again."

"I'm calling my lawyer."

"What's your lawyer gonna do?"

"I don't know. It's gonna get me incriminated."

"You are incriminated! What do you mean *getting incriminated?* You kicked her during this swarming, and then you and Kelly go over and kill her. Possibly rape her."

"I did not kill anybody. I did not rape her."

Brown spoke less sternly now, contemplatively, as if a new idea had just occurred to him. "Maybe that's why you're having a tough time with this. Because you sexually assaulted her. Maybe you're disgusted with that."

"Accuse me of whatever you want, okay?" Warren said.

"There's no accusing of anything," Bond said. "We're saying we've figured out what happened. Your friends are lining up to say Warren did this. Warren did that. Warren did the kicking. He wore white pants. He went to his girlfriend's place. Blah, blah, blah. But everyone seems to be on the same page: you and Kelly went to the other side of the bridge with Reena, who was alive, and when you both came back, she was dead. Doesn't matter who threw the final punch. It's like two people going out to rob a bank. I may be the one that talks to the teller and my partner may be the guy that drives the car. We both robbed a bank. Hey, both of you guys went over there. I think Kelly was leading you, and said, 'Hey. I've had it with her. I'm tired of her shooting her yap off. I'm gonna go deal with her. Hey, come along.' You come along as the good guy. I don't think when you went over there you necessarily thought she was gonna get killed. I think you thought she might get punched out a little more."

"The only thing I thought was that she was going to find out everything that happened from Reena's point of view. And what happened after, after she'd been punching her like that, that shouldn't have happened."

"Well, did you say *stop?*" Bond inquired.

"When she was dragging her down to the water, I said, at least three times, 'Stop. Let's go.'"

"And do you think she was dead or alive when that was happening?"

"Probably alive."

"How far was she dragged?"

"Twenty feet. Thirty feet."

"By her feet or by her hands?"

"By the feet."

"So Kelly had one foot, and you had the other foot?"

"No. I didn't even have a foot. I didn't help."

"Don't forget. DNA, fiber, trace fiber," Bruce Brown said. "Do you know about the Atlanta child murder case? The guy, Wayne Williams, they found his fibers on his victim's clothing weeks after."

"I know."

"You've read about him?"

"No, I know though, even a small bit, just a hair. . . ."

"You've got some problems here."

"I know," Warren conceded, at last. "I know."

"I think your story has got the room to improve in certain parts," Bond confided with an instinct that Warren was about to stop "calibrating" his story. "You're not being totally clean. But some of it makes sense. Kelly was leading the attack on the other side. You weren't. She was the one that wanted to get things done. When you said, 'Let's get out of here,' if you would have went and phoned 911, well, all you would have had to say was, 'There's a girl that's been beat up and she's at the beach.' You wouldn't have even had to give your name. And when you went to court, you know what they'd say? Maybe the guy didn't deal himself in to kill this poor girl. But now what they'll say is two people go over the bridge with Reena, she ends up dead. There's no effort by you to do anything. It doesn't matter if you ended up punching her in the head or you dragged her in the water. The bottom line is, you're gonna be held accountable for—"

"Her murder," Warren said.

"That's right. There's one spin you can put on this thing right now. You should say, 'Bruce. John. I haven't been quite up front with you. This is what happened. Hey, this thing went crazy. It went sideways. It happened so quick.'"

"What happened under the bridge," Warren said softly, "it was crazy."

"Oh, I know. There's so many people that want to tell us about what happened under the bridge that I'm running out of goddamned tapes. That's not the thing. You're lined up for that. That's a no-brainer."

"You see, what happened on the other side, Kelly," Warren paused, "beat her up, okay? I'm calling her. She was puking." He began to sob. "And choking on blood. And Kelly was. . . ." His words were muffled by sobs. "Kelly might be a small girl, but she is strong."

"Do you think Kelly's gonna get up in court and say, 'Yeah. I went over there and personally punched the shit out of her 'til she was throwing up and puking and then I dragged her in the water and tried to drown her. And Warren, my friend, was saying, 'Hey, let's get out of here. This isn't right. Let's go.'"

"When she was dragging her in the water, I said, 'Let's go.'"

"But prior to that, when she was getting beat up, they're gonna say, hey . . ."

"Why didn't I offer to come and help?"

"Oh," Bond predicted, "Kelly and her lawyer are

going to be eating you alive. You think this is ugly? Hey, we might as well be having a cup of tea here. It's gonna get uglier for you because Kelly's got some high-flying lawyers now, and they're gonna say, 'Hey, my client was there, but this kid Warren, he's got the bad temper. He's tough. He's lean. He's quick.' It's going to be half-true, half-false, but it's going to be enough for the jury."

"It's going to be a lot of b.s.," Warren said.

"Oh, I know. They're just gonna do a number on you like you wouldn't believe."

"Kelly doesn't have any blood on her clothes," Bond said.

"You go check her Calvin Klein jacket."

"Okay. We'll try and help you out and come up with this jacket. But do you think she's gonna end up taking the whole rap for this? What do you think?"

"She's gonna point the finger at me."

"Yeah," Bond agreed, his voice suddenly sympathetic. "So let's make sure we get the portions of liability right. The person that did the bulk of it should take the lion's share of the punishment. The person that just played a 10 percent or 20 percent role should make sure they get their story told. Because the hardest part is dealing with this in court. It's not dealing with Bruce and me. We're easy guys to deal with."

"You're nice guys. I know that."

"Hey, Warren," Bond said, as if speaking to a good friend, "if she's done the bulk of this and you've done a little bit of it, tell us right now what you've done so we can assess and just see how much trouble you've got yourself in here."

"The shoes," Warren admitted. "I put them with the jacket. So there's gonna be two fingerprints right there."

"Okay, that matches up," Bond said, encouragingly.

"And where did you put them?" Brown inquired.

"Right by the white schoolhouse."

"She was ordered to take the shoes off, wasn't she?"

"Yes."

"And who was doing the ordering?"

"Kelly."

"Did she resist?"

"No. She said, 'Take them.'"

"And what did Kelly do next?"

"She started beating her up again."

"So why didn't Reena resist taking her jacket or shoes off? Was she injured from the fight earlier?"

"She had a little bit of blood on her face."

"A little bit?"

"But she was still talking fine. She was walking fine."

"What did she say to you?"

"She didn't say anything to me."

"I'm sure there were some things said there."

"But she didn't even know us. I don't know that girl. That was the first time I met her in my life. And the last."

"Well, you won't be meeting her again," Bond said gravely. "I agree. That's the last time you'll meet her because she's dead."

He paused. The men were quiet, and so was the boy. Bond watched Warren attentively. He looked at the clock, and let some minutes go by. He then spoke, his voice friendlier, even more respectful, than it might ever have been. Anyone listening might have thought he was speaking to a person whom he greatly revered: "Warren, I can tell right now that you're about thirty seconds from saying, 'Guys, this is eating me up. I just want to tell you my involvement. Something happened that was bad. I wasn't the one that caused the most grief.'"

"I wasn't."

"I know you've got something to say to us right now about what happened down by the beach and you want to say it right now. I can tell that right now."

Warren sighed, and because he felt understood, even accepted, for the first time, by the two men, the nice guys, he said he would speak now, if only they turned off the tape. Bond's instinct had been correct. Warren was ready.

He told his story then, through tears, in a whisper.

"After Officer Hodginson came, we left Shoreline. We turned left. We went under the bridge. Everyone was down there and there was all this screaming noise. I was close enough that. . . ." He began to cry. "Twice."

He paused, as if overcome by the darkness of memory.

"After that, everyone left. I don't know if she was unconscious but she was sitting up. She was down by the water. They all left. Kelly's like, 'Well, we're gonna talk to her. I want to find out exactly what went on tonight. I want to find out if that Reena girl is sorry for all the trouble she caused.' So we went over the bridge, and then we stopped to order her to take her shoes and jacket off. When she took them off, I threw away her jacket and put her shoes on the steps. And then beat her up more until she was woozy, and Kelly grabbed her head. Her head was smashed against a tree."

"Smashed against a tree?" Brown said, incredulously.

"Yeah. So there's probably blood all over the tree. And then . . . then she started kicking her in the head and the ribs. I didn't kick her when she was on the ground. And then she, she started choking on blood. And that's why, Kelly. . . ." Still sobbing, he looked down at the wood table, away from his interrogators. "I dragged her for about nine or ten feet, but I couldn't. I didn't want to drag her. I said, 'No. Let's go.' At least three times. I was telling Kelly, 'Come on.' At least three times. Why don't we leave. 'Cause I don't want to do any of this. And then I'll have to deal with it right now . . . but there's no way I can get rid of it. . . ."

"Hard to do, huh?" Brown asked.

"I can't," Warren said, still sobbing.

"Well," Bond said, "with what you've told us, you know, you could be charged with being part of the homicide just because you were there. And first-degree murder is when someone is sexually assaulted and then murdered, but I don't think that's the case here."

"I didn't murder her. And sexual assault? I mean, that's sick. Seriously sick."

"So where's all her clothes now?" Bond asked.

"They were right by her."

"Did you go down later and pick up the clothes because you were worried about fingerprints?"

"No."

"Who have you told about this?"

"I didn't tell other people about it."

"Well, you told somebody."

"I didn't tell any friends. I didn't tell anyone."

"You know exactly who you told."

"I may have told Maya."

"And how about Syreeta?"

"Hmmm."

"How about Syreeta?" Brown repeated.

"I haven't told her anything."

"You're stalling for some reason here. And don't be stalling just because you don't want to give up a name. This is your life we're talking about. There's one person you told, Warren. I think you know the answer. You have to tell me. Show me you're being truthful and honest."

"I didn't tell anyone else as far as I remember."

"Syreeta has met with an officer. So this is your chance."

"I don't remember, honestly."

"Do you think there's anyone that actually saw you and Kelly that night?" Bond asked.

"Saw us walk over the bridge?"

"Yeah."

"Dimitri and Marissa."

"On a scale of ten, with respect to the death of Reena, how do you think you're responsible? Like, is Kelly eight out of ten responsible and you're two out of ten?"

"Three and seven," Warren said.

"Three and seven?" Bond said, staring at Warren. "Okay."

"I know what I did was wrong."

"Okay."

"I know I'll get punished for it."

"Hers is seven. Yours is three," Bond said, returning to the fraction of responsibility. "What would your three consist of?"

"Kicking, dragging her that ten feet, and being around."

"How about being in the water?"

"I was never in the water. I never went in. I know I should have—I wish I had—stopped her. I should have left before any of this happened."

"Oh hey," Bond said, hoarsely. "Hey, I would have loved it not to happen because I wouldn't be here. I'd be home with my family. But that's not the case. This has happened." He sighed and looked down at his notepad. He could sense his partner's desire to end the interview now that they had closed in and won.

"How do you feel?" Bond asked Warren. "You feel okay talking to us?"

"Yeah. I feel a lot better. It's just—I know I'm going down for something that I didn't have a major role in."

"You feel okay talking to us?" Bond asked again.

"I'm being truthful."

"You are being truthful," Bond agreed.

"You guys are being honest with me," Warren said.

"Yeah, and hey, just between the three of us, and guy to guy, I think there's absolutely no way you sexually assaulted her or intended to sexually assault her. That's guy to guy. I also feel that you, as a rule, don't go around hurting people. That's not your style. And I think you want to deal with this situation. You think, 'Hey, now that I'm talking to Bruce and John, I feel better.' You feel better in the last ten minutes, don't you?"

"Yeah. It's still eating me away, what happened."

"Well, that's good," Bond said. "It's been eating me away too."

"I'm scared of *everything*," Warren said, and his eyes returned to the surface of the table, as if he could will himself to be swallowed up by the dark and sturdy wood. His interrogators were quiet, containing their contempt, and he made a sudden request.

"Can I phone my girlfriend?" Warren asked.

"I think your girlfriend is being interviewed right now."

"She's here?" Warren said, and he turned his head, as if looking for a nonexistent window.

"I'm not sure."

The room was silent and airless, and Warren wondered suddenly if he could pass Syreeta in the hallway, just see her one last time. The two men seemed impatient now, and he worried that they no longer liked him. He thought of the police officer, years ago, who had sneered his name, *Glowatski*, as if to say, "Oh you're one of them."

"I just really wanted to talk," Warren said. "And tell you guys what happened."

"Do you want to speak to a lawyer?"

"It's too late now."

"It's not too late now."

"I'll speak to a lawyer later on, yes." He seemed about to speak again, and looked down at the table, and then up at the two men to whom he now confessed.

"I don't have it in me to kill a person. I know what I did is wrong and I shouldn't have done it and I should have phoned the cops as soon as it happened."

"So when you were by the white schoolhouse, were you thinking, 'Hey, geez, I might have a problem if Reena rats on me'?"

"Yeah, but I'm not gonna kill a person just 'cause I can get charged with assault."

"Did it enter your mind that you were deep into this and it would solve your problem if she died?"

"No. It never ran in my mind that I'd kill a person."

"But how did you feel when you saw Kelly killing her? I mean, did you think 'That's the end of my problem as well'?"

"No. I couldn't handle watching her. I said, 'Let's go. Stop. Let's go.' I tried to stop her."

"Is this the truth?"

"I swear on my grandpa's grave."

"Your grandpa's grave, eh?" Bruce Brown stood up now. His movement was decisive, final, hinting at his contempt. He felt exhausted, as he often did at the end of an interrogation. This too was an odd reward. He now had what he wanted, and yet what a terrible thing to have procured.

Wanting to leave, he turned to the paperwork and told Warren to sign a form, and after Warren signed it, Bruce Brown said the words he was legally obligated to say, words that contained neither hostility nor sadness, though he felt both of these things, greatly and endlessly, then, on that Saturday afternoon. "Warren, you've signed this sheet, you understand the ramifications and the jeopardy that you're in, right?"

"I know I'm in jeopardy. I'm in deep shit. I'm in over my head."

"Yeah, you are," Bond said, standing up, refusing to look in the eyes of the small boy. "There's no question. I think that's pretty evident today. But you're in better shape than Reena is," he said, and he turned off the tape recorder, and headed, directly and rapidly, toward the door.

RIGHT OUT OF PLACE

The Victoria Youth Custody Centre, known as YCC, or more informally, as juvie, is located around the corner from a small corner store owned by Chinese immigrants, a purveyor of candy and lottery tickets. The detention center itself, an unremarkable slab of a building, stands somewhat camouflaged by the Department of Public Works office building. Despite its purpose, YCC has no barbed wire or electrical fence surrounding the property. In fact, the only sign of law and order is the daily arrival of a white sheriff's van.

On November 22, in the late afternoon, seven new residents would arrive.

The guards were given special instructions in regard to the new girls: Maya, Willow, Laila, Eve, Dusty, Kelly, and Josephine. They were to be kept separate; they were not to speak to one another.

The guards observed the new girls, the schoolgirls.

"Most of the kids in here have been in and out of juvie since they were twelve," a guard named Floyd explains. "They all know each other. They're from the same milieu. But these new girls, you could just tell they had never been in trouble before. They probably grew up having barbecues together. And now they're here. They were right out of place and they knew it."

• • •

Newspapers and television news were banned suddenly. This censorship increased the interest in the arrival of the new girls, and it took only hours for rumors to move through the hallways and classrooms.

"When I found out what they'd done, I just said 'Holy Shit!' It exhausted everybody's brains," Floyd, the guard, recalls.

The kids in juvie found it "weird" when seven girls came in together, and soon began their own investigation into the crime since the newspapers were missing and the guards were unusually tense and silent. In juvie, days are divided into blocks and in those blocks of time the residents attend arts and crafts class or woodwork or gym. But at 1:30 and 3:15 and 5:30, they're granted free time, and in these moments of free time, several girls discussed their findings.

"Warren started the fight," a girl named Sidra said. "That's what I heard."

"No, Warren told Craig that he didn't do anything," insisted Annie.

"I heard this!" a red-haired girl with a Chinese tattoo on her breast declared: "The girl who died was Warren's girlfriend and she screwed around on him and Warren got pissed off. So, he got Kelly mad at the girl and then there was a fight and the other girls took off because they were scared."

"Why would they take off?" Sidra asked.

"I don't know. They all beat the girl up and they were scared they were going to get charged. They're standing there, like, 'What are we going to do? What are we going to do?' And Kelly goes, 'Don't worry about it. Don't worry about it.' And then Warren and Kelly followed her. They went over the bridge after her and they burned her with a cigarette and they drowned her. They kept it secret for a week. This all happened last Friday."

"No, I asked Dusty. I go, 'What are you all in for?' And she goes, 'We beat the shit out a girl and then she died.' Just like that. Exactly like that! She's all proud of it."

Arianna, a girl with black roots and a sly smile, a girl who'd lived on the streets near Chinatown since she was twelve, was thoroughly disgusted by the revelation. "I was high as a kite when I did my assault," she sneered. "These girls were stone-cold sober. But I like Laila," Arianna said. "She's cool. I talked to her in arts and crafts, and she said she doesn't even know those girls. She just met them that night. She said she tried to stop the fight."

Lily spoke up now, "I heard Kelly ask the girl with the braids, Eve, she asks her, 'Why'd you rat me out? My lawyer told me you gave a statement against me.' And Eve goes, 'I'm not going down for murder. *You* did it, not me.'"

"Yeah, Kelly's got a lot of attitude. I wouldn't be acting like that if I was going down for murder," Arianna said, and all the others nodded.

"She's sick," Lily said. "They're all sick. They killed a fourteen-year-old girl."

"Yeah, at least I can change the things I did," Arianna said.

Lily, too, contemplated redemption and the consequences of murder. "I can go back and apologize to the people I've hurt, but once you *kill* somebody, that's it. You can never change that. Kelly thinks she's getting out of here too. She told me, 'I've got a good lawyer. I'm getting out any day now.'"

The girls laughed and wondered how long Kelly would last if she found herself cornered by eight others. How long would she last if she was the cornered one?

"The blonde Josephine is a little princess. She looks like she should be doing ballet."

"What was the name of the girl they killed?" Annie asked softly.

"Elly something," Lily said. "That's what I heard. I think her name was Elly McBride."

• • •

Though they were forbidden to do so, Kelly and Josephine found a way to whisper.

"Did you give a statement?" Kelly asked. The stud in her nose had been taken away.

"Fuck, no. Of course, not."

"Well, don't give a statement against me, and I won't give one on you."

"Of course not, Kel," Josephine said, truthfully. "I would never do that to you."

The girls hugged and held one another, and then Floyd, the guard with a brush cut and a wrestler's physique, came and brought Kelly back to her cell.

"Tell these girls in here to stop messing with me," Kelly ordered, as if he was her personal bodyguard. "Tell them I know karate."

He held back a laugh and opened the door with a key attached to the chain on his hip. "Take a good look at the company you're in," he said to her, without sarcasm or irony.

THE FIREMAN'S SON

John Bond knew the man who showed up at the station that Saturday evening. They'd both been volunteer firemen together for the View Royal Fire Department. Doug was a good man, Sergeant John Bond thought, still married to a nurse, and on the weekends he'd take tourists on fishing trips around the bays of the island. The fireman had brought in his son.

The son seemed slightly hesitant. The young boy held his skateboard to his chest, as if it was a shield that could ward off dangers about to come his way.

The fireman's son was seventeen. When he was at Shoreline, he was one of the "cool" boys, who seemed effortlessly possessed of a certain and elusive charisma. Colin Jones thought the fireman's son was "hilarious . . . he has an awesome sense of humor," while even Warren would later admit, "I've got a lot of respect for that guy."

Billy, the fireman's son, was now a senior at Spectrum School and thus had heard no rumors of the murder. He nonetheless arrived at the Saanich station soon after his father saw the commotion near the Gorge. Bond would later speak of Billy's information as "the nugget."

"You get all these false leads, and all these kids giving you what I'd kindly call carefully calibrated versions of the truth, and then you get a kid like Billy who's just totally forthcoming, and it's an interview, not an interrogation."

Billy's crewcut was bleached blonde, in the style later favored by Eminem. Dimples appeared in his cheek when he smiled, which, until this moment, had been quite often and constant. Like Syreeta, he was about to step away from the innocence of his youth in View Royal, all because of what occurred on the evening of the Russian satellite.

Billy had not seen the satellite fall. He'd been at his friend Craig Smith's, watching a movie with his girlfriend, Annika. The movie was called *The Relic*, and later, he would remember how silly they'd all been, so goofy, just watching the monster in the horror movie and screaming and laughing.

At eleven o'clock, Billy and Annika left because Annika had a curfew of 11:30, and Billy planned to walk to his place, get his dad's black truck, and drive her home. Only something very unusual occurred as he crossed the Old Island Highway. He saw Kelly Ellard— he'd known her "for most of my life." He was friends and classmates with her older brother; he knew her stepsister; she lived down the street from him and he'd been to her house a few times. He felt neither friendly nor hostile toward her; he felt largely indifferent. She was just a little sister, another girl from the neighborhood.

And then that night, after watching the horror movie, he'd bumped into her and it was a little weird because her pants were wet up to the knees. It got even stranger, even creepier, even the strangest thing that had happened to Billy in his young and carefree life.

Kelly had walked up to him, seeming "stressed out," and had asked him for a cigarette. She then told him that she had just held a girl's head under water in the Gorge waterway.

"What should I do?" Kelly had asked him. "What should I do?"

When he heard this, Billy thought she must be kidding around. "I just thought it was a complete joke," he would later admit.

Bond asked him if he had told anybody about the conversation with Kelly.

Billy said yes, he had told his father when he got home that night. His father had also thought the story of Kelly drowning a girl in the Gorge couldn't be true. It was only on this Saturday when he'd seen the divers in the Gorge and heard from other firemen that a young girl's body had been discovered that he realized his son had important evidence.

"My dad," Billy would later say, "made me go to the police."

"Well, we appreciate you coming forward," John Bond said. "That's pretty significant information."

Billy nodded, and he pressed his skateboard back to his chest.

• • •

Erna Anderson greeted John Bond at the door of her apartment. She was a talkative woman, a cashier at Thrifty Foods supermarket. "Well, I thought the coat was my friend's grandson's," she said, chatting nervously. "And then at work today, my co-worker, well, he took the training test to be a police officer, and he told me on the news he'd heard about a girl found in the Gorge, and I told him, 'Well, jeez, I found a coat down there last Saturday,' and he says, 'Erna, you got to call the police.' Her apartment smelled like carnations and apple pie. John Bond smiled, and she kept chatting to him as she offered him some coffee. "And when I got the coat, it was covered in blood."

Hearing this, he asked to see the coat, which she had retrieved from her friend. He touched the cloth. The coat was large and ordinary, just a black and white Adidas jacket with a few cigarette burns in the sleeve.

"The blood was there, and there," Erna said, pointing at the clean cloth. "And I thought, well, whoever stole this from Robby must have got in some fight." She shook her head.

He saw no blood on the coat, and looked at her quizzically.

"Oh," she said, blushing. "I washed the coat."

She was still chatting away, for it was nice to have a visitor, especially someone like John Bond whom you just wanted to talk to for as long as possible. "You noticed the blood more on the white part," she said, pointing at the stripe on the sleeve. "I put it in my car after we took it from the jogger and it was soaking wet and—"

"Can I take a look at your car?"

"Sure," she said, and she led the detective outside, where her car was parked under the awning of a cherry blossom tree. The detective cut out part of the carpet on her car floor, leaving a dark and rough hole. He told her they would need to send the carpet to the lab. Even at this early stage, John Bond knew if there were to be convictions in this strange case, the detectives better hurry up and find some real and tangible evidence.

A MORALITY DRAMA

On Monday morning, the public spectacle began.

In Youth Court, all eight teenagers appeared and were formally charged before a judge. The atmosphere of the courtroom was charged and frenetic, for the hearing was attended by a large number of journalists, from countries as far away as Sweden and Japan. Never before had so many journalists crowded into a courtroom in the small and lovely town.

Teenagers too arrived at the courthouse, a square box of a building located near the tearooms and tartan shops of downtown Victoria. Teenagers sat on the steps, not far from the sheriffs', but farther from the plaque engraved with the blessings of Queen Elizabeth, for courts in Canada are still under the monarch's domain. Across the street, satellite trucks were parked in the lot of the Cherry Bank Hotel, and beside the sign announcing barbecue ribs—"all you can eat—10.99"—cameramen wielding telephoto lenses smoked American cigarettes and paced, furious that they were not allowed into the courthouse.

"I feel kind of quivery," a girl named Millie Modeste, a Shoreline student, confessed to a reporter, unaware that her words would appear in *The New York Times*. "I'm really surprised," Millie Modeste said. "I go to school with them and they don't seem like those kind of people."

From the back row, surrounded by the cadre of media, Dusty's sister showed no concern for protocol. She screamed out to her young sister, who stood teary-eyed and startled beside her more regal and proud former cohort Josephine. "I love you!" Dahlia screamed to her little sister.

After his appearance in the courtroom, prosecutor Don Morrison went outside the courthouse and held an impromptu conference. Don Morrison, a seasoned prosecutor with silver hair and a quick smile, was known for being neither timid nor bland, and yet he was momentarily startled by the large crowd surrounding him. It was another kind of swarming, one far less dangerous then the swarming of Reena Virk, but a swarming nonetheless. The journalists shoved each other, pressed forward, elbowed away photographers, raised their microphones into his face.

"A young woman was brutally murdered," he announced. "It appears that a group of women assaulted the girl. The assault ended. There was a second assault. This ended in death."

"Why'd they kill her?"

Don Morrison did not reply, for such details were not to be revealed to the media. He didn't even recognize most of the crowd. He heard foreign accents; he saw only one local reporter looking rather perturbed by the presence of so many pushy interlopers.

"Why'd they kill her?" the crowd screamed, but Don Morrison turned and went inside.

I've prosecuted many more horrible crimes than this one, Don Morrison thought, and there have never been so many reporters. What was the big deal here? He'd prosecuted the "ice queen" case in which a young girl stabbed her boyfriend's mother to death, and there'd only been the few regular crime reporters in the courthouse for that one. He hadn't even recognized half those folks swarming him: the Asian lady with stiletto heels. Who was she? The vicious-looking lady with too much blush, in a black silk suit—never seen her before. He even thought he'd glimpsed the letters CNN on one of the cameras, but there was no way that could possibly be. Then he remembered. APEC. The prime ministers of Canada and Japan, the presidents of the United States and elsewhere were all in Vancouver. The reporters must have caught wind of the Virk story and come hopping over on the helijet. They were probably bored out of their minds hearing about the near collapse of Yamiachi Securities and South Korea asking the IMF for a $20 billion bailout package. Here was something a little juicier, a little sexier, a little more human interest. Grisly Slaying of Girl, 14, Startles Small Town. Brutal Murder in Beautiful British Columbia. The Schoolgirl Killers. She Thought They Were Her Friends, But They Killed Her. Lonely Misfit Attacked by Female Gang. Or the headline might merely be the question they had screamed at him, the question to which he had given no answer. Why'd they kill her? Why did Reena Virk die?

*

In the Major Crimes office, Don Morrison found a stack of messages from reporters and flipped through the pink notepad, still surprised.

"Did you see the circus out there?" he asked his secretary.

"You're loving this," Stan Lowe teased, wandering into the office, still dressed in the black gown all lawyers wear in Canada's courtrooms.

"What's the big fascination?"

"I don't know. Maybe it's the kids killing kids angle."

"It's APEC," Don Morrison said. "APEC must have been really boring."

If he'd talked more to the media, he might have told his view: that this case was about *peer pressure* and the values of a *particular* group of kids. Bullying was a school district problem, and maybe *parents* should be a little more concerned. But from a legal point of view, the case was rather dull. He liked forensics: the bone in the bathtub, bullet residue on the steering wheel. In the courtroom, he could present elaborate but clear charts to the jury outlining the intricacies of the forensic case. But this case lacked any such fascinating elements. His first priority would be to make sure Ellard and Glowatski would be tried not as youths, but as adults in the Supreme Court. He could hear himself before the judge: "Due to the seriousness of the offense . . . the viciousness of the crime. . . ." With such public attention, he didn't foresee a problem in having the accused murderers tried as adults.

As for the six girls, they were to be charged instead with aggravated assault, not murder. He'd tried to make this clear to the media. There were two separate incidents here: an assault under the bridge and then a murder. But by now, it seemed the public wrongly believed that all eight kids had killed Reena Virk under the bridge. Oh well, soon enough the truth of the narrative would be public knowledge, probably when the assault trial of the six girls took place. Until then, he wasn't going to talk to the media about anything. The media weren't really his concern.

"This file is going to be huge," Stan Lowe said. "You've got eight accused. You're looking at a massive investigation."

"I know," Don Morrison said. "We've got the dream team on it, Bond, Brown, and Poulton. And there are *thirty* investigators working on the file. They're executing search warrants right now." He thought as well that the Dive Unit should go back into the Gorge. There might still be a weapon, some real evidence. Maybe one of these kids would have blood from the victim on his or her clothes. So far, the strongest bit of evidence they had was Billy, the boy who'd seen Kelly Ellard on the evening of the murder. The kid was reliable and sober. That was some solid, eyewitness evidence. Hopefully, more kids would come forward who had seen both Glowatski and Ellard right after the drowning.

"What was it? Some kind of thrill kill for the two of them? Was it a 'kick' kind of thing?" Stan Lowe mused.

"Ellard's got Adrian Brooks," Don said, pondering the significance of the girl's defender.

Don Morrison, like most everyone in the chummy legal community, would speak reverentially of the man. "I have the utmost respect for Adrian Brooks," those who wore black gowns would say. Brooks, as a young man, had learned his craft under the tutelage of two of Canada's most famous lawyers, Eddie Greenspan and Clayton Ruby. He was a worthy adversary, Don believed, and he enjoyed courtroom battles with the man, who had vast knowledge of the intricacies of reasonable doubt and evidence, and an intellect, Don believed, on par with his own.

His secretary came rushing in then, her face rather flushed.

"My mother just phoned. She saw you on CNN! And there's a reporter on the phone. From *GQ*. He's coming to Victoria and wants to set up a time to speak to you."

"Take a message," Don said, and he looked at Stan, and shook his head.

"APEC must have been really boring this year," he said again, for this seemed the only explanation for a bunch of Americans trying to find out about the secret story behind a young girl's death.

The two men spent the afternoon reading through the thick file of transcribed interviews. They read of Polo Sport and Calvin Klein, of the smoke pit and the stolen phone book, of stomachaches and a rap song and a boy named Jack Batley and jealousy and beauty and longings and gossip and tears.

While some prosecutors believe their role is merely to

"present the evidence," Don Morrison saw each trial as the presentation of "a morality drama." You need drama in the courtroom, he'd say, to reinforce the morality of society. A trial then, like a drama, needed both characters and themes, and above all, a clear narrative. The essence of the case needed to be conveyed in a phrase both concise and evocative.

The two Crown prosecutors would later not recall who exactly coined the phrase, only that they had come up with a rather haunting choice. On the bridge, three went over, two came back. Perfect, Don Morrison thought, and with this the men now had the linchpin of their strategy.

Three went over. Two came back.

CALVIN KLEIN AND
RALPH LAUREN AND A FAIRY TALE

In three teams of four, the men entered the bedrooms of the teenage girls. They were armed with search warrants to allow them entry into this most private realm.

Sergeant Bond, together with Sergeant Kroeker and two members of the Ident team, drove to the home of Kelly Ellard's father. Her father was unsurprised by their appearance at 8:15 in the morning. "Adrian Brooks said you'd be coming," he said gruffly. He believed quite fervently that his little girl had been wrongly accused, and the police seemed to him like misguided interlopers. He handed them a paper bag full of Kelly's clothes. John Bond looked into the bag. He wanted to collect the Calvin Klein jacket, for Warren had told him this was the jacket Kelly wore as she waded into the water with murder on her mind, but the Calvin Klein jacket was not in the bag of clothes Kelly's father had prepared.

Twenty minutes later, while searching through a closet near the laundry room, Sergeant Kroeker, in this place of domestic normalcy, attained the first piece of possible proof: the Calvin Klein jacket with some telltale marks. On the sleeves there was sand and even small pieces of seashells. And there were white stains as if the jacket had been immersed in saltwater. He handed the jacket to his partner, with his eyebrow raised. Something real. At last. When the men touched the jacket, they could smell the tart scent of saltwater stronger than the faint fragrance of a soft lilac perfume.

Other men moved into the bedrooms of the young girls and searched uneasily in the piles of denim skirts and white bras. Surely they had never done this before, rifled through the possessions that signified innocence. The men touched and took Willow's diary. The men touched and took Maya's pillowcase. "A small drop of a dark foreign substance is evident on the pillow case," the men would later note, explaining why they removed it from the girl's bed.

The men took photographs, capturing the bedrooms. On the walls, there was no evidence of a criminal lifestyle, only photographs of cherished best friends and adored heartthrobs. Suntanned girls laughing on the beaches of Hawaii. Posters of rainbows and Snoop Dogg and Michael Jordan. Yearbooks inscribed with promises. "I'll love you forever, Maya." "You're awesome, Willow." "Let's party together this summer."

The men took away and marked hoodies and black leather purses. In Laila's basement bedroom, they seized a pair of Tommy Hilfiger jeans, for "there appear to be blood drops on the thigh."

Warren's paltry duffel bag was now less a totem of an unstable life and more a source of potential evidence. Bruce Brown wrote that Warren's belongings consisted of "some CDs, some clothes in the dresser, and three pairs of white jeans." He seized the white jeans and Warren's Crip

Mafia Cartel baseball cap, which sat atop a speaker.

After the searches were completed, the seized items would be driven by Scott Green to a forensic lab in Vancouver. There, they would be dusted and coded and analyzed. Bullets and machetes and syringes and shotguns were the usual telling tableaux in the forensic lab, but now the gowned experts waded through a very modern and ordinary collection. With gloves and microscopes, they conducted tests on black high heels and Club Monaco sweatshirts, on a Guess handbag and Nike sneakers and a tube of Nivea cream. The evidence in the Virk file seemed less like evidence in a homicide investigation and more like the purchases from a particularly bountiful shopping trip at the seemingly wholesome environs of a suburban shopping mall.

On the day of the searches, Frances Olsen, the principal of Shoreline, contacted Bruce Brown to express her concern that there might be something connected to the murder in the high school hallways. "And maybe," she said, anxiously, "there is something in the lockers that could jeopardize the safety and security of the school or other students."

"I have the authority to open the lockers at any time," she told Bruce Brown, "and I think I'll do it this evening. Can you be here?"

In this way, he found himself in the halls of a high school at 6:45. Principal Olsen touched the locks. She said, "Due to the nature of this offense, I feel this is. . . ."

"It's fine," he reassured her, and her hands trembled, as if anticipating a dagger to emerge.

"This is Kelly Ellard's locker," she said, as she turned the silver wheel on locker 120.

The seasoned and very proud police officer found himself staring at a piece of adolescent artwork. Kelly had drawn the scene of the murder of a police officer. Beside a bank, a man in gangster gear (pin-striped vest and black armband, tilted fedora) aimed a black gun at a cop. Bullets flew toward his chest, drops of blood rose from his heart. On his hips, handcuffs dangled, unused. From his mouth, the words he said were, "Oink. Oink. Squeal. Squeal." On the street by a fire hydrant, a disembodied head lay in blood, near a severed hand. Beside the bank, there were drawings of windows with gathered curtains.

"I think I'll take this," he said to Frances Olsen.

In Maya's locker, there was nothing of evidentiary value, nothing to threaten the students, as she had feared, only another drawing by Kelly, which, as Bruce Brown noted, "shows a stoned-out guy smoking what looks like a marijuana joint." On a piece of paper, attached to the steel door, he read various writings that were vaguely foreign to him, their meaning unknown. *B.K. 4 Life. Westside Wigger. CMC Crew. Crip. R.I.P. What'z up now Bitch!*

In his notebook, he wrote, "I will seize the last paper with the words, 'Should've never fucked with me,' and the one with, 'So you wanna be a gangsta.'"

"In a Land Called Funk" was the title of the school essay found in locker 701. Written on July 21, 1997, the "essay" was Warren Glowatski's assignment for English class. In fact, it was not an original piece of prose, but the borrowed lyrics from the song "Ghetto Cartoon" by the rap star Coolio. The song, a revision of childhood cartoon episodes, features Minnie Mouse getting shot down, a crime witnessed by Kermit the Frog, who was too "scared" to testify.

Warren's teacher corrected his misspelling of "drive-buy" and had circled "glock," adding her own question mark.

Bruce Brown wrote in his report. "I seized the fairy tale; a sort of gangsta/rap type story about somebody being shot using characters such as Goofy, Mickey, and Bugs Bunny."

Bruce Brown and John Bond found themselves at the Tillicum Mall perfume counter. The two men, both wearing leather jackets, might have been mistaken for husbands buying a gift for their wife. They surveyed: Opium, White Diamonds, Happy, Eternity.

"Can I help you?" the salesclerk said hopefully.

Sergeant Bond flashed his badge.

"Is this about those girls from Shoreline?"

He nodded and produced some shards of glass from a plastic bag in his pocket.

The small shards of glass had been retrieved from the concrete of the parking lot behind the Comfort Inn.

"Do you know what kind of bottle these might have been from? What brand?"

She looked down at the shards, observing the blue letters. The small line of an L. The faint curve of the S.

"Oh sure," she said, proudly. "That's one of our best-sellers. I have it right in the Ralph Lauren section. That's Polo Sport."

ON THE BRIDGE

Two detectives from the Ident team stood at the scene of the crime. Both men were examining the bark of a tree with a magnifying glass. The white schoolhouse remained incongruously surrounded by yellow crime scene tape. How pristine the empty and antique schoolhouse remained, the boards still white and clean. The homes on the other side of the Gorge too remained elegant and envied locales with their view of the shimmering Gorge. How strange it seemed that no one in any of those homes had witnessed the murder in their midst under the light of the full moon.

The bridge now was covered completely in bouquets of flowers. The place of passage had become an ad hoc shrine. Those who had never known Reena now gathered on the bridge and held each other and cried and cried. Her photo was propped up amid the flowers. Lines from a Robert Frost poem, placed at the site by Reena's family, were on a piece of white paper, above the words, "Reena, forever in our hearts." The true memorial would have to wait until after the autopsy results were complete. Photographers aimed their cameras down toward the flowers, then traipsed under the bridge to capture some images of the dark place of attack.

The two detectives were inspecting the bark of the

tree as, according to their notes: "Sgt. Bruce Brown informed us Glowatski said the victim's head had been smashed into the trees."

The sky was gray and yet soft with the plumes of mist and mountains the color of smoke.

The men tried to be furtive, for the media and public were not yet to know the specific details of the last moments of a girl's life. The secrecy, as it is wont to do, only created more curiosity. Sergeant Archer saw no sign of red on the gray and wet ancient bark. Surely the rain had washed all the blood away. Sergeant Archer found the day's assignment particularly frustrating.

"Everywhere I turned," he would later testify, "there were cameras in my face."

The cameras bothered Tara as well. She would later recall how on her walk to and from school, "There were 500 reporters trying to talk to you. They didn't look at us and see that we were so young. They don't think about how they make people feel. We couldn't concentrate in school. Only our teachers didn't judge us; they were the only adults that understood that we weren't bad people."

To the world, the boy she had once called Speedy Gonzales was now a "savage killer." Warren, her friend, who had once called Marissa munchkin and called her a Care Bear. She'd already gone to the police station and given a statement about the friends she'd known and loved. "Thank you very much for coming in, Tara," the detective had told her. "It showed a lot of courage for you to come in here and talk to us. I hope there're more people like you rather than the people who were cowardly enough to be involved in this thing."

Still, she felt neither brave nor honorable. She'd been there. Under the bridge. She would see the moment again and again when she was trying to listen to her teacher discuss the chart of elements. Under the bridge. She would see the moment as a flurry of such frightening and troubling savagery. It was the most horrible thing she'd ever seen. "Especially when friends whom you've known forever are kicking, pulling hair, punching, smashing heads against railings."

And now those friends whom she'd known forever were locked away and their desks were empty and their names were not read or mentioned by teachers, as if they too had gone missing into some eternal place of absence.

In the hallways, Tara noticed Syreeta walking like a phantom with her hair lank and shadows under her eyes. "Syreeta used to always be high class, but after what happened, she just wore track pants and sneakers and she was just so sad." Syreeta and Tara had gone together to the place below the old schoolhouse, and they'd placed two single roses on the sand for Reena. Then the reporters had come rushing down to ask them if they knew the girl who died, and they'd both run away together, chased by the unknown adults.

"After the arrests, The Five of us just stuck together. We talked about it all the time. We were just there for each other. 'Do you want to go for a coffee?' People didn't know what to do with themselves. Our whole big group split up; the whole dynamic changed. No one wanted to go out anymore. Other people couldn't understand what was going on. We talked about it all the time on the phone. For us, that was all we could think about. Before I went to bed, that's all I could think of. When I woke up, that's all I could think of."

All that Tara could think of was this:

"The fact of seeing something so horrific.

"The fact that your closest friends could be capable of what they did.

"The fact that someone had lost their life *for no reason at all.*"

• • •

A Shoreline student named Jodene Rogers walked over the bridge to her mother's home after school, and instead of doing her homework or calling her boyfriend, she asked for a drive to the police station.

Sergeant Poulton met with the girl. She was dressed in flared denims and a Calvin Klein hooded sweatshirt. Her eyes were a pale violet-brown, and some strands of her hair were tawny while others were almost gold.

"I have a few questions," Jodene said. "The only thing I'm really worried about in giving this statement is the confidentiality. I don't want anybody to know that I've been in here and given this information. It's because of personal safety. There's certain people, who are not involved, but if they knew I was ratting on Kelly, they wouldn't like it and I'd have to deal with them. That's the one thing I'm worried about."

"Well, that could be a problem. If necessary, you would go to court to say what you'd seen or heard. I mean, it may be absolutely crucial to the case against Kelly."

Worry shadowed Jodene's eyes and the pale violet seemed to turn to a steady and dark brown.

"It's tough," Sergeant Poulton said. "We understand these are hard decisions you and all your friends have to make right now. We're in a position where we're dealing with a murder investigation of a fourteen-year-old girl who's been killed and it's our responsibility to get to the bottom of it. For your own peace of mind, telling us what happened might be better for you. Basically, Jodene, if everybody gave information to us about Kelly and then didn't show up in court, well then Kelly would get out of jail tomorrow and she'd stay out."

"Well, can't you use my recording? Can't you play that in court?"

"That's the way our justice system works. People have to stand up and give their evidence, and be subject to cross-examination. That's the fair way of doing it."

"See, the thing is," Jodene said, biting her already bitten nails, "I *want* to tell you this. I know it's the right thing to do, and I pray to God that I do not have to go up on that stand. I'm not the only person who knows this exact story. I know others know it, but they don't want to tell you guys because they don't want to go on the stand."

"Well, as you say, it is the right thing to do."

Jodene sighed.

"Okay, well, I was talking to Kelly outside the school last Thursday. We were having a smoke on a break from our peer counseling class. She mentioned to me that the cops had been phoning her friends, and I asked her why. She told me her and her friends invited Reena out and told her they were just going to go out and party with her and have fun, but all along they planned to beat her up. And that's what they did. They just beat her up and everybody was in on it, and then they left her. They went away, and somehow she managed to walk over the bridge, and Kelly wanted to go after her. She wanted to have a talk with her to make sure she wouldn't rat, and Warren went with her, and Kelly said she began kicking her. She pushed her on the ground, began kicking her in the head, took a stick, and messed with her face somehow. She said she snapped or broke one of her arms, and she hit her with some sort of object, in the head. I guess Reena got up, and they knocked her over, and she fell in the water. She was bobbing in the water, and Kelly said she held her head under the water for a good two or three minutes, and she told me she lifted her foot up, like, 'Whoops,' you know, and then, I guess they left. She never once mentioned that Warren did anything. It was all her, she said."

"What did she mean by 'whoops'?"

"She had her foot on the girl's head, and she made it as if it was a joke, like 'whoops' type of thing. I don't know. I didn't take Kelly seriously. I know she told other people this, because we sat on the phone the other night. We just talk about it all the time now, and nobody really knows. A couple of my friends think that her arms may have been broken, but we don't know for sure."

"Did you have any conversation with Warren?"

"I saw him every day at school during that week, but he really kept it quiet. If someone came up to him, he was just like, 'Get the hell out of my face, get away from me,' type of thing. People were asking him what was wrong with him. Something was wrong with him."

"Have you known him to be involved in other fights?"

"No. I know he's in that little Crip thing at school. I've never heard of him fighting before."

"You said she told you Josephine and Dusty were involved in the fight. Do you know them? Could you describe them?"

"Josephine's real tiny. Other than that, I don't have a clue. Dusty, she's quite big with wavy black hair. Other than that, I don't know her."

Before she left, Jodene was asked by the detectives if there was anything she'd like to add.

"I don't know. The main reason I came down here is because I thought about what Kelly told me, and I re-played it in my mind, and I guess I came down here because I do not believe Warren did that. I'm sorry. I can't even picture him doing that. He's a nice guy. I mean, I can picture him standing there, like this is my mental picture: I picture him standing there, just going, 'Oh, you're crazy,' you know, and it's not clicking what she's doing. I just can't picture him killing her and leaving her in the Gorge to die. Kelly, I don't know. Kelly's messed up in her head. I always thought she was really weird. She's the kind of person who destructs things, gets herself in trouble. She's been in trouble so much at school she should have been expelled from Shoreline by now. She's either ripping things off the walls or punching people in the face. I can't see either of them doing this, but it shocks me about Warren most of all."

• • •

Dimitri no longer walked over the bridge because his father had taken him out of Shoreline. His father drove him to the police station, avoiding the bridge, but it did not matter because for years, and perhaps forever, Dimitri would see Reena on the bridge and replay it in his mind and think if he'd only followed her, if he'd only grabbed Warren a second time, if he'd only. . . . A rash of pimples now marked his once-clear skin, and he'd pretty much given up on trying to play basketball. He could barely talk to Marissa now because she too was a part of the memory. He knew no one at his new school, and he walked through the hallways, an outcast where he once, as he told the *GQ* reporter, "pretty much ran Shoreline." He was over six feet tall, but he felt as if he must be still growing because every one of his limbs ached and he'd curl up with his knees banging into his chin just trying to still the anxiety.

There was this too: he knew more than he'd told the cops. He knew more about Warren's activities on that terrible evening. As his father's car drew closer to the station, he thought of the Decision, as Sergeant Poulton had referred to it—"the Decision you all have to make." The Decision, however, could get him in deeper, cause his complete exile from the youth of View Royal. So many guys know shit, he thought, why must *I* be the one to tell what happened?

Then, as he recalls, "I just decided I'd keep some things out of my story. I wanted to help Warren. I just wanted to keep some things to myself. Before this all happened, me and Warren ended up getting really close and hanging out, and I didn't want him getting in trouble, because he was my friend. I didn't know what to do. I was up and down all that week after the arrests. I didn't know if I was coming or going. I did not know what to do."

Sergeant Bond could tell that Dimitri was being "selective." He could tell from the boy's uneasiness that he was holding back some knowledge about his best friend.

"Make sure you're telling it straight, Dimitri," he said. "To be blunt about it, I think only certain areas of your story have a ring of truth. I'll cut to the chase here. You've washed a pair of pants worn by someone who's murdered. You're the first person Warren talks to after the murder. You've seen your buddy and Kelly pursue this girl across the Craigflower Bridge. Now I know you don't question your friends about a little scuffle down by Mac's, but I think this is a significant event. I've got some problems with your story, Dimitri. I've got major problems with it."

Dimitri sighed. "If you've got a problem with my story, then I'm sorry."

"I see you as being a bit uncomfortable with yourself."

"If you don't believe me, that's your prerogative," Dimitri said, with the certain sullenness and defiance common to all confused and pimply boys.

*

When Syreeta walked on the bridge, she saw Reena's face in the photograph. When she arrived at school, she could not focus and was told by her teacher that it looked like she would likely receive a failing grade in math. Though this once would have been of great concern, she could now not deal with the rows of numbers in her textbook. She spent most of her time in Mrs. Smith's office. "I practically lived there," she would later recall.

We don't think you deserve to have any guilt at all, the cops had said. *We think you're a nice person. You don't need to feel guilty about this,* the cops had said.

"But I do feel guilty," she told Mrs. Smith. "Warren wanted to walk me home that night, and I said no. If I had just let him, a girl might still be alive. Or I could have just stayed with him. I don't know why I left him. If I had stayed there that night, I can 100 percent guarantee you Warren wouldn't have done anything."

"Syreeta, you can't blame yourself for this."

There were geometry exams and the study of the human genome. Surely, she would fail every test and remain forever in the ninth grade, a girl with her lank hair and a blind eye.

I think you'll find yourself feeling a lot better, the cops had said.

I think you'll find this is the worst week of your life.

She wanted to write Warren, just to see if he was okay, but the cops told her he could not receive her letters because she would be a witness against him. A witness *against* him. "You're going to be subpoenaed," they told her. "You're going to have to go to court."

"But what if I don't want to? Can't I say I don't want to go to court?"

"This is murder," they said, with great disgust, unable to comprehend the bond of a young girl's first love.

Who could she talk to about her strange and sudden fate? She could read her horoscope or talk to her friends. She could drift through the pages of *Seventeen*. Could anyone know what to say to the girlfriend of an accused killer? Mrs. Smith thought she should go visit her grandparents, get out of town, just go somewhere without the whispers and the talk.

She talked to the police for a second time. They came and picked her up after school. She wasn't sure why, since she'd told them, again and again, everything she knew about the conversation in the bedroom. They just kept asking her for more details, as if they suspected she was holding back something because "of your love for Warren."

She'd heard so many stories in the hallways and smoke pit since the night of the arrests. She'd heard Kelly had told Tara and Jodene and Maya that she alone drowned Reena. That she put her foot on Reena's head, holding it under the water, while she calmly smoked a cigarette.

"I thought maybe Kelly might have done it all by herself, and Warren might have wanted to look like he *could* do something like that, even though it's an awful thing to do."

On that Wednesday night, she slept, or thought she slept. She was afraid to sleep, and she left the radio on, as if the songs would soothe her or lull her to dream. She woke up and she was shaking and there was cold sweat all over her arms. She'd kept a bucket beside her bed because since this all happened, she'd seen the scene in her mind and awakened nauseous and trembling. What time is it? She looked at the red numbers on her clock and it was 11:00 and then it was 3:00 in the morning. She no longer saw Warren's face in her mind, though sometimes she could hear the sound of his voice. It was Reena's face she saw. "Every time I closed my eyes, I saw her face."

Everyone at Shoreline was grounded now. Everyone at Shoreline had been told by their parents, "You are never going out again."

Under the bridge, there might have been discovered some malevolent spirit. There were dark forces who could beat and attack your daughter, or who could turn your daughter into a brutal and careless thug. *Stay away from the bridge,* parents said, as if it was a place, an abyss, holding all the savagery.

THE MECHANISM OF DEATH

Dr. Laurel Gray is a scholarly looking woman, with cropped gray hair and gold-rimmed glasses. She might be taken for a librarian or an academic, as she drives to work dressed in tweed suits or cashmere sweater sets. Yet she has authored articles such as, "The Coronary Artery Luminal Narrowing in the Young with Sudden Unexpected Death." As a young woman, she learned about signs of drowning by studying the lungs of drowned cats; she learned how to recognize stabbing by staring at puncture wounds in pig skin. Her hands often shake when she performs autopsies, for out of the morgue, she smokes cigarettes.

Like the Dive Unit, she often can't see anything when she examines a body. The heart blurs; the organs are too decomposed. And often she observes shimmers—fleeting colors that are translucent, temporary—and these shimmers either blind her from the search or offer illumination from the dark.

On November 24, when she looked at the young body of an unknown girl, she saw a shimmer of gold and removed a single earring, for the piece of gold caught itself, became tangled in the girl's black hair.

• • •

The burden was on Dr. Laurel Gray to provide proof more tangible than the stories being told in interrogation rooms. She was to find the cause of death. Her report would, it was hoped, hold something more scientific than cartoon drawings and hip-hop fairy tales. Blood had been washed away by rain and washing machines. The truth was fading fast in the web of loves and lies and gossip, and it would only fade faster when the lawyers began to try to protect their clients from punishment. By looking at blood, bruises, the heart, Dr. Laurel Gray might be the only one now able to establish the truth about the death of Reena Virk.

In the morgue, Reena is now a girl without opinions or dreams. She is a Deceased Female. She is Case No. 97-2749-33.

"The morgue is very sterile," Sergeant Poulton, in attendance, explains. "The body is on a metal table, and there's a metal stand as a head support. Everybody's gowned and gloved and in little slip-on boots so you're not introducing new elements into the area. The pathologist does a narration as she's doing the autopsy. I was taking notes and another officer was taking photographs."

"Measured, the girl is 5'6. She is 182 pounds." Dr. Laurel Gray said. In her external observation, she saw no needle marks, no signs of drug use or disease. "She's a very healthy girl."

"The body is intact, but the skin on her hands and feet is starting to slip away. I would estimate she spent a week in cold water."

Dr. Gray took a number of swab samples, and then removed Reena's bra and the camisole tangled up around her neck.

"It is certainly apparent that she received a very severe beating. The following observations regarding bruising are:

—bruising and swelling under both eyes

—very bruised cheeks

—a large laceration on her lips

—nose bruised; bloody discharge in her nostrils

—red marks on tops of both shoulders (an odd symmetry to the bruising on shoulders, almost a circle)

—bruising on collarbone

—"thermal burn"—circular red mark—above right eyebrow

—on left side of back of head, a mark that is textured in a manner consistent with a sneaker

—also pattern of footwear on the left side of her back

—a large bruise on left side of voice box—this bruise appears to come from a "karate chop" type blow

Opening the girl's mouth gently, Dr. Gray says: "Her teeth are clenched. Her tongue is clenched in her teeth."

"The body was X-rayed and examinations showed no broken bones. No fractures. No dislocations. This further corroborated by physical examination. Examination of body for sexual assault indicated no obvious signs present and no genital trauma."

An incision was then made. "It's a Y-shaped incision," Sergeant Poulton says. "From one shoulderbone to the other, then straight down to the belly button. They peel that open, and then they snip all the ribs out. That comes out in one big slab."

Dr. Laurel Gray noted: "Damage to the liver and pancreas. Multiple blows sustained in the abdominal area. The layers of her abdominal wall are deeply bruised in a number of locations. Mesentery *torn away*. Organs crushed. Separation of fatty tissue from muscle tissue. A 'crush convulsion' injury, as often seen in car crash victims.

"Most severe damage at torso. Evidence of internal bleeding in the chest and lower abdomen. This consistent with a forceful kicking or stomping in the abdomen area."

Dr. Gray removed Reena Virk's heart and she weighed it on a sterile scale.

"The heart is about the size of a hand," Sergeant Poulton says.

Dr. Laurel Gray would later testify, softly, that "Reena Virk had long, luxurious hair." Now the hair was shorn. On the bare scalp, there was evidence of "severe bruising. Most severe at the back and front of her face. Extensive bruising under the skin of her face. Multiple bruises under the tissue. This bruising is almost a complete mask right up to the skull bone.

"There is a substantial degree of general hemorrhaging and trauma. Brain is swollen. No indentations or abrasions to the skull. Sufficient concussive injury to cause unconsciousness."

Dr. Laurel Gray motioned to the photographer. "A bruise in the shape of a sneaker print is on the back of the brain."

Another incision was made. The brain was removed and, like the heart, was weighed. The brain was sliced for further observation.

The lungs too were weighed, and here, in the place of breathing, the most crucial evidence was discovered.

"Internal examination of the lungs shows a white frothy substance. This would be consistent with the mechanism of death by drowning."

Death by drowning, was the conclusion written on the report. "Alive when she went into the water."

Dr. Laurel Gray, when looking closely at the lungs, finds something delicate and hidden, below the telltale white froth. This too is telling of Reena's agonal gasp—*agonal* meaning the last breath before death. Reena's last breath had been in the dark waters of the Gorge, and she had taken in this before her lips were forever closed. *This.* Dr. Laurel Gray removes this carefully, as carefully as she can, in the same careful way the men floated the body. She holds this in her hand. This is soft and curved and so tiny. She counts these small pebbles, which had once been on the bottom of the waterway. There are eighteen pebbles, and before she will finish, she will hold these pebbles in her shaking hands and count them, very carefully.

A GIFT IN THE GORGE

Sergeant Gosling was back in the darkness of the Gorge. By the bridge, he was careful, for there were rusted nails near the wood beams, and he did not want to spike himself. He felt slowly, his hand touching the cold underneath, where he felt the roughness of gravel and silt. The pages he found were loose and floating, no longer white, but a certain kind of ivory, and they wavered and lilted, out of his reach. He touched something sturdier then and brought this discovery up with him as he rose toward the sun. This object was, to his surprise, "pretty pristine."

The words were not yet gone, and he knew they would dry and be legible, for most ink is permanent, and most words survive. It was strange, he would say later, because he was looking for her clothes or a weapon: those were the objects he'd been sent to find. Yet under the bridge, as he floated and touched, he found this undestroyed gift. Though he was not looking for it, in the cold waters, he found Reena's diary.

THE DEATH OF A TEENAGER

At the Saanich station, Sergeant Chris Horsley held an extraordinarily well-attended press conference.

Though the media had not yet learned of how or why Reena Virk died, the interest was nonetheless relentless. For the next few weeks, the *Times-Colonist* would run daily front-page stories on any related issue: bullying, the shrine on the bridge, the yellow ribbons— "a pledge to nonviolence" worn by students at Shoreline. These stories appeared under the headline: DEATH OF A TEENAGER. Above DEATH OF A TEENAGER, Reena's yearbook photo was shadowed, so her face appeared merely as a black silhouette.

"We have many, many more people that still need to be interviewed and spoken to," Sergeant Chris Horsley said, surely sending a chill through the youth of View Royal, many of whom tossed away the business cards of detectives because they "didn't want to get involved."

"Any murder investigation is huge," he continued, "but we're dealing with eight accused in this case. It puts an incredible burden on investigators. And there could be more arrests. Other names have come up in the rumor mill."

"Was the murder gang related?" a journalist asked.

"Police agencies recognize gangs as those that are

organized and criminal, such as you'll see in the southern United States. That's not what's going on here. All of these teenagers live in the same area, and they all hang out together, but they're not a gang per se."

"What are their parents saying?"

"Well, a lot of them are in a state of denial that their children have been involved in what someone described as a horrific incident. A lot of detectives have teenage children, and they're experiencing disbelief themselves. It's been a bit of a shock, not just for us but for the community. I think there are going to be a lot of people in this city and across the country who are going to shake their heads tomorrow and say, 'How did this happen? How did juvenile fourteen-year-olds come to be implicated in the death of another young girl?'"

BRING BACK MR. KUCEY

The townspeople discussed the question endlessly. "How did this happen? How did juvenile fourteen-year-olds come to be implicated in the death of another young girl?"

Because morality is lost, Alice Klyne believed. When a city turns its back on God, the end results are, sadly, all too predictable. We have lost our moral compass, and our young people are raised in a moral vacuum, where sex and violence are the norm both on television and in real life. We have forsaken our godly heritage, and there are no longer any moral absolutes in our society, nor is there any fear of a God many simply no longer believe in.

Since learning an explanation for a scene she witnessed on Saturday from her window, Ruth McVeigh thought about what has happened to teens since she was one, half a century ago. To begin with, there was no television. "In my first decade, I hadn't watched hundreds of thousands of people being murdered in the guise of entertainment." Her mother was there when she came home from school. She listened. She hugged. But now the family is disintegrating, and if youngsters don't feel like important members of a family group, well, they look for another group to belong to, a gang. "I sense these children are filled with a global anger. They are missing something they'd never had. Those were the ones who commit vandalism, get into fights, seek to escape unhappiness through the abuse of drugs." Those were symptoms, rather than a disease.

Rosalind Karadimas didn't think the problem was television or loss of God. A fourteen-year-old girl's body was dumped in the Gorge! Where are the parents? All this money was being spent curtailing youth violence, and a fourteen-year-old girl was killed. Well, the government should get tougher and "show these abusers that we're serious about shutting down youth crime." And the question really to be answered is: Where are the parents? All this talk about "it takes a community to raise a child," that was flat-out wrong. A father and mother would be sufficient.

Ron McIsaac disagreed. MP Keith Martin was looking to get tougher on youth crime and throw more kids in jail, but didn't he realize that almost all violent criminals were sex abuse victims in childhood?

These kids were not normal, Mrs. Kirk believed. All these people saying Reena Virk had "normal" teenage problems. But, normal kids go to school. They participate in sports. They work. They live at home. My deepest sympathy goes to the Virk family, but really, as a society, we need to reevaluate what is normal.

*

Michel Murray, well, he'd warned people. He'd written a letter to the *Times-Colonist,* and they'd published it, although they'd spelled his name incorrectly. It was Michel, not Michael. Anyway, he had hardly expected such brutal confirmation of his warning to come so soon. He warned people about what was going on in the schools! The district chairperson should be let go immediately before another penny of tax money was squandered on her. And the rest of the school district bureaucracy and most of the Ministry of Education should be given the boot too. They were all utterly incompetent. Schools should provide safety, not "grief counseling" when one student was murdered by a group of others. Get rid of the district chairperson, and bring back my old elementary school principal, Mr. Kucey. Roust him right out of retirement, and give him absolute authority over all schools in the district. He can't undo all the damage of this so-called progressive education, but by the end of the year, I predict he'll restore discipline and safety. And maybe next year, he could restore genuine learning in subjects like English and math. Of course, I don't expect my suggestion to be even entertained, much less followed. I expect more hand wringing, more grief counseling, above all more yadda, yadda, yadda. Oh yes, and more violence.

My God, C.J. Charlebois declared. How many more children must die before we wake up? The brutal slaying of Reena Virk is the ultimate outcome of a government that murders children and gets away with it. I worked for the Youth Services Bureau in Ottawa twenty years ago, and I had four young boys as my caseload. Four! I was out on the streets at 3:00 A.M. searching for runaways. I was at the hospital with parents poisoned by drugs and alcohol. I intervened in severe physical abuse. I searched for guns hidden in bedroom drawers. I dealt with police frustration and brutality. Now I've read about social workers who have caseloads of thirty or more clients. Thirty! I read about children dying on a regular basis. I read about expensive reports written by politicians and academics that lead nowhere. Enough is enough! Listen. Do you hear the children crying? Do you hear them screaming?

Gary Allen was surprised there weren't more of these beating deaths. Hey, he'd been a probation officer for twenty-three years, and he'd seen a half dozen of these teen murderers. It's not like these are the first ones. These kids these days, they're obsessed with violence. If you listen to their conversation, it's all about violence. They say, "I'm going to kill him," or "I'm going to beat her up good." And the parents, say, "My kid's not capable of killing someone." "I dealt with David Muir's family. You know, he was a teen killer. He was convicted of killing his buddy's grandmother and mother for the insurance money. And his parents didn't believe it. If there was ever one kid on the surface who didn't look capable of killing someone, David was it. My sense is these kids are way beyond their parents' ability to control them."

*

These stupid kids, Denise Helm wrote in her column in the *Times-Colonist*. Try Los Angeles if you really want to join a gang. As the cruel drama of Reena Virk's murder unfolds, it is fueling the same sick play-acting that cheapened her death. Every time anyone likens the vicious violence to Los Angeles gangs, they are giving these stupid kids exactly what they want. Attention. And for all the wrong reasons. It's time to shut this game down. To the punk shaking his hand in a "gang" symbol in the background of a television broadcast at the murder scene: Why don't you go to LA's bleak, desperate ghettoes and see what it really means to be a gang member?

Denise Gemmel felt really angry at the local media. She was angry and frustrated with all this sensationalized TV coverage resulting from Reena Virk's senseless murder. And it really bothered her that the media were focusing on Shoreline School. It was true that some of the accused did attend Shoreline School. But the reality is, there are 360 students at Shoreline, and those accused are a very small percentage. In a community trying to come to grips with the horror and trauma of this incident, we need not have all our children included under the same terrible banner. There are good kids in Shoreline School—kids who work hard to be on the honor roll, kids who have jobs and perform community service, kids who have respect for their teachers, who have parents who care about them, kids who have morals and values and who are having a hard time living through this nightmare that has become their daily existence.

The painful process of trying to make sense of this tragedy is made even harder under the microscopic glare of reporters and news cameras. Because let's face it, whatever happened under the Craigflower Bridge is not a school problem. Whatever happened under the bridge is a problem within our society.

BAD GIRLS

At the University of Victoria, Dr. Sybelle Artz checked her voice mail. NBC had called yesterday. She sighed to herself, counting the pink slips. Twenty calls she had to return, and a photographer was scheduled to arrive in her office in a few minutes. It's madness, she said to her secretary. Since the death of Reena Virk, Dr. Sybelle Artz had found herself described as: the hottest expert in the country.

Her ethnography for the past decade had been among the sudden scourge: the Violent Suburban Schoolgirl. Dr. Artz had identified such tribes as the Beastie Girls, young women who listened to the Beastie Boys and engaged in antisocial behavior. She was no mere pop psychologist; she offered no sound bites, but rather sentences such as, "Violence is a rule bound and purposeful activity engaged in to redress the intolerable balances girls perceive in their largely hierarchical social world."

The good fortune of Dr. Artz was due to her publication, this very month, of a book with a title both alluring and academic: *Sex, Power and the Violent School Girl.*

As the media called, every day and constantly, she was quite happy to oblige, for as she warned, "Youth violence is more intense, vicious, and deadly than ever before."

Searching the hallways of a high school in East Vancouver, Suzanne Fournier, a *Vancouver Province* reporter, located some specimens of this current scourge. A seventeen-year-old honor student named Donna let her know that "chicks can do a lot more damage than guys—they're a lot more violent." Monique agreed: she just "lost it" after a girl left taunting messages on her pager. "I just felt this kind of uncontrollable rage and I went for her neck—I could have hurt her bad." Honor roll student Donna was another potential menace to society, for she was "a slow burner, but when I get mad, I go right to rage."

Overnight, it seemed, in cafés and in offices, in newsrooms and in bars, a new preoccupation was born. The attack on Reena Virk could not be written off as a single aberration, for there were *seven* girls fighting, and so many more who watched, who did nothing. These girls—they broke arms and legs, they stubbed out cigarettes on flesh, they set hair on fire. And these girls were not just on an idyllic island but inside everyone's daughters perhaps, just waiting to rise and go right to rage.

A national magazine published a story called "Bad Girls" wherein reporters examined the case of Reena Virk and announced the fact that violence among young girls was "sharply on the rise." Often, the article warned, "the fever seems to rise because of boys. To a chilling degree, very young girls are desperate to be mated."

Dr. Ray Corrado, an expert on violence, cautioned

the public not to panic: "The vast majority of young girls are doing what young girls have always done: attend school, pursue hobbies, flirt."

Prior hysterias had gripped the nation. Satanic cults. Yuppie greed. Pedophiles in day care centers. Latchkey kids. Bad girls were the latest concern, as exaggerated and distorted as past menaces that emerged, shimmered, and vanished so suddenly. No one spoke to the vilified girls now in cells, and the girls now in cells spoke to no one. Their stories stayed unknown. "Are these gang girls or cheerleaders?" a movie producer asked a journalist, inquiring into the potential for an M.O.W.—Movie of the Week. It all became so simple to comprehend. Reena was an "overweight misfit," while her attackers were "remorseless" and "troubled." The reality of all their lives, the reality of why girls erupted and kicked and screamed, seemed destined, despite the 2,679 media articles, to remain as hidden and dark as the red codes of graffiti under the bridge.

• • •

What would the academics have made of Lily?

Lily who was pale and famished, still a little dazed from her daily dose of Ativan.

On the day Dr. Sybelle Artz dealt with her phone messages and Don Morrison contemplated charts and strategy, Lily sat cross-legged in her cell in juvie, braiding the loose threads on her blanket.

Like Nadja and Anya she was not a fan of police, and yet she did not know who to turn to now. She could not stop shaking. There were goosebumps on her arms. Arianna would be disgusted if she told her what she was about to do. Maybe. Maybe Arianna would agree, but she couldn't risk asking Arianna for advice. She'd been trembling since the night before, since she'd heard what she'd heard in the bathroom.

She called out for a corrections officer, late at night, after lights out, when she knew the others were all asleep. By 11:00 at night, she sat in a room at the Saanich Police Department, talking to Sergeant Poulton.

Lily, by all official records, was a certified bad girl. A person of bad character, a criminal. Her offenses were solicitation for the purpose of—a crime in which the solicitant is set free but the solicitor is arrested. Lily had been busted twice under the rather arcanely worded law, a formal phrase for prostitution. Lily was sixteen.

• • •

Her boyfriend told her to try it; he was the one who pushed the needle into her skin. She was fourteen then, and she was addicted by the time she was fifteen. She did things for the heroin, and then she did heroin to forget about the things she did for the heroin.

In juvie, they gave her Ativan. When she was in the city cells in Nanaimo, they'd given her something stronger; she wasn't sure what it was called. Lily looked very much like the girl in *Alice in Wonderland;* her hair was fair and straight and framed a face that was classic and pretty. The pills got lighter and lighter. When she was first withdrawing, they gave her "a really, really strong sleeping pill." She slept for ten days in city cells, and then she started to withdraw from the strong sleeping pill. She thought she was losing her body; her body seemed a separate pale white sliver; she shivered and craved. So then they gave her something lighter. And in juvie, they gave her only Ativan now, at night, because she had trouble sleeping when the sky was dark. During the day, she no longer craved or shivered, and after three weeks in juvie, the guards even told her that she seemed transformed. Lily was in juvie when the Reena Virk girls arrived.

She was with Arianna and Sidra when they decided they should do something.

It wasn't much really. She just tripped Kelly, and Arianna poured juice on Kelly. They just bugged her. They told her, "Kelly, you'd look good in red. Red's a good color for you, Kelly."

But then something terrible happened in the bathroom, which was why she now sat here with a cop. He sat before her, waiting, with his tape recorder poised. It was 11:30 at night, and the detective had spent his days in bedrooms, touching and taking the black jeans and black shoes of girls who were no longer in their bedrooms. He read a diary full of words he couldn't fathom. Hook-up and hoochie and hottie. He talked to girls named Laila and Marissa and Melody. And now he was listening to Lily, who was, in police terms, a junkie and a prostitute.

"I was in the bathroom last night. When we go to bed, we brush our teeth. I was brushing my teeth, around 9:00, when Kelly came in. I looked at her, and I said, 'You're sick.' And she said, 'Listen, I feel bad enough already about what happened.'

"And I said, 'You should feel bad. A fourteen-year-old girl is dead because of you.'

"She goes, 'It wasn't only me. I'm getting all the blame for this. It was Warren too.'

"She said, 'Maybe I was the one who held her head under water, but I didn't mean to kill her. You don't think I feel bad?'

"And then, she goes, 'You don't have to treat me like this. I'm not scared of you.' And she walked out. And after that, it's just, I don't know." Lily looked away from the detective, hugged herself. "I've been getting goosebumps up my arms and stuff. Because my assumption was that they beat up a girl and she accidentally died. And then, when I heard out of her mouth that she drowned her . . . it just scared me . . . really bad. I thought about it for a long time. She said she felt bad, but she didn't show any sympathy. It was more like she was trying to prove something to me, trying to, I don't know, get in good with us, because we don't like them. She didn't care. She totally didn't care about what she did. Her face was just emotionless. And I just keep thinking about it over and over again in my head. The girl she killed, that could have been my little sister. That could have been anyone's little sister.

"I thought she died because of her injuries, because they beat her up so bad, and there was eight of them. I thought maybe it was an accident. Maybe they didn't mean to do it. And then, when she said that in the bathroom, said that she held her head under water for five minutes. . . ."

Lily looked at the detective, and he seemed confused, so she tried to explain again. "It's just the way she said it too. Every time she comes into the room, I get goose-bumps up my arms and I feel sick to my stomach. She laughs about it. We'll get mad at her, and she just starts laughing. She's not the most popular person in juvie. And . . . she just *laughs*. Every time we say something to her, she just smirks and walks away.

"She doesn't feel bad. I don't understand that. She doesn't show any emotion at all. She doesn't look like she feels sorry for it. She just wanted to do it. She set out to do it, and she did it. I think that she should get in trouble for what she did. I don't think she should get away with it. I think she should pay for what she did. Because it's wrong. It's wrong. Murder is *wrong*.

"I've done things in my past. I can change them. I can say sorry to the people that I've hurt, and I can say that I'm not going to do it again, and that I'm going to change. But once you take somebody's life, you can't say sorry for that. You can't take it back. There's nothing you can do. That's not right. It's horrible.

"I talked to my little sister after that on the phone. It's just so real now. It's changed my whole outlook on life. If I was sitting at home, watching it on TV, it would be totally different. You know, you go, 'Oh my God. That happened. I can't believe it.' But when you meet the people who've really done this, it's so different. It's real. It's too real. It's just too real.

"It's overwhelming that someone could do that. When you see it on the news, it's like a fictional charac-ter, so it seems like it didn't really happen, not in your world anyway. You think, 'Oh, it can't happen to me.' And then, when you meet the person, face to face, and you know what their hands have done to someone, it's sick. It's beyond the imagination.

"I can't even sleep across the hall from her. If you met her, if you've seen her, everything she's put on in front of you is a show. But when she comes in here, she's smirking and smiling and laughing, and she just *killed* someone on Friday. What's she happy about? I don't understand it. Nobody does. If you can, talk to the girls in here. Everybody thinks it's pretty sick. I'm sure if anybody heard anything else, they will tell you too. I'm pretty sure if they heard anything, they would. Because we were thinking about doing something ourselves, but I'm going tomorrow to assessment, and I want to get into a treatment center. I want to get my life straightened out. I don't want to be in jail ever again. I'm not going to put myself down to her level and be in for assault or something, like she is. I'm not.

"Another girl, Arianna, she gets out soon too. And she wants to get her life straight. She's got her own problems. We thought about doing something, but it's not worth it. The law will take care of it. If they did it, they'll pay in some way. God, the law, whatever. I don't know. You had to be there just to see the look on her face. When I said, 'You're sick,' she just blew up. She got so mad. She said, 'I didn't mean for it to turn out the way it did. I only held her head under for five minutes. I didn't mean for her to die.' I said, 'Whatever,' and I walked out of the bathroom, but it just sent chills all through me, just to think about it.'"

She stopped talking, and the detective noticed she was trembling.

"Are you on any medication?" he asked the trembling girl, for he'd seen her police file.

"I get Ativan at night, for sleeping. It's not too much different than Tylenol."

"Okay. You've used heroin. You were obviously addicted at some point."

"Yeah," Lily said, wondering why this question now.

"How long were you addicted to heroin?"

"For about a year and a half. Off and on."

"Do you hope to gain anything from talking to us?"

Lily thought about this, wondering what she could gain. "I guess I hope that she'll get what she deserves. A couple of days ago, after she met with her lawyer, she said she was going to get released soon. If she did do this, she should get punished for it. There's no way she should get away with it because somebody is not here with us, today, anymore."

"And that's your reason for telling us?"

"Yes. It makes me feel bad. It's real. It's too real. It happened. I couldn't live with myself if I didn't say something, and she really did do it."

"All right," the detective said, and he shortly after arranged for a sheriff to drive Lily back to her place of custody.

• • •

Dusty wrote poems. She gave them to guards. She wrote letters to boys, like Jack and Nick and Brian. She wrote a letter to Warren:

Hey, hon, whad up? How are you feeling these past few days? I'm o.k. I need a lot of questions answered right now, but I can't say in this letter but I think you know what I'm talking about. I know we don't know each other but I think we have a bond that can't be broken and I don't think what's happening to you is fair but just keep on praying and it will be o.k. and if I get out before you I will send you letters all the time but only if you write back. I don't know you very well but I think about you all the time because I don't think you deserve this kind of punishment and I hope you don't hate me after all that happened but anyways this jail food sucks huh! I haven't seen you or been able to talk to Kelly. Kelly has a no-contact order with all of us. I feel sorry for her but what can I do right. Here is my address. I've got to go. Stay strong and have faith in God because he can help us all through.

P.S. Don't forget to write back!

Dusty drew a heart with an arrow. The guards seized the letter and sent it to the police. The love letter would become Exhibit 345 in the Virk case. Warren never received the letter, and from all the boys she wrote to, Dusty received no letters in return.

Dusty's sister, on her drives to Yellowknife, would think of her little sister and feel more than regret. ("When I saw the story on the news about a girl killed in Victoria, I just knew somehow that Dusty was involved.") She wondered if she'd been at fault for sending her little sister away, her little sister who, as she told the police, had known no love, no caring. She needs help, she'd pleaded, someone has to please help her. But who was helping Dusty now? she wondered. Surely not the experts she saw on TV—those who talked about peer pressure and hierarchy.

• • •

"Feel my ass," Laila said to Warren, and he laughed.

He said, "What the hell for?"

"It's rock hard," she replied, and she told him about her kickboxing finesse. Warren now lived in the Honor Wing. "I liked Warren a lot," Floyd recalls. "He never caused any trouble at all." Warren was roommates with a boy who was in juvie for murder also. High on many drugs, he used a jackhammer to, quite literally, bash in the brains of a DJ who'd stolen his Ecstasy.

His roommate, like Warren, was attractive and well behaved, and had it not been for the grotesque and terrible nature of their acts, the boys might have been mistaken for the sons of the wellborn, spending time at a boarding school. Warren often wondered how they both could have ended up like this, and he could find no answers, and still, very often, he would contemplate the fate of the boy beside him, the other killer who seemed to be possessed of neither malice nor hate.

In March, a girl named Coral arrived, and she fell in love with Warren, and he was not sure what to do because he still loved Syreeta but he was very lonely. Grace Fox brought him hair gel, which was not allowed. She brought it for him concealed in bottles of shampoo. Once, while hugging him, he felt her slip something in his pocket, and she told him to wait until he was alone.

When he was alone, he found it was a letter Syreeta gave to Grace to pass on to him. He read the smuggled letter. She'd sent him a photo of herself with Tara and Marissa. The three girls were laughing, sitting on the back of a blue pickup truck. Once he was watching TV and a shot of the bridge appeared in a news flash, but the guard quickly turned off the TV. Still, he'd seen the bridge, and the moment he saw the image, he felt a shiver go through him. It seemed to him that he'd been here before, or he'd always known he would be here. There would be a bridge. He would see the bridge from his past, the bridge he'd been under. He would be in juvie for his crime, watching the bridge, knowing he'd been in that dark place. "It was kind of like déjà vu."

His mother came to visit him but she was raving and reeked of alcohol, and the guards would not let her in to see her last son. His father phoned him from California, and while Warren sat in the phone booth, his father said, "I love you," and that was the first time his father had ever told him he was loved and he didn't know why, but he just cried, maybe for an hour, or maybe even more.

Lily left. She took a bus alone and left the island where she'd done all the things she didn't want to do anymore, ever, ever again. The bus brought her across the waters on a large ferry, and then she took another bus to the town of her mother. *I want to get my life straightened out. Her face was just so emotionless. It's so real. It's too real. It's changed my whole outlook on life.* She lived in a valley, full of pear trees and orchards. All the poisons left her system. She wandered in the orchards with her little sister, holding her sister's small hand, too tightly at times. Several months later, the staff at juvie would receive a grateful letter from Lily's mother. "I don't know how to thank you," she wrote. "You've done so much for my daughter. She's so kind and strong now; she's just completely changed."

THE MOST IMPORTANT WITNESS

The Crown knew the case was high profile and important to the community. ("We're called the Crown in Canada because we represent the Queen. We don't say the People vs. So and So. We say Her Majesty the Queen vs. Glowatski.") The investigators accepted that they probably wouldn't find any forensic evidence to build a case against either Kelly or Warren. Stan Lowe knew "you're in trouble when there's no direct witness to a crime."

Don Morrison had assigned Stan Lowe the case against Glowatski. Kelly's skilled lawyer, Adrian Brooks, was fighting her elevation to adult court and had plans, if he lost, to take her case all the way to the Supreme Court. It seemed highly likely that Warren would be tried first, and so Stan Lowe began to assemble his list of witnesses.

When he'd watched the tape of Syreeta's first interview, he clapped. A first-class interview, he thought. Constable Brian Cameron just slowly got her to give more and more details, by having her tell the story again and again. He didn't lead her or suggest. A textbook brilliant interrogation. Brilliant!

That girl's going to be the most important witness, he thought to himself.

He decided, on the last day of November, that John Bond should interview Syreeta. "I just wanted to make sure, absolutely sure, we'd gotten everything right," Stan Lowe recalls.

Several hours later, Bond returned his call, informing him that Syreeta was no longer in Victoria. "She's gone to stay with her father's family, in Grande Prairie."

"Well, I need the answers now," Stan Lowe said. He authorized Bond and Cameron to take a Lear jet to the prairie town across the Rockies.

In this way, Bond, an aficionado of airplanes, found himself on the rather lavish aircraft. The jet had been purchased at auction and once belonged to Hank Snow, a country and western singer known for his appearances on the Grande Ole Opry, and for discovering Elvis Presley. "There were leather seats," Bond recalls, with wonderment. "And this plush red carpet."

In the posh jet, the men flew over the rugged mountain range, on a strange chase after a girl who had committed no crime and been in her bedroom on the night of the murder.

"The trip was just incredibly fast," Bond would later recall. "I think we got there in a few hours. Going over the Rockies, that was just really beautiful."

THIS IS NOT A HOUSE
THAT'S BEEN BROKEN INTO

Far away from View Royal, on the banks of the Peace River, Syreeta now sat with her grandparents, Gloria and Jim. She returned to the place where her mother had been born and where she had been born as well. The town was a place of oil and fertile soil, a town without mountains or beaches but with flatlands, full of bales of hay. She was not running from the law. She didn't know the law was after her. She only wanted to get away. For just a while. The house was warm, with a fireplace in the kitchen, and Syreeta was thinking maybe she would sleep again here, for in View Royal she was afraid to close her eyes.

Her grandfather had just brought in some firewood on the afternoon when the police arrived. Her grandfather was an ex-RCMP officer, and he decided he'd sit with her during the interview. "He didn't look so well," John Bond would later recall. "I think he was having some heart problems. Cameron thought he was about to have a heart attack."

• • •

The conversation started out quite well at first, because she liked John Bond. ("Bond was an all right guy. I didn't have a problem with him. He had a little compassion.")

He asked her about her job at Brady's. He asked her what her favorite subject was at school. It was slightly awkward, the way it always was when adults tried to make small talk, but still, she thought it was decent of him to not treat her as if she was the criminal. "What type of fun things do you and Warren do together? Do you go to the movies?" he asked.

"We usually go to the beach and go for walks," she told him.

"Which beach?"

"The one by my house," she said, and she did not tell Bond that on the beach, Warren asked her to please, I'm serious, marry me.

But then Bond asked her to explain exactly how she became involved in this case.

"I'm not involved," she said. "I was involved because you guys got me involved in it."

"You're not in any trouble here," Bond reassured her. "You're one of fifty people we've spoken to."

"Have you talked to other people three times?" Syreeta wondered.

"Yeah. That's where these white hairs come from," Bond said. "Marissa, Tara, Dimitri, you know, everyone's been spoken to. You may not like doing this, but I've got to tell you, we've got a dead girl here. I've got a lot of explaining to do to everyone in Victoria."

"I know."

And she told them again about the blood on the pants. The 187 conversation in the bedroom. She told them all this again.

"I bet it probably made you sick hearing about it,"

Bond said. "Did it bother you? I mean, you've got to be thinking that something is not quite right here. This isn't the guy I know."

"I didn't think anything like that because I didn't think it was true."

"So what did he say that you didn't think was true?"

"The whole thing. I didn't believe any of it. I didn't think he could do it. I didn't think it could happen."

"What exactly did he tell you?"

She sighed. "He got on his knees and he whispered to me. He asked me if I'd known the girl was missing. I said no. He said something about him and Kelly went back. She's dead. The Gorge. She's dead. Kelly. Beat her up. And more. And then. She was thrown. In the Gorge. Or she was dragged."

"Well," Cameron said, "in your earlier statement, you recall *exactly* what his conversation was in regard to who dragged her into the water."

"No, in my earlier statement, I recalled what I pictured in my head when he told me because I was asked what I *pictured* in my head when he told me."

"We'll just give you a second and you try to remember more details. This is important. We're not dealing with somebody stealing some celery from a grocery store here. Somebody was killed!"

"I'm well aware of that," Syreeta said.

"This is not a house that's been broken into. If you think these questions are difficult and uncomfortable, wait until you're in court, in front of a jury and a judge. It probably won't be as comfortable as being here in the kitchen with your grandparents."

Syreeta looked near tears, and Bond suddenly felt very sorry for her. He softened his tone. "You haven't done anything wrong here," he said. "I know you and Warren went out for seven months. I can appreciate that no one wants to be in a position where they have to come to court and testify against their boyfriend. But we have got to get this while it's fresh in your memory. In a year, when it goes to court, it may not be as fresh. And in court, Warren's going to try and put it on Kelly. Kelly's going to say, 'Hey, it wasn't me. I'm not an aggressive person.' And everyone's going to be looking at you, Syreeta, because you heard it directly from Warren."

He drank some of the coffee Syreeta's grandmother had brought him.

"Now if I asked you: 'A month ago, who ordered fish and chips at Brady's at 6:30 at night?' you're not going to remember because it's not that big of a deal. But when your boyfriend is kneeling down in his bedroom indicating that he's responsible for a homicide, I would say you'd probably remember pretty closely what he's saying."

She tried then to explain to the older men the way she'd felt but it was seeming to her more futile trying to explain. "It's not like I was like, 'Oh tell me.' I was sitting there, trying to be stubborn, acting like I didn't care."

"Well, what was his emotion like when he was on his knees, telling you this? Was he crying? Was he upset?"

"He wasn't proud of it."

"Did he look like he had sorrow?"

"He looked like he regretted it."

"You've been dating him a long time. You know him better than most people know him. So when he's on his knees, showing remorse and he seems quite upset, didn't this lead you to believe he was telling the truth?"

"I think it was that I didn't *want* to believe." It was funny then because she'd spent so much time trying to understand Warren and what *he* might have done. Now, for the first time she understood herself, and it was very clear to her finally: I didn't want to believe.

"But I think inside you did believe him," Bond said, gently. "Is that fair of me to say that?"

"I can't say for sure."

"I think you had two sides to you. One side said, 'What I'm hearing sounds true.' But in your heart, you didn't want to believe what he's telling you. It's like hearing something bad about a member of your family. One side of you says, 'Hey, my brother or sister couldn't have done this.' Is that the kind of feeling you had?"

Syreeta nodded, struck again by Bond's understanding. He seemed to know her so very well.

"We investigate lots of these types of crimes," he said. "It's hard for the family or the relative when they hear something like this." He looked at her now. "When he was on his knees, was he praying to God? Was he saying, 'God, I made a mistake'?"

"He had his hands on my knees like this," she said, and she pressed her palms against her grandmother's knees to demonstrate.

"What was he whispering? Take your time. Go slow."

"He told me that she was dead, and, I think, that she was dragged into the Gorge."

"So in your first statement, you remembered more than you do now?"

"I've been trying to forget."

"Do you wake up thinking about it at times?"

She nodded. "I've been having nightmares. Every time I close my eyes, I can see Reena's face. I've been scared to turn the light off. I can't go to sleep without the radio on."

"It's posttraumatic stress," Bond said. "It usually goes away in a few months, but it's common when you hear something this terrible. It overwhelms you. One side of you says, 'He's my boyfriend. I've been going out with him for seven months. He's a good guy. This isn't like him.' And the other side says, 'Well, the newspaper says it's true. The police are picking me up. There's something to it.' Is that how you feel?"

"Yes," she said, and she nodded several times.

"Did you ever ask him, 'Why the heck did you do this?' You must have wanted an explanation."

"I think it's like you said before: I didn't want to believe it."

"You realize that he's ruined his own life. You haven't ruined it. Reena didn't ruin it. He's ruined it himself."

She began to cry then, and under the table, her grandmother squeezed her hand.

"Did he ever tell you why he screwed up? He was sort of mixed up in his family. Did you guys talk about that?"

"Well, I know his dad didn't want him. His dad left him and went to San Diego. I knew then that his dad was just an asshole and his dad didn't even care about him. And I know his mom's an alcoholic. He was supposed to go out there for Christmas, but then she started drinking again."

"Did he ever discuss what put him over the edge here? Why he did it?"

"He won't tell me details. I know he's had his share of b.s. in his life."

She felt guilty suddenly. She shouldn't be telling these strangers the things Warren had been so ashamed to admit.

"When I first talked to you," Constable Cameron said, "I could tell that you were obviously very much in love with Warren. You were quite emotional that day. I don't think you stopped crying through the whole interview. I could tell that there was still just a little bit more that you wanted to say, but because you loved Warren so much, you didn't want to say it all. Well, that's what we're looking for today. That little bit more that you didn't tell us before."

"Well, my love for him doesn't have anything to do with it. He murdered someone my own age. That could have easily been me. So I don't care that I love him. I'm telling you everything I know."

MEMORIAL

The high school gym, crowded now with a community, grieving. A table, set up like an altar, displayed an assembly of photographs, entitled "Reena's Life and Her Loving Family." Photos of: a little girl, no more than five, with her hair in two ponytails, a bright blue pinafore, smiling, and behind her, the white chrysanthemums in fragrant bloom. This was a Reena most of the audience had never seen. In the past week, Reena, to strangers, was a girl in the newspapers, described in the shorthand of a simple story: "a misfit," "a chubby girl," most of all, "a girl who got in with the wrong crowd." She was even more misunderstood in death, merely a warning sign, a victim, a symptom.

Below the photographs of a beautiful child, fresh daffodils lay with petals loose and frail, emerging from the stems so long and green.

Suman wore a thin white veil over her hair, a black jacket; her eyes were very red, and all who observed her would later use words to describe her, words like *grace* and *dignity*.

Through a spokesman at a press conference earlier, she stunned many of the townspeople by offering, publicly, her sympathy to the families of the accused. "The Virks have no feelings of vengeance or animosity toward any of these people, neither the accused or their families."

Sitting at the memorial, Amy did not yet know that the diary she had given Reena was both discarded and rescued. She thought now only of the gifts exchanged. The ring Reena had given her "because you've helped me so much." The diary she'd given Reena because "it's important for you to have a voice in all this." Now, help and a voice seemed abstract concepts, both futile and given too late, taken away. What mattered now were stories.

There were so many stories. The stories made her head spin. There were stories in the newspaper of the "awkward misfit." There were the stories told to detectives of "some Indian chick," of "Rhea," of "Trina," of "Elly McBride." There were stories in the autopsy report, stories of bruises and footprints on a skull, and a body literally crushed. There were stories in the Bible told now by the Jehovah's Witness elder. There were stories of an ordinary night turned terrible, soon after the lights in the sky blazed and broke from a falling satellite.

But the story of the memorial seemed wrong and untrue to Amy, for no one spoke of Reena as she had known her, and she wished she could have stood up there, told the strangers of a young girl who was so young, who didn't know the ways of the world. Yet she was emerging, as if she no longer wanted to melt into the walls behind her, as if she was ready to be. Amy would have said Reena was determined; she was not awkward or shy, not anymore. True, she didn't belong anywhere, not really. She didn't belong in the traditional world of her grandparents or in the modern world of thugs and contrived sexiness. She didn't belong with the strict and severe JWs, because she was fourteen and wanted birthday parties and rebellion, and she wanted to celebrate. But she was trying to be a girl who would belong somewhere, not yet, but soon.

Reena told stories in the last year of her life that surely were untrue. Stories of probation officers and pimps, stories of romance with boys named Nick and Jack and Dan, stories of a girl named Josephine who really painted on her eyebrows and was not so pretty with her makeup off. But were these stories, Amy wondered, any different from the stories in the songs all the kids loved? Invented tales of mayhem and lovers, boastful braggings that earned that most elusive quality: something they all called respect.

There were girls who teased her, girls who stole from her, girls she wanted to be.

"Why do you lie?" a teacher once asked her.

"Sometimes I have to lie to get people to like me," Reena had replied.

After the memorial Amy thought, *There are all these stories now, and there will just be more stories about Reena. The stories at the trial. The stories in magazines.* The truth in these stories would hopefully surface and shimmer, borne forward like the pieces of glass Reena discovered in the sand.

More memorials would follow, for Reena was now everyone's daughter. In the park she had loved as a child, a petition was signed by many who vowed to honor "nonviolence."

"Reena's death is a wake-up call," said the chairwoman of the Greater Victoria School Board, "a wake-up call that we must listen to in order to honor her memory."

Shoreline students presented roses to Reena's mother. Among these students were Tara and Syreeta. John Bond, in the background, observed the presence of Syreeta, cynically. "Now there's a person who could have helped us," he scoffed. Mrs. Virk hugged Syreeta, and thanked her for this gift. But her stoic composure could not be possibly maintained at the private funeral.

"My baby, my baby, don't do this to my baby," she screamed as the coffin moved toward a rather dark place of flames. She tried to throw herself on the coffin, to hold her daughter, but she was pulled back and the casket receded into the place for burning.

PART IV

The Trials

"Which way ran he that kill'd Mercutio?
Tybalt, that murderer, which way ran he?"

—citizen, *Romeo and Juliet*

THE COLOR OF RIGHT

First to appear before their judge were the six girls who had been under the bridge. The media invented the moniker for these girls: "The Shoreline Six." The name was slightly erroneous, as only three of the girls had attended Shoreline. Yet the name suggested some romantic troupe of rebels, and truth be told, the name was rather catchy.

If the townspeople were hoping the assault trial would be cathartic and sensational, their hopes were dashed, for the trial was cursory and quick, and the convictions of all six girls seemed from the start a fait accompli.

Mayland McKimm, Maya's lawyer, was neither surprised nor pleased that the assault trial took place less than three months after the arrests. Neither was he surprised nor pleased that the Crown hired a special prosecutor from Vancouver, a "big gun" lawyer named James Wesley Williams.

"In this case, society needed an answer immediately, and they needed to put closure on it. There's a huge social value to that. Everyone knew the odds for any of the girls walking out free were zero. In a case of this magnitude, the state has all the machinery in place. Those girls were hooped. Those girls were doomed. Even before

344 • Rebecca Godfrey

we went to trial, I wanted to say: 'There is no way you're walking out of here.' There was just no way."

The Crown had changed the charge from aggravated assault to assault causing bodily harm after reviewing the evidence. This seemed a more appropriate charge for the punches and kicks that had felled Reena Virk. Perhaps because of the lesser charge, perhaps knowing they were doomed, Josephine, Dusty, and Laila all pleaded guilty.

Maya, Willow, and Eve chose to plead not guilty, and their trial would last for only three days. The girls' names could not be printed since a law called the Young Offenders Act prevented the identification of any minor under the age of eighteen. The public never got a chance to see the faces of the supposed savages, and though sketch artists attended the trial, the portraits they drew appeared in the newspapers as girls, literally, rendered unrecognizable with blank faces.

The public never heard their voices, their stories, their explanations.

Judge Filmer listened to the youth of View Royal during the course of the trial. He heard witnesses* speak somewhat reluctantly of seeing their former schoolmates and friends surround Reena Virk "in a semicircle" and pummel and kick and punch the girl until she "was bruised up pretty bad." Judge Filmer heard as well of the bragging during the week after the night of the Russian satellite, when the girls boasted of "kicking the shit out of some girl."

---

* Witnesses in Youth Court cannot be identified.

The prosecutor, James Wesley Williams, a former police officer, was a stern, imposing, and convincing teller of the tale. He stripped away all the talk of love and beauty and jealousy, of bitch fights and likes and Omigods and maybe, yeah, whatever, something. Told in his austere manner, the events under the bridge nonetheless made for a dreadful and disturbing narrative. After the teen witnesses spoke—haltingly, reluctantly, with mumbles and slang—he made a forceful and clear summary of his case. "Reena Virk was a young girl who appears to have a certain social awkwardness about her and may not have been enormously well accepted by others. The evidence shows that Reena Virk was essentially trapped, with persons surrounding her, and that she was there struck and kicked a number of times. She was not able to extricate herself from that predicament and she was struck a significant number of times and effectively covered herself up and cried out for the others to stop hitting her."

Away from the courtroom and out of his black robe, James Wesley Williams was less formal when speaking of the attack. "It was a nasty bit of business. They swarmed her. Can you imagine the insane cruelty? It's breathtaking."

James Wesley Williams often reflected on the difference between those who were violent and those who were not criminal. He himself believed the factor that allowed some to cross the line was, simply, conscience. For conscience allowed you to stop yourself from harming others — it "acts as a brake upon your conduct."

During the trial, as he was able to establish, with little

theatrics and even less doubt, there had been no brake in action on the night when the Furies released themselves like so many pairs of dark wings beating.

The day before Valentine's Day, Judge Filmer returned with his verdict. He found all three accused girls guilty. He spoke less of the beating and more of the aftermath when the girls grabbed Reena's knapsack and ran with it to the parking lot of the Comfort Inn. This gesture seemed to him to reveal the real reason for the savagery.

"Why did Laila take Reena's bag? Was it a theft or a robbery? I do not think so. I think she took it because she had what adults know as a 'color of right,' a belief that there was something in the bag that did not belong to Reena Virk and that somehow in this rather bizarre scenario, these young people felt that they had the right to do what they did to get the object that was in Reena's bag. Her perfume was in that bag and a diary or journal was in that bag. We hear nothing more of the journal, nor do we hear anything more of the pajamas. But we do hear that someone rather casually or cavalierly broke or dropped the bottle of perfume.

"The inferences that I choose to draw from this particular narrative, if I can call it that, is this: that what occurred that evening was some form of punishment. The punishment was aimed clearly at Reena Virk. It was based on something some of this group believed her to be responsible for and that in fact the book or the diary was to be recovered in the process."

Josephine was the one who had reason to search for "a book or diary." As James Williams had stated in his opening, Reena used the book to call friends of Josephine's and make statements that were "defamatory or untrue," and this caused Bell "to remark that she was angry and she intended to cause harm to Reena Virk." Thus, the judge sentenced Josephine to one year, the harshest sentence possible, and a sentence also handed to Dusty. Maya, Laila, and Willow received sentences of six months, while Eve received only sixty days, for as far as anyone could establish, she had only slapped Reena Virk once or twice, and she seemed, to the courts and the psychiatrists, the girl most remorseful and least culpable.

Hearing of her sentence, Josephine was outraged. She did not mind so much that the judge had spoken of her "bizarre mafia fantasies" and announced to the world that she "has displayed all the elements of sociopathic conduct." No, what enraged her was the sentence of a year. "A year?" she raged. "I got a year for one shot. I only gave Reena one shot and everyone else kicked the shit out of her. That's nice. A year, for one fucking shot! Reena was fine when I left. She only had a black eye. If it hadn't gone to a murder, I probably would have gotten a month, maybe, not even. They would have looked at me and said, 'Oh, first offense. It's serious, but it's not that serious.' I would have gone on probation, but that's about it. And instead, because of all the media and all of that, *I* get fucked around. That judge is smoking crack!"

Maya and Willow and Eve held hands and cried when their verdict of guilty was read aloud.

Mayland McKimm read to the court of Maya's "atrocious" family background in the hopes the judge would grant her leniency. "Your Honor is aware that Maya was present when her father was murdered during the course of a prolonged beating and that she was then abducted by the culprits of that crime and kept out of contact with the police or any authorities for some five or six days. Your Honor will notice that I have filed a letter from a detective, which talks about the little girl that he found at the age of six, devastated and traumatized, having been locked in the basement of a drug house for a period of time. Her mother is in court today, that's her adoptive mother, Ms. Belle Longet, and she has been extraordinarily supportive through the process. She feels now that her child has seen the inside of a jail, that she sees the hardening process taking place, because that's how you survive in a youth detention center. If we increase the jail sentence, Maya will simply harden more. We have jailed a number of young people in this matter who were the more serious instigators. They were the people who had the problem with Ms. Virk, and they're the people who led her to her untimely demise. We're at a crossroads here. She can go to the Youth Detention Centre and become brilliantly tough, or the court can show some compassion and allow some latitude for her to deal with the issues before her."

The judge listened attentively, and then sentenced Maya to serve her full time in youth custody.

Josephine returned to "juvie." Kelly, released on bail, was back in View Royal, under house arrest. Alone, Josephine suffered indignities. She could not watch MuchMusic, the Canadian version of MTV. Dean Melanson, the Director of Programs, explains: "We didn't think the videos were giving the right message. With rap music, it's all 'ho,' 'bitch.' We're trying to change attitudes." Certain magazines were also banned, in particular those that "depict females in a non-positive way." The list of contraband magazines read as follows: *The Source, Vibe, Details, Glamour, FHM, Maxim,* and *Low Rider.*

Josephine, one evening, ate her dinner of grilled ham and cheese, split peas, and fries, and then went to the games room where she could play Super Nintendo and Donkey Kong. Above the raucous machines, there was a reproduction of a Van Gogh.

A boy named Barrington was reading Tolkien's *The Fellowship of the Ring,* and others were playing Ping-Pong and shuffleboard.

Suddenly, on the television, a reporter said something about the murder of Reena Virk. It was difficult to hear his words. The imagery, so often played, of a black shapeless bag being removed from the Gorge, of the rainy skies, of the flowers on the bridge, appeared and the boy reading Tolkien asked Josephine, "So how did you kill her?"

"I didn't have anything to do with the murder," Josephine said, definitively.

Warren was in the games room as well, and though the two youth of View Royal rarely spoke now, Warren suddenly began to talk to Josephine. "He got mad," she recalls. "He said, 'I don't want to talk about it. I don't want to hear about it. I don't want to think about it.' He kind of had a little spasm or whatever, and I was like, okay. Sorry. I won't talk about it anymore. And he just said, 'I hear it *every single day*. You turn on the TV and there it is. I turn on the radio and there it is.' He goes, 'I swear, every time I turn around somebody's talking about it. Every time somebody looks at me, they're thinking about it.' He goes, 'When I go to sleep, I dream about it. I can't get away from it. Everywhere I go, I turn on the TV, I turn on the radio, I go to sleep, it doesn't matter what I do. . . . If I was in a room all by myself, it would be there no matter what. It would *always* be there.' He said his bad dreams were something to do with the murder and he woke up crying and the bad dreams wouldn't stop and that he was scared and he wished he didn't have anything to do with it and he wished he'd never met Kelly. He just said that he wished that he never met her, and he said, 'Oh, I shouldn't have been there that night. I wish I wasn't drinking. I wish I wasn't there that night. I wish I wasn't such an idiot. I don't know why I did those stupid things.' He said stuff like that and I felt kind of bad for him, and I said, 'All right, we won't talk about it anymore.'"

Josephine slept in her cell, under a quilt purchased at Wal-Mart. She thought about Warren's "spasm" and she "felt kind of bad for Warren." She thought again of her former friend, and wondered if Kelly had bad dreams now. "It was weird that it never bothered Kelly," she says. "She never seemed to have any bad dreams about it or anything. Warren seemed really bothered by it." If she was asked about the presence of bad dreams, she would say, "Who knows? Maybe Warren had a conscience. Maybe he has more compassion for people."

Of Warren, she thought, "He's a smart kid. He probably could have done something with his life."

• • •

In his BMW, Warren's lawyer, Jeremy Carr, drove to juvie and gave Warren the bad news: the letters he had written to Syreeta had been discovered and confiscated by the police. More bad news. Here was the list of Crown witnesses who would testify against him, a long list, a list of all those he'd loved and been loved by: Dimitri, Marissa, Richie D., Maya, Willow, and mainly and mostly this, Syreeta.

"Syreeta's going to testify?"

"I don't think she has much choice. She gave statements to the police."

Warren knew this already, but he was not too concerned about Syreeta turning against him. "Our bond was too strong," he would later explain.

Jeremy Carr was a portly man with a gentle, soothing voice. He was a senior partner in a small law firm, and Warren's trial would be his first murder case. Maya had recommended him to Warren for he'd helped her when she was first charged. Before the trial began, Jeremy Carr brought in Dale Marshall, a lawyer with more expertise in murder cases. On this day, Jeremy Carr suggested Warren forego a trial by jury and have his case heard by a judge alone.

"You'll have a better chance for an appeal if you're found guilty," Jeremy Carr advised.

"That's a stupid idea," Warren's dad told him. "Go with a jury."

"I think the guy knows what he's talking about; he's a lawyer," Warren reasoned, before asking his father to come for the trial in April. His father promised to be there.

A few weeks before his trial for the second-degree murder of Reena Virk, Warren received a package from his father, and inside he found a double-breasted pin-striped suit, two sizes too large. "I can't wear this at my trial," he thought to himself after trying the large blazer on. "I'll look like a little hoodlum."

His hair was no longer bleached or curly, and he'd grown several inches, but he still was neither tall nor with the physique of a man. Often in juvie, he seemed content to strangers, though he was not content. "Hey," he'd say, "don't worry about me." He painted a scene of rainbows in arts and crafts class and sent the drawing to Tara. He liked arts and crafts most of all. "The teacher, Glo, she's an awesome lady. She was like a mother to me."

Many of the girls in juvie may have had crushes on him, may even have fallen in love, and Warren may have loved them in return, but he would not, could not, forget about his love of Syreeta Hartley.

"Where do I start?
What should I write?
Hugging my pillow tight
Just trying to fall asleep.
Holding in my tears, not wanting to weep.

It all started back in the day.
I had a boyfriend who thought it was o.k.
To take a young life away
And still to this day he's in jail
And can't even receive my mail.

Just as things started to straighten out
My mom went to the doctor and he told her about
The cancer in her body that has started to sprout
She went through chemo and lost all her hair

I'm only sixteen
My life is too much
All the pain that I've seen
I go to court next week to testify
Just thinking about it makes me cry
Sometimes I wish I had the strength to die
But I'm too scared
I can't even try."

   from the diary of Syreeta Hartley,
   April 18, 1999

THE MEANING OF ANIMOSITY

Of a young woman, once it was written that she possessed a "beauty too rich for use, for earth too dear." The same might be said of Syreeta as she arrived in Courtroom 54 to testify at the trial of her first love.

She chose not to swear on the Bible. ("I didn't want to dig myself in that deep.")

"Please state your name in full," the clerk said, as Syreeta sat in the seat surrounded by a square of mahogany.

"Syreeta Chandelle Hartley," she said.

"Ms. Hartley, it's very important that everyone in the courtroom be able to hear you, so please project your voice as much as you can."

Hearing this, Syreeta suddenly looked very glum, and she dropped her chin.

Stan Lowe rose to face his most important witness. ("Those men were all so scary," Syreeta would later say. "All those men in their black gowns.")

"I'm going to ask that you pretend that I'm hard of hearing so your voice is nice and high," he said to Syreeta, for he could tell she was uncomfortable.

And so he raised first the subject of her first love.

"In November of 1997, you were in a romantic relationship with a person named Warren Glowatski?"

"Yes."

"How long had you two been together at that point in time?"

"Six months," Syreeta replied softly, her tone reluctant, as if to say to the men in the room, "I would rather not speak of my love to you."

"And on November 22, you were interviewed by police with regard to the investigation of the death of Reena Virk."

"Yes."

"Did your romantic relationship with Warren continue after his arrest?"

"Yes."

"How long did it continue for?"

"Two and a half months."

"Objection!" Warren's lawyer announced. "I'm not sure what the relevance of this is."

"Well, her relationship with Warren Glowatski is potentially an issue in this matter," the judge said. "I'm going to let your learned friend proceed."

"I'll repeat the question. Last summer, did you still have romantic feelings toward Warren Glowatski?"

"I had feelings," Syreeta said, raising her chin for the first time, and staring at Stan Lowe directly.

"What kinds of feelings?"

"Memories, and just . . ."

"Did you have any animosity toward him?"

"I don't know what that means."

"Let me try another word. That's my fault. Did you dislike him last summer?"

"Sometimes."

"While he has been incarcerated at the Victoria Youth Detention Centre, did you ever receive letters from him?"

"Yes."

Stan Lowe nodded, and then having established their illicit and questionable conduct of staying in touch when the law had forbidden them from doing so, he moved away from love and to the night of the Russian satellite.

"Did you work that day?"

"Yes."

"Where did you work at?"

"Brady's Fish and Chips."

"And what did you do after work?"

"Went down to Shoreline School."

"Did you see Warren Glowatski that night?"

"Yes."

"Now how were you feeling that night."

"Sick."

Though no one could tell, for he seemed outwardly pleasant, Stan Lowe was frustrated with her monosyllabic replies. "It was like pulling teeth with her," he would later recall.

"When you say sick, what was your problem? If you don't mind me asking?"

"Um, I just had a really weird feeling in my chest."

"When you were feeling sick, did you go somewhere?"

"Yes, I went home," Syreeta said.

"What time would that be around?"

"Nine o'clock," Syreeta said, with the dull voice of someone indifferent or drugged.

"Would you like a sip of water?"

"I'm fine."

"What did you do when you got home?"

"I went to bed."

"Prior to going to bed, did you do anything to prepare for bed?"

"Not besides brushing my teeth and washing my face."
If Stan Lowe sounded as if he was speaking to a very young child, Syreeta had started to speak back to him as if he were a particularly ignorant and bothersome adult.

"What do you recall next?"

"Receiving a phone call."

"What time?"

"Around 11:00."

"What were you doing at the time?"

"Sleeping."

"Who was the phone call from?"

"Warren."

"How long did you talk for?"

"Thirty seconds."

"What was the conversation about?"

"There was no conversation. I said I was asleep, and I'd talk to him in the morning."

"Did you see Warren Glowatski the next day?"

"Yes. In the afternoon."

"He came over to your house. Did he not?"

"Yeah."

"I'm sorry. You have to say yes or no. Now, where were you when he came over?"

"In the shower."

"Okay. I want you to take your time. Think back.

Describe as best as you can what the conversation with Warren was then."

"I just told him that I heard he kicked a girl in the head the night before. I asked him why he did that, and he told me not to worry about it, and that was the end of the conversation."

"What was his demeanor . . . I mean, what was he acting like?"

"Normal."

"And is that all you recall from the conversation?" Stan Lowe said, incredulously.

"Yes."

"Okay," he said, trying to maintain a friendly tone, despite his growing awareness that she was most definitely and certainly becoming a hostile witness.

"You mean today you can't remember word for word everything that was said with Warren on the 15th of November?"

"Yes."

• • •

"Did you do some laundry for him?"

"Yes. I washed a pair of white jeans and a cream-colored sweater."

"How dirty were they?"

"There was lots of mud on them."

"Was there anything else on the pants?" he said, both hopefully and hopelessly.

"A bit of blood."

"Can you describe what that bit of blood looked like?"

"It just looked like splatters off a paint brush maybe."

• • •

"What happened in the bedroom?"

"Um, on the CD player came a rap song that said '187' and he pointed to the CD and said 'Exactly that.'"

"Did he say anything further about this 187?"

"I don't remember in what terms, but somehow it came out that she was missing, and that's where the 187 came in."

"What did you take that to mean?"

"Um, personally, I didn't believe him. I thought, you know, being a boy, that he was trying to make up stories, and you know. . . ."

"Was there any other conversation in the bedroom?"

"No," Syreeta said, rather languidly.

"Do you recall today if he said anything else in the bedroom?"

"No."

And Stan Lowe then sank, almost fell down into his chair, as if he'd been flayed by a scythe.

Court took an afternoon break.

Warren, at night in his cell, wondered, "Why didn't she look at me?" He had forgotten that her right eye was blind. If she had wanted to look at him, she would have had to turn her face dramatically toward him. When he saw her after so much time, it startled him slightly, and he felt both the stab of disbelief and loss—disbelief that he'd once held on to that beauty, that he'd once been so close to such beauty, and for no reason, he'd lost it forever. Lost her, lost so much, all because of the darkness of that single moment, under the bridge, after she'd left him, and after she'd walked away and not let him walk her home. All in the darkness when he'd walked across the bridge and gone to an even darker place, away from the light, and nearer to the place where the moon pulled the water with some invisible force.

You fucking fool, he told himself for the millionth time. What had he done? And why? The girls he'd dragged into the darkness, the girls, the one he didn't even know and the one he loved.

He'd been in a slow haze of his own making all during the trial, a self-induced and perpetual numbness, but seeing Syreeta, he'd been roused back to this reality. He'd heard the words around him for the first time. She was telling those who would decide his fate about the words he'd said to her in his bedroom, but she was telling them reluctantly, and regretfully. He could hear the regret in her every pause and every breath. She didn't want him to go to prison, he thought, and she didn't want to lie before Reena's family. What was she supposed to do? She was in a terrible position. He wished he could fall back into the fog. Once he'd thought their bond was too strong for her ever to betray him. "Our bond is too strong," he'd told himself on the night of his arrest. He thought back onto her earlier answers and found himself dizzy with the vision of his cell wall through tears. "I had feelings," she'd said, in her way, sort of haughty and sassy. "Memories, and just. . . ."

Round Two. That was how 2:00 P.M. felt to Stan Lowe. A bell might have rung. He might as well have sucked water from a clammy bottle rather than drinking the last of his stale coffee. He grabbed his black cape of the courtroom.

He often said: "You gown up, the battle's on." Stan Lowe did not need to review Syreeta's statements, though the junior prosecutor, Ruth Picha, had underlined the pertinent lines from Syreeta's police interviews:

He told me that him and Kelly killed the girl.

He told me that she had kicked her and stepped on her head or something, a couple of times, and then she stuck her head under the water for about five minutes and then they dragged her into the Gorge.

"I've memorized every friggin' word in her statement," he told Ruth, and he returned to face his adversary.

She has to tell the truth, he thought, even though she seems to still be in love.

"Syreeta, besides what you've told his Lordship this morning, is your memory exhausted as to that conversation you had with Warren in the bedroom?"

"That's all that I remember," she said, and he then tried another tactic.

"Okay, Syreeta. I'm going to ask you to turn to page 11 of your police statement. Are those portions that I've outlined accurate?"

"It is surely what I told them, but all I know now is that I don't recall Warren saying those things to me."

"Explain that to the judge."

Still in a voice somewhat distant and almost sleepy as if she'd been roused from her dreams, Syreeta tried to explain: "I think rumors got mixed in, and the questions being asked over and over again by the police, sometimes you add a little bit each time, and I'm not sure if that's what happened in this situation, but I don't recall Warren saying those things to me."

"Have you exhausted your memory as to any further conversation with Warren?"

"I've pretty much exhausted my memory to every conversation."

She said this with such finality that no one was surprised that Stan Lowe soon thanked her and let her be.

Warren's lawyer moved toward Syreeta. Like a jealous lover, Stan Lowe bristled. "She's smiling at him," he thought to himself. "I bet they met before this."

"Syreeta, I just have a few questions for you," Jeremy Carr said solicitously.

"When you got Warren's pants on Saturday morning, do you recall if they were wet?"

"They weren't wet at all."

"You've had a chance to review three statements you gave to police, and correct me if I'm wrong, but you don't recall Warren Glowatski giving you a lot of details, is that right?"

"That's right," she said, tucking her hair behind her ear and raising her chin.

"Is it correct to say that Warren would always want to protect you by not telling you things?"

"That's right," she said, nodding.

"How would she know?" the judge interjected.

"Thank you, my Lord. Now, you're clear that Dimitri used bleach. You have not used bleach before, though, is that correct?"

"Yes."

"Thank you. I have no further questions."

Syreeta left the courtroom now. She could not look at

Warren, not only because her blind eye made a glance futile, but also because of her guilt. "I felt as if I'd betrayed him. He didn't have anyone there for him, and I should have stood by him."

• • •

The trial would proceed with testimony from Dr. Laurel Gray and Dimitri and Maya and Dusty. Dimitri and Marissa could establish that Warren and Kelly were on the bridge after the fight, around 10:40 following Reena into the darkness of the faraway north side, while Maya could verify that she'd seen Warren and Kelly returning, heading south, together, around 11:10. Three went over, two came back. Even more damning was Dimitri admitting something he had never said before. Stan Lowe was proud of Dimitri, grateful for the boy's betrayal of his best friend. "He did the right thing," Lowe said. Dimitri finally admitted he'd seen Warren later that night, "pumped up" and boasting of his fight with the "Native guy." His pants were splotched with mud and blood and water, as they had not been when he was under the bridge kicking Reena in the head. The boys at John Wear's crash pad too testified of Warren's appearance at sometime around 11:15, and Chris Fox said that Warren got home sometime after 11:00 and they sat on the porch and talked about the "Russian thing that went through the sky."

The Dive Unit recalled their discovery of Reena's pants and underwear in the silt near the water's edge, while Dr. Laurel Gray spoke almost mournfully of the pebbles in Reena's throat, her half-naked body, the bruises and trauma as if she'd been stomped on with all the force of a car.

A DARKER PLACE

On the third day of May, the defense opened its case. It would call only one witness: Warren Glowatski.

Warren didn't feel prepared for his time on the stand. He turned to a friendly guard for advice. "Just tell the truth," the guard said before escorting him out of his cell.

Warren wore a shirt by Tommy Hilfiger as he had on every day of the trial. Teary-eyed and trembling, he told his story of the evening, and he told what had occurred after he'd left the dark place under the bridge.

He told of the brutal acts by Kelly Ellard and his own panic and pleas for her to stop and of coming home and calling Syreeta and she'd told him she was sleeping and he'd said good-night and he'd gone out to the porch and talked to Chris Fox about the Russian satellite.

• • •

"There was nothing real about his story," Stan Lowe thought to himself disgustedly as he reviewed his notes that evening. Pieces of paper were all over his kitchen table, near the drawings by his own children and the photos of a costumed family on Halloween. Stan Lowe prepared for his cross-examination of Warren. "There was no Reena in his story. It was just all about minimizing his own actions. You have to get him to break it down. You have to get him to explain how he got Reena to the water. Why? What did he think was going to happen if he dragged her down there?" His strategy was to force Warren to admit to the consequences of his actions, the utter lack of any reason for his movements beyond the most simple one: he wanted Reena to die.

"Don't take him through the night chronologically," he told himself. "Throw him off. Shake him off. Keep going back to his actions because those are the actions of a person who is guilty. Making up the story about the Native person. You have to get into his mind. 'What were you thinking, Warren? When Kelly punched Reena, what did you think?' Keep bringing up Reena because there was no Reena in his story. 'Was Reena crying? Was she begging for her life?'"

He couldn't prepare much more. "I always say 90 percent of cross depends on what they say on the stand. You can't prepare for that. You just have to listen really hard. Think on your feet."

And this: "I wanted to peel him down. I wanted to wear him down."

• • •

Had there ever been a person not somewhat moved by the lovely and frightened face of Warren? "I did feel a bit sorry for him," Stan Lowe recalls. "He was very, very nervous. He was crying. I asked him if he wanted some water. Taking the stand is not easy for anybody. I didn't envy his position."

He began by asking Warren about his explanation that he'd dragged Reena "only to get her to a darker place."

"You say you were pulling Reena to a darker area? Why?"

"I thought Kelly wanted to take her away from the road because cars were driving by."

"But the lights from the road weren't shining on you," Stan Lowe said, pointing at a photograph that proved he was correct. "*You were already in a dark place. So why did you drag her to an even darker one?*"

"I don't know," Warren admitted.

"Did you ever say, 'Kelly, where are we going?'"

"No."

"Well," he said, his tone harsh for the first time, "you must have realized you were heading toward the water!"

"I never thought about it."

"You never thought about it?" Stan Lowe repeated, incredulously. His manner had changed dramatically, from the gentle and patient way he'd been with his own witnesses. Now he was aggressive, mildly sarcastic, and even menacing. One could see why convicts called him "The Undertaker."

"You never thought about it," he said, strutting toward the boy. "Warren, did you sit on Reena so Kelly couldn't drag her in the water?"

"No, it's the worst mistake of my life that I didn't do that."

"I'll agree with you there. Did you try to push Reena's pants up after they fell down—give her a little dignity?"

"No."

He then produced a pair of jeans, and he brought them over to Warren. With his gloved hands, he also handed the boy Reena's underwear. Warren flinched and shivered. He cast his eyes at some invisible sight. For the first time, Reena seemed to be in the courtroom, at least some pitiful and lost part of her. And for the first time, those in the audience seemed to viscerally understand there had been a real girl, for she was evoked by the tangible sight of her clothing in a way that all the mentions of her name and "her" and "that girl" had never really evoked an image or a reality.

"When you were dragging Reena toward the water, it never entered your mind that something would happen to her?" he said, his voice a hostile reprimand.

"I didn't think she was going to die," Warren whimpered.

"Well, what did you think was going to happen when she went into the water?"

"I don't know."

"Did it look like she needed a swim?" Stan Lowe sneered.

"Objection!"

"Mr. Lowe, please refrain from the sarcasm," the judge intoned dryly.

"I'm sorry. Mr. Glowatski, I suggest to you that you and Kelly dragged Reena into the water. You were in the water up to your knees, and Kelly Ellard was in the water up to her waist. You watched Kelly hold Reena Virk under the water until she died."

"No," Warren said, but Stan Lowe found his denial unconvincing, for as he described the final moment, he scrutinized the look on the boy's face. He was standing as close to Warren as he possibly could, with a vantage point no one else in the room could hold. So close, and he looked right into the eyes of the boy.

"He'd started to relive the moment," Stan Lowe would

later recall. "There was this eerie look in his face, and I knew he was going back there. He seemed almost excited. There was an excitation in his face. You just knew when you looked in his eyes, he *was* there and more."

Stan Lowe looked up at the judge and saw he too seemed to be struck by the look in Warren's eyes. The judge was looking down at the boy, and though his own face remained stiff and unreadable, he was noticeably observing Warren very, very carefully.

"No further questions, my Lord," Stan Lowe said, and he returned to his seat, and sat very straight. He smiled then, very slightly.

• • •

Though they had classes, Syreeta and Marissa returned to the courtroom to hear the verdict. The girls believed Kelly was guilty of the murder and Warren was guilty of *something*, but not of drowning and not of causing a death. But this was not the smoke pit at Shoreline, nor were they members of the tribunal. This was the court of law, where words of Latin were on the walls and these were words they'd never learned.

Diana, Tara, and Felicity also sat in the courtroom for the first time, and Warren turned his head briefly before the verdict was read and saw The Five, there for him. Their attendance both comforted and subdued him for he knew, whatever the verdict was, he'd brought about their loss of innocence. ("My trial was really traumatic for all those girls; it messed them up. I was like their big brother, and then all of a sudden, I was involved in a murder.")

So many people arrived in the courtroom to hear the

verdict that speakers were set up in the lobby of the courthouse. "I've never seen so many people in the courthouse in all my life," a sheriff said. "I thought we might have a riot on our hands if that Glowatski kid was found innocent."

Stan Lowe glanced at Warren's lawyer, noting he was writing with his special good luck Mont Blanc pen. He himself wore good luck bulldog cufflinks, a gift from Don Morrison.

"It's 50/50," he told himself.

"It was such a nail biter," Stan Lowe would later say. "If we'd had a jury, we would have known immediately, but we had to sit through the whole judgment before we got his decision."

The judge read: "Reena Virk died on November 14, 1997, after a vicious beating. Warren Glowatski is charged with second-degree murder. Another individual, Kelly Ellard, faces the same charge but will be tried separately at a later time. All three were teenage students at the time as were most of the Crown witnesses. The Crown must prove the charge of second-degree murder beyond a reasonable doubt."

The girls shifted in their seats as the judge went on and on about "objective determination" and "fundamental guiding principles."

"The Crown must prove that he or Ellard would cause bodily harm to Virk of a kind that he knew was likely to result in death and that he was reckless whether death ensued or not.

"Virk drowned in the Gorge on November 14th, 1997, following a savage beating that occurred during the two hours before her death. She suffered severe internal injuries from blows and stomps to her front and back torso area. The pathologist compared the force involved to a crush injury if run over by a car. These blows would have caused immobilizing pain and severe shock. I consider it highly unlikely that Virk would have been able to walk across the bridge if she had received the blows that caused the internal damage at the south end of the bridge. In my view, the inference is inescapable."

Stan Lowe glanced at Warren's lawyer, for he was making an odd motion with his good luck pen. He was shaking the pen, and his wrist jolted back and forth.

"His good luck pen has run out of ink!" Stan thought to himself, and he smiled then, for he was a believer in such omens.

Though she was not on trial, the judge spoke first of Syreeta. Clearly, he did not agree with Jeremy Carr's description of her as "honest and forthright."

"During her evidence in chief, Hartley was at best reluctant, and, at times, almost indifferent. She was a bold liar at trial, but not a sophisticated or clever one. I also take into account her demeanor as well as her relationship with Glowatski, including her current feelings for him, in reaching my conclusion that she lied to protect Glowatski whenever she thought she could get away with it."

Syreeta could not understand the harsh condemnation. She believed she'd done no lying on the stand. "That judge didn't take five minutes to talk to me! How do you base an opinion without talking to me?"

*

The judge then turned to his verdict on her ex-boyfriend, Warren G.

"On the whole, Glowatski's evidence was incomplete and improbable. I did not believe him nor do I have a reasonable doubt about the truth of his evidence. I conclude that he actively participated in the further beating at the north end of the bridge and then helped drag Virk, while she was unconscious, to the water, where Ellard probably drowned her. I am satisfied beyond a reasonable doubt that Glowatski intended to cause Virk bodily harm of a kind that he knew was likely to result in her death and also that, by then dragging and abandoning her near the water, he was reckless as to whether death ensued. I find Warren Glowatski guilty of second-degree murder as charged."

As soon as he heard the verdict, Warren turned his head to the public for the last time before he was taken back to the cells. He could not see The Five, for they had fled the courtroom. He could not see his father, for his father sat in the back row, alone, behind his dark shades, with an air of stoic misery. His father spoke to no reporters and seemed out of place in the grand courtroom, like a cowboy who'd wandered into the palace. Warren could not see his friends or his family. In the front row, when he turned, he saw the Virk family. His eyes met those of Reena's little brother. They exchanged a glance, and the young boy looked only sad and not angry. When he looked at the little boy, it was then that Warren knew, as if for the first time, what it was that he'd really done.

• • •

Through the chaos of the reporters screaming into their cell phones, The Five were heard to utter their own verdict, as they hugged one another and drifted, stunned, from the hated courtroom. "That's so unfair!"

The Virks moved to thank Stan Lowe, though there was nothing celebratory or vengeful in their hearts, for they felt almost pity for a boy so clearly lost and without reflection or knowledge or faith. As for Stan Lowe, he found the verdict, as they often were, "anticlimactic."

"Reena's mother is just an amazing lady," he would later say. "She was gracious through the whole thing, and she must have such a strong faith to survive in the way she does."

Another mother behaved with less dignity. Surrounded by reporters who had figured out her identity, the red-haired lady scowled while her companion pushed a photographer suddenly. "My son never killed anybody," Warren's mother said. "I know him, and he doesn't have it in him. There's just no way that he killed that girl," she said, and she left the courthouse to see if she could catch sight of her son through the dark glass of the sheriff's van.

AFTER THE TRIAL

Syreeta considered what she should do with the box marked Warren G.

From a new and unmarked box, she retrieved her diary.

All her youthful years, she'd never kept a diary of any sort, and then, one day, in the midst of the sad days, Mrs. Smith gave her the gift.

After her time on the stand, she had written: "Being a witness is the hardest thing I've ever done, and I hope it stays that way."

The newspapers on the day of the verdict were full of her face and her name. How could that be? she wondered. Those who had punched Reena and kicked her, those girls like Dusty and Josephine, were protected and sheltered, while everyone in the country was reading of her name. GIRLFRIEND TIPPED OFF POLICE, the headline said in the *Times-Colonist,* and a photo below showed Syreeta trying to shield her face from the photographer. On the day of Warren's verdict, she'd skipped the articles, knowing her name would appear, followed by the words: "a bold liar, but not a sophisticated or clever one." Would that have been better, she wondered, if she'd been a sophisticated liar? Skip it, she told herself. WARREN GLOWATSKI:

GUILTY. Leave it be. She turned to the horoscopes, finding them near the cartoons. *Once I was naive and once I was carefree. And everything just changed in an instant, for no reason at all.*

Syreeta believed in her heart that she was the reason Warren was going to jail. Warren's father agreed. When asked his opinion of the girl his son so loved, he would scoff before taking a drag from a Marlboro Red. "She pretty much hung him," he'd say, bluntly.

Her horoscope meant so much to her on the day after the verdict. She cut it out and memorized every single word. April 25, the horoscope for Aquarius. "Whatever else you do or don't do this week, you must not allow yourself to feel guilty for what happens to other people. You are not responsible for the world and its woes and those who say you have no right to be happy while others are suffering should be shown the door—as quickly as possible. The best way to make the world a better place is to demonstrate how easy it is to enjoy it."

At school, Syreeta still found herself spending most of her time in Mrs. Smith's office. The cancer in her mother's body had subsided for now, after months of chemotherapy, but still her diagnosis was: terminal. ("April 9: She is so important to so many people, especially me. I can't live without my mom. I hope I am as much help to her as she has been to me, always.")

Mrs. Smith offered her the articles about Warren's trial. Syreeta wished instead to thank Mrs. Smith for the new job at the Royal Colwood Golf Course. After two years, thanks to the efforts of Mrs. Smith, she was finally moving on from Brady's.

"Thank you so much for getting me that job," she said to her guidance counselor. "They said I could work at banquets."

"It's a very fancy place," Mrs. Smith remarked.

Syreeta wanted to ask Mrs. Smith if she thought Warren would be sent to a federal institution and put away for the rest of his life with cruel and crazy men. But Mrs. Smith would only tell her what the horoscope said: "You are not responsible for the world and its woes."

Finally, she read the articles.

One entitled "A Moral Blind Spot" was written by a man named Chris Wood. Syreeta had never spoken a word to him.

He wrote: "Syreeta Hartley's hair is glossy and dark, like the victim's, but the 16 year old is also thin and model-pretty. According to prosecutors, her slender young boyfriend confessed to Hartley at least twice before his arrest a week after Reena Virk's Friday night death. She never bothered to inform police. Call it a disconnect from reality. Call it alienation, marginalization, a moral blind spot. Hartley has shown an apparent indifference to Virk's murder that has troubled and perplexed courtroom observers."

Christie Blatchford, Canada's most high-profile columnist, also wrote of Syreeta. Syreeta had not spoken with Christie Blatchford. She'd never even heard of the reporter from Toronto.

"Ms. Hartley, her exquisite, perfect oval of a face, perfectly blank, was in the courtroom at the same time that two young men were gunning down their former classmates at a Denver high school. The link between these soulless youngsters is not imaginary. Ms. Hartley likely would have no difficulty talking to the young men any more than she had trouble talking to Mr. Glowatski, after he had, allegedly, confessed to killing Reena Virk."

Soulless. Indifference. Syreeta knew the meaning of these words no more than she knew the meaning of *animosity.* She tried to laugh it off. "Wow," she said to Mrs. Smith. "I had no idea everyone thought so low of me."

Under her pillow, she kept the diary. After the trial, she would write: "Today I got fired from the Royal Colwood Golf Club because they saw my name in the newspaper. They said that since they are a private club, they didn't want all the whispering."

• • •

"Violence is not a recreational activity," Judge Macauley told Warren on the day of his sentencing. "The death of a young woman and the many shattered lives are a testament to that." The judge said he had taken into account Warren's "immaturity and physical demeanor and size" as well as the fact that he'd caused "no significant problem in the Youth Detention Centre" when considering whether Warren should stay in a youth detention center or serve his time in an adult prison.

"Warren Glowatski, please stand. You are sentenced to life imprisonment without eligibility for parole before November 21, 2004. I order that you serve the balance of your sentence within the federal penitentiary system."

• • •

Soon after arriving at the ("dirty as hell") medium-security prison, Warren was surrounded by his fellow prisoners. He knew what they were going to do. A few of them were "keeping six"—just watching out in case the guards strolled by.

Travis, this "overweight guy, around thirty-three, with a Caesar cut and long sideburns," who was inside for "something petty," offered to do it to Warren. He used a motor from a Walkman and needles stolen from the arts and crafts classroom. The black art wasn't really an initiation, just more of a ritual way of killing time.

Travis placed the onion paper onto Warren's back and began to tattoo. The words would be written in Olde English style; Warren was never sure where he got the idea for that style of writing, but probably from some picture of Tupac or some gangster. He wasn't into that stuff anymore; he saw his former heroes as some scared kid's fantasy. Travis pressed the onion paper into Warren's skin; soon the letters came onto the skin of his back. Travis lifted the needles to pierce the skin, to engrave the two words Warren chose to have forever on his body: First Love.

Finishing the job, Travis rolled some Old Spice onto the tattoo, allowing the alcohol of the cologne to work as a de facto curative.

"Boy, did that hurt," Warren would later recall.

THE VILLAGE IDIOT

Josephine, almost sixteen, sat in the room of the police station, curious, suspicious, intrigued. She was dressed in a gray sweatshirt and gray sweatpants, and she bore the resigned and malcontent attitude of one who'd been confined for many months. Why did the cops want to talk to her now? Six more months of jail time faced her. What could they want with her?

The cop who arrested her sat across the table from her in their private meeting room. "We went up there to talk to Josephine because the Crown asked us to. They were hoping she'd be a little more forthcoming. We suspected that there was more involved in the planning of the murder by Kelly. We weren't sure where her loyalties were."

This meeting would be an attempt to shatter Josephine's loyalty.

To Josephine ("She still had a lot of attitude, but she seemed more resigned. She was looking a little more mousy."), Sergeant Ross Poulton said: "Now, I understand that Kelly's your best friend. She's been a good friend for a long time."

"Since I was eleven."

The cop pointed at a tape deck. "Well, we wanted you to have a chance to hear this tape."

"Fine, go ahead," she said, shrugging her shoulders. "Play it."

He pressed Play. Kelly said:

"Josephine's got some psycho problems. She says weird, demented things all the time."

"Oh, really, that's nice," Josephine said, crossing her arms over her chest.

"She says weird and demented things, all the time, all the time. She said, 'I want to kick the living crap out of Reena, that stupid bitch!' She's always saying stuff about burying people."

Sergeant Poulton stopped the tape, and looked to see how Josephine reacted to the words of her former best friend.

"She was scared," Josephine said rapidly. "She just said those things because she was scared. I can hear that was scared. Was she crying?"

"Nope, I was right there. She was talking to me. There were no tears."

"None?"

"None at all."

"Well, she *was* scared. I could tell."

"She was scared of getting caught for something she knew she'd done, and she was trying to load it on to you!"

"Well, it's a pathetic lie, if you ask me. I have alibis. The chick at Seven Oaks signed me and Dusty in at 11:03, so I'm really not too worried about what Kelly has to say."

Josephine was silent for several moments, and then, as if forsaken, she inquired of her captor: "When did she give that statement?"

"The night she was arrested."

"Are you serious?!"

"Absolutely."

"The night she was arrested? Are you sure you're serious?"

"Of course, I am. Listen, that statement is going to cause some problems for you. The problem you have right now is Kelly's trying to say the responsibility for the murder lies with you." Hearing this, Josephine gasped aloud.

"How can she possibly do that?"

"Well, she can say that she did it because you persuaded or coerced her."

"Kelly has her own opinions."

"Well, why don't you tell us about the discussion between you and Kelly with regard to killing Reena. We know about that phone call, Josephine," Poulton said, alluding to the sworn statement in which Elaine Bell had detailed the chilling phone call she'd overheard.

"I don't remember any conversation about killing Reena. I had a lot of telephone conversations with Kelly, but I don't sit there and tell her who should die."

"Do you recall ever saying that Reena should be buried alive?"

"No, I *never* said that she should be buried alive."

"Well, you know what happened the day after the murder."

Josephine sighed and looked at her bare and boring nails. The restrictions on cosmetics sickened her immensely. How was makeup hurting anyone? She yawned, perhaps enjoying the position of power she was clever enough to realize she now occupied.

"The morning after?" She smiled sweetly at Sergeant Poulton. "I probably did my makeup in the morning. I probably had a cigarette. I usually have a coffee." She squinted her eyes, looked to the ceiling, gazed at the cop through her dark eyelashes, and smiled once more. "What else did I do? I probably went downtown."

"Well, Dusty says you found Reena's shoes and threw them in a garbage can."

"I don't remember that. Maybe Dusty has a better memory than I do."

"Personally, I find it unfortunate that you'd want to cover for people."

"Who says I'm covering for anybody? I saw Kelly that Saturday. We talked about parties. We talked about cigarettes. We had stupid conversations. She said, 'You should smoke Players. Du Mauriers are gross.' See, we don't talk about murders and stuff. We just talk about cigarettes and makeup. We don't talk about violence."

She smiled once more, rubbed a finger over her dry lips.

"When did you find Reena's shoes?"

"Can you charge me if I tell you?"

"No, I can promise you that."

"Can you charge me with accessory to murder?"

"No. You haven't had any charters or warnings or any lawyers. Nothing you tell us is going to incriminate you."

"That's good."

Then suddenly she stopped toying with the cop. "Reena's shoes were black. We saw them at the schoolhouse. Somebody said, 'Get rid of them.' I put them in my Guess bag. I think Kelly's mom paged her, and she's like, 'Oh, I've got to get home for dinner.' So me and Dusty took the shoes and ditched them downtown." She rolled her eyes, as if to say, *What is the big deal?* Of the cop, she inquired: "How is any of this useful?"

"Well, we don't want anyone to point fingers at you."

"I don't care, though. You guys could give me a hundred years, and I'd tell you to go to hell. See, jail's done me a lot of good, huh? Look at the positive outlook I have on life now. Every single day, every time something pisses me off, or I get locked down, or I get yelled at, I just go, 'Fuck. I hate the fucking cops. I hate the judge. I hate everybody who put me here. Everybody.' Because I know that I don't really deserve to be here. I'm not downplaying my role. I know what I did was wrong, okay? I know that I shouldn't have done it and I'm not going to do anything like that ever again. I didn't even like violence. I've never been a violent person. Never. I've seen too much of violence. Normally, I wouldn't have touched her because that's not my style. But I was just like, 'Hey. I have to do something because people are going to be talking about me and saying I didn't do anything about Reena fucking with me.' It wasn't peer pressure. I chose to do it. It was my fault, but I had to."

"You're not here because you hit Reena. You're here because they murdered her."

• • •

Again, Sergeant Poulton pressed Play.

Kelly: "Josephine is so demented. She worships Satan. . . ."

Hearing this, Josephine laughed, and then, tilting her little chin upward, she laughed in a rather dismissive way. "I'm not a big Satan worshipper, so I don't know what she's talking about there."

"No pentagrams tattooed on you anywhere?"

"No, I do have a tattoo, but it's nothing to do with Satan. It's a flower, okay, a fucking flower!"

"We don't think you're as callous as the impression you give sometimes, Josephine. Even your mom said you sounded so tough and callous when she talked to you on the phone about Reena. But we don't believe that's the case."

"I acted a little," Josephine conceded.

"Exactly. It's a tough situation. You're under a lot of stress, and it was clear to us you were probably surprised and upset."

"You guys all wanted to see me cry so I wouldn't cry. I wouldn't let you see that. And I don't consider myself part of the murder. I don't."

"We don't consider you part of it either," Sergeant Poulton reassured her.

"Sometimes it feels like everybody does," she said, softening.

Observing the shift in her demeanor, Poulton seized the opportunity, and encouraged the girl to reflect upon her own morality. "How do you feel about what happened?" he asked her, compassionately.

"I think I was a fucking moron, and yeah, I feel bad.

I thought she'd just go home and have a black eye, and I thought I would apologize to her if she was in the hospital and maybe I'd bring her flowers. I probably wouldn't have gone that far, but you know, I didn't think she was hurt that bad because I saw her get up and walk away."

"So you must have been absolutely freaked out when you found out she was dead."

"You think? I kind of lost it."

"What did Kelly tell you?"

Josephine shook her head, realizing she'd fallen into a trap. She paused, but then returned to her denial. "I don't know."

"You *do* know. You just don't want to tell us."

"Even though Kelly fucked me around, I just don't want to fuck her around."

"Even though the reason you're doing a year is because of Kelly's stupidity?"

"Maybe it's meant to be that I'm supposed to be in jail right now."

"A noble thought, but it's all Kelly. It's not karma."

"I guess so."

"Doesn't it bother you that she's implicating you?"

Josephine was silent for a while. She reflected and considered, and her thoughts turned back to Kelly's moment of betrayal. "Can I ask you a question?" she asked Sergeant Poulton. He nodded. A certain camaraderie had developed between the two. She was no longer toying with him, no longer trying to appear invincible. She looked, for a moment, very sad.

She asked, "Did Kelly have to be interviewed by you, or did she choose to be interviewed?"

"At no time did she have to be interviewed. We told her that. At any time she could have stopped talking, but you know, she seemed to want to tell us that you're the one who's somehow responsible." He mimicked Kelly's insistent, girlish, bratty voice: "'Oh, it's not me. It's Josephine.'"

"That's something else to hear that," Josephine admitted, and once again, she seemed to change and become more reflective, more open to conversation, even confession.

"It's funny because she never blamed it on me when we were together after we got arrested. I saw her before we went to jail, and she was just like, 'Are you in as much trouble as I am?' I told her I wasn't in half as much trouble as she was. I told her they'd dropped the murder charge on me and everybody but her and Warren. And she just said, 'Oh.' That was all she said to me! And then, the last thing she said to me, before we left the cop station, was, 'Don't write any statements on me. I won't write statements on you.' She told me she didn't even bring my name up in her statements."

"No kidding," Sergeant Poulton said, whistling.

"She told me she would never write a statement against me. I'm her best friend."

"Oh, she's such a loyal friend."

"Yeah, and I wasn't even worried about her writing a statement. I didn't think there was anything bad she could say about me."

"Except that you set the whole thing up. That it was all your fault."

"When you're in that much shit, you really look out

for number one, huh?" Josephine mused, sardonically.

"But *you* don't. You take responsibility for what you've done. That's actually pretty noble. Kelly's a piece of work. And I feel sorry for Warren. She's sucked him in big time."

"Yeah, I guess so. She really is a good person, although . . ."

"You're obviously pretty disappointed."

"Yeah, I am. She's like my sister."

"That's too bad."

"Yeah, it is too bad, but I can find more friends. I have lots of friends."

"Did she ever say she was sorry about what happened when you were at the Gorge the next day after the fight? Did she ever seem sorry?"

"She seemed like she was on top of the fucking world. It seemed like she was having a great day."

"That little bitch," Poulton said, shaking his head, scornfully.

"Yeah, it didn't seem to bother her at all. When I was in jail, I felt bad and I apologized to Reena a billion times in my head. There's nothing I can do to make it okay. I'll just have to live with it, I guess."

"Kelly's mistake."

"It's hard for me not to like her, though. It's hard for me not to care about her. I remember when we were in jail, she's like: 'I'll never write a statement against you. I'd never do anything to hurt you.'"

"Other than try to pin it all on you."

Josephine laughed. The two might have been friends now, discussing a ridiculous co-worker. "I know," she said, shaking her head. "She's like, 'I won't do anything to hurt you.' Oh, I'll try and put you in jail for twenty-five years, but that's all."

"Did you say that you'd do anything for her?"

"I said that to her *lots* of times. I said I'd always be there for her. I told her she was my best friend and I'd do anything for her, and you know what? I would have if she'd never given that statement."

Knowing now was his moment, Sergeant Poulton leaned toward the young girl with an expression of great fascination: "When did she first actually tell you that she'd killed Reena?"

"She just kind of implied it."

"How so?"

"She just said stuff like, 'Maybe something will be floating down the stream pretty soon.' She just joked around about it: 'She's floating around somewhere.'"

Josephine looked at her nails but kept on with her surprising revelations. "Part of me just thought, 'This can't be happening.' Maybe Reena's just in the hospital. Maybe she hit her head and got amnesia. Maybe she's in New York. I looked at every explanation I possibly could. Me and Laila thought maybe she was ashamed because she got beat up. That would definitely do something to my ego. So maybe she ran away. Maybe she met some guy at the hospital. There were a million explanations but none of them really fit. They were all kind of long shots."

"When did you know that Kelly was actually involved?"

Josephine sighed. Her eyes seemed to become more blue.

"Well, she told me from the beginning, but I just didn't believe her. I didn't think it was humanly possible for her to kill somebody. Or Warren. I mean, Warren really didn't seem like he could do that. Did Warren see Kelly's statement?"

"I would think so."

"I'm kind of like the village idiot, huh? Everybody knows she's blaming me, and no one says a thing? God, I feel like the village idiot." She shivered upon realizing the implication of this indignity.

"Did Kelly ever phone you in the morning? Nadja told us she did."

Josephine finally admitted for the first time, "Yeah, she phoned me and she said, 'She's dead and I drowned her.'"

"Did she say why she did this?"

"She didn't say why. I don't know. I don't think it could have been just because of me."

"Kelly did it for Kelly," Sergeant Poulton said consolingly, for Josephine looked near tears. Her closed and perfect face gradually had grown rather mournful and tight. She rubbed her palm over her eyes wearily.

Josephine said, softly: "She told me what happened."

Sergeant Poulton nodded. More revelations came then, suddenly.

"She said she went up to Reena, and said, 'Don't fuck around with my friend.' Reena said she was sorry."

"So how did it go from that to her being dead?"

"They beat her up and beat her up."

"After Reena apologized?"

"Kelly didn't want to hear an apology. She didn't care

what Reena said. Reena would have got it one way or another."

"Do you believe that?"

"Yeah, I do."

"Did she say that?"

"Pretty much."

"How so?"

Josephine sighed before revealing her final and significant secret: "Kelly said, 'I did it for you. I did it for all of us. I did it as a favor to all of you.'"

"When did you have that conversation?" Sergeant Poulton said, leaning forward, alert.

"When we were in jail, I said, 'Why did you do it?' I was mad at her. Everybody was pissed at her. We all thought, 'Kelly got us in here.' And she just kept saying, 'I did it for you guys. I did it for you guys.'"

"What did you say?"

"I remember Laila said, 'You still shouldn't have done it.'"

"Well, you've told me a lot of information today, Josephine. I appreciate it." Sergeant Poulton stood up suddenly. He couldn't wait to phone his superiors. If Josephine would testify to this conversation, there was a chance Kelly could be convicted of *first-degree* murder. At the very least, the revelation established a motive for the murder, and up to this point, no one had any idea why Kelly would have killed a girl she'd never met before. Some strange kind of desire to please the group, the clique, the Furies: *I did it for you guys. I did it as a favor to all of you.*

"You've been very honest with us today," Sergeant

Poulton said appreciatively, but Josephine was not listening to his words of gratitude. She looked up at him then, and she looked very forlorn.

She made one last request of the blue-eyed detective. She asked: "Can I hear Kelly talk again?"

THE MANY TRIALS OF
MISS KELLY MARIE ELLARD

There were three versions, at least, of what happened to Reena Virk on the other side of the bridge. One was the version Warren Glowatski had told on the stand. ("I kept saying, 'Kelly! Stop! Leave her alone.'") There was the version told on the streets and school fields of View Royal. ("Kelly said she had a smoke and stood on her head for five minutes or something.") And the third version was Kelly Ellard's version. She had never crossed the bridge. She had neither touched nor murdered Reena Virk. The youth of View Royal had framed her, conspired against her, and so, on March 18, when she stood before the judge, she softly pleaded, "Innocent."

• • •

The Honorable Madame Justice Nancy Morrison is a well-known figure in the elite circles of Vancouver society. Perhaps this is due to her prominence as a "groundbreaking feminist legal advocate," or because of her famous soulmate. For years, she'd lived and dined and traveled with the actor Bruno Gerussi, a Canadian television icon, and the rugged and salty star of the popular show *The Beachcombers*. Judge Nancy Morrison would take center stage, literally, in the first trial of Kelly Ellard, perched high above the girls and boys of View

Royal, in her black robes. With brown curls neatly and tightly arrayed and with her face slim and austere, she seemed like a most proper ladyship. A more sensual and pleasurable side is evident in the introductory words to *A Love of Bruno,* her memoir and cookbook: "There has always been time for friends and cooking in her life, but never enough hours for sitting under the tree reading, golfing or learning French."

"The Law presumes Kelly Ellard to be innocent," she cautioned the jury, on the first day of the first trial. "Keep an open mind." And she added this warning. "Pay attention to the young people. I caution you to scrutinize these witnesses with care."

Surely, as the days went on, the judge was an exemplar of caution and scrutiny of the young people.

"There was this weird thing in the sky," Tara said, on the stand, when asked to recount the night of the satellite. "I don't know how to describe it. . . ."

"There was something in the sky," Maya said. "I don't know what it was. . . ."

Thirty witnesses would be called to testify against Kelly. The young people, the youth of View Royal, composed the bulk of the Crown case. Fifteen teenagers would provide evidence against Kelly Ellard. With so many witnesses, the Crown might have confidence, might have thought they had a very solid and convincing case.

Yet teenagers, as Don Morrison once noted, "can be difficult witnesses. They're nervous. They've got loyalties. They're emotional."

And after Kelly's lawyers were done with them, they also seemed to have drug problems, anger problems, problems with rules, with sex, with heroin, with honesty, and, most of all, problems with Kelly.

Almost before it began, the Crown's case began to fall apart with the eviscerating cross-examinations by Kelly's two lawyers. ("You'll find Adrian Brooks is highly intelligent, always well-prepared," says Mayland McKimm. Mark Jetté, at thirty-five, was already acclaimed for his legal prowess, and was already partner at one of Vancouver's top law firms, housed in a sprawling loft in Vancouver's trendy neighborhood, Yaletown.)

The Crown was represented by Derrill Prevett ("a DNA kind of guy," says Sergeant Poulton) and Ruth Picha ("an academic"). Kelly's lawyers, possessed of an almost wild energy and dry wit, would rivet and enthrall, while the Crown lawyers often induced a certain lethargy.

Maya could say she saw Warren crossing the bridge with Kelly. Yes, she had seen them at 11:10, and yes, that was unusual, to see those two together, and yes, they were walking back over the bridge, and yes, she had waved. And she could tell the judge and jury that Kelly had told her that she was "happy" about "killing Reena" and Maya observed her to be quite "proud" of what she did.

But Adrian Brooks could simply ask Maya this, with so much condescension and insinuation, enough to imply, if not outright declare, that Maya was framing Kelly for one reason only: the love of Warren G.

"Do you accept collect calls from Warren Glowatski?"

"Yes."

"No further questions," Adrian Brooks said, walking away from the girl as if she had just spat on his face.

"Jodene," Adrian said incredulously, "did you in fact tell the police that 'the only reason' you came down to give a statement was because you thought 'Warren was a really nice guy!'" Tara too must have been another girl desperate to save Warren G. On his birthday, while he was in juvie, Adrian Brooks revealed, Tara went so far as to put up a birthday card for him at Shoreline School and asked everyone to sign it. And that was forbidden! Forbidden because Warren Glowatski was in jail for murder!

"Did you have a crush on Warren?" he asked Tara, smirking, as if the question was rhetorical.

"A crush?" Tara said. "I just thought of him as a really good friend."

Richie D., after the murder, many months after the murder, finally came forward and told the cops this: he'd seen Kelly and Warren on the night of the murder. They were coming up from the schoolhouse, and Kelly's pants were soaking wet, so wet he'd asked her "if she pissed herself." But Richie D., despite his damning evidence, was just another miscreant. He was liquored up that night; he was drunk most every day. Weren't you? Yeah, I guess so. Worse still, he was a Crip. He was part of a gang. And who else was in this gang of roving thugs?

Warren G.

*

Willow could not be reliable though she saw Warren and Kelly crossing the bridge together around 11:10, and Kelly had told her the next day that she "went back and finished off Reena so she wouldn't rat." Well, Willow smoked weed every day, and she too wrote Warren letters in jail and still, still to this day, still thought of him as "a really good friend."

Lily had no love for Warren, but Lily, who told the jury of Kelly's admission in the juvie bathroom ("She said, 'I held her head under water for five minutes. I didn't mean for her to die'"), Lily shot heroin at fifteen and turned tricks in Nanaimo and refused to obey the terms of her probation. Next came Dusty. Well, Dusty had a "little problem with anger," Adrian Brooks said sarcastically. Dusty before the murder was on a one-woman crime spree. It took Adrian Brooks five minutes to read out her list of prior crimes. You held a knife to the throat of your twelve-year-old cousin! You threatened to kill her! You chased a girl named Melinda out of the recreation center! You were told not to return to the recreation center so you followed Melinda and you hid in the bushes and you told her to watch her back! You stole your sister's car! You trashed your mother's house!

And Dusty, you had reason to be angry with Reena Virk, didn't you? She'd been with your boyfriend. And let's face it, Dusty, you do seem like the kind of person who holds a grudge. Dusty, it was you who crossed the bridge, wasn't it? You were the girl Maya and Willow saw with Warren. Dusty, it was *you* who killed Reena Virk, wasn't it?

"No," Dusty said, rather cheerfully.

Well, what's the special bond with Warren then?

"The special bond?" Dusty said, wrinkling her brow.

"You wrote him this letter, did you not? 'Hey hon, whad up. I don't like what's happening to you and I don't think it's fair. You and I share a special bond.' What's the special bond, Dusty?"

"I don't know," Dusty said, looking ashamed. If she was ashamed by the discovery of her love letter, read before the courts, her blushing face only assisted Adrian Brooks's conjecture.

"Dusty, it was you who crossed the bridge! And you killed Reena with Warren! And that's your special bond, isn't it?"

"No," Dusty said, and she seemed for the first time in her life, so very tiny.

Rarely did the Crown try to re-examine their witnesses. As the days went on, Adrian and Mark flayed the youth, shamed them, confused them, and the youth felt as if no one came to their rescue.

Only Billy, the fireman's son, could not be tied to the alleged conspiracy. He had no reason to make up a story about Kelly, certainly no loyalty to Warren. He hadn't been drunk or high, and he'd been walking his girlfriend home to make her curfew, so he seemed a perfectly respectable and dutiful type of guy. Nonetheless, Mark Jetté kept asking him over and over again. How long was the conversation? Did you say five minutes? Well, when you just repeated it here, it only took you thirty seconds or so to tell us. Did you say she looked stressed out, or did you say she looked distressed? Which one is it? Did you say your girlfriend didn't hear this conversation? But I thought you said your girlfriend was standing beside you. Did Kelly say to you, "Later on her head was put under water"?

"Yes," Billy replied, and only later he realized his mistake. Kelly had told him, "I put her head under water," which was quite different from "her head was put under water."

"I got tricked," Billy realized. He'd missed a day of work, gone over to Vancouver, had his name in the paper, and now they'd tricked him. His dad said: "You did the right thing." But since he was seventeen, he'd lived with this case. He'd testified five times, at preliminary hearings and Warren's trial, lost some friends for doing so, received less than pleasant treatment from some men in the Ellard family. All he'd done on November 14 was try to make sure his girlfriend got home for curfew. And now everyone in View Royal was saying the Crown was fucking up the case, and Kelly's lawyers were just destroying all the kids, and everyone was saying, "It looks like Kelly Ellard is gonna walk."

• • •

During the breaks in the trial, Kelly, Nevada, Kelly's mother, stepmother, father, stepfather, stepsister, aunt, grandmother, and grandfather formed a large and very blonde and white contingent. They would sit near the end of the long hall, far away from the pack of media and the Virk family. As she was waiting for Dr. Laurel Gray to testify of bruises and froth, Kelly walked away.

Nevada was reading *Vibe;* Nevada's hair still fell to her shoulders in strawberry blonde ringlets.

There was a carpeted platform along the bottom of a stairwell.

Kelly began to walk across this platform as if it was a balance beam. Suddenly, she did a pirouette. And then she turned, smiling, to see if Nevada and her sister were watching, for the two girls sat together, slumped and restless, on a sofa.

"Stop dancing!" her father ordered, aware the inappropriate image might be observed by the media. But Kelly continued to raise her leg, and she raised both arms, as if testing her balance, and she did not tremble nor did she fall.

• • •

The jury was not present when Warren was brought into the courtroom before Madame Justice Morrison. For months, he'd been so nervous about being brought back before a judge that he'd begun eating food voraciously. "I packed on about thirty pounds," he would later say. "I was a fat motherfucker." His head was shaved now, all his curls gone, and the court artists who'd seen him at his own trial were startled by the disappearance of the doe-eyed elfin boy. He looked miserable, he looked surly, he looked like jail hadn't been good to him at all. Large shadows darkened the skin below his eyes; a black tattoo was visible through his pale T-shirt. He still did not look like a thug, but he looked more thuggish than he ever had before. Derrill Prevett did not look kindly on the young boy. He'd brought him in so he could be charged with contempt.

Perhaps the boy would reconsider when he found himself facing two more years locked up. Perhaps he'd have a change of heart.

"I don't want to testify," Warren told Judge Nancy Morrison. "I don't understand why I'm being brought here. Me being here puts my life in jeopardy."

This was not an idle excuse. The code against ratting was even stronger in prison than it was at his former suburban high school. He was no longer in the presence of wannabe gangsters like Erik and Rich, but instead he shared his days with necrophiliacs and pedophiles and Hell's Angels and white supremacists. A man who'd literally cut the heart out of his wife lived down the hall. A man who'd doused his daughter in gasoline and watched her burn lived in a cell near his own.

Warren did not tell Nancy Morrison this: the guys inside more or less told him he'd "be taken out" if he committed the transgression of being a Crown witness. "They told me, 'You'll be going out of here one way or another, either in an ambulance or a body bag.'"

• • •

Kelly took the stand in her own defense, and her hair was cut in a demure pageboy. She spoke in a voice a little like Dusty's—a little girl's voice, the voice of Betty Boop or Shirley Temple. Her manner was both aggrieved and bewildered, the manner of someone truly dismayed to find herself in this unfortunate predicament of being on trial for second-degree murder.

"We saw the meteor shower going over us," Kelly recalled softly, "and we talked." The night at Shoreline School had begun so innocently on the field and under the falling lights. "We were just mingling," she said sadly.

Under the bridge, she'd punched Reena only because Reena had tried to hit Josephine. "I was just protecting Josephine," she said apologetically.

"Reena fell into me, almost knocking me over. I pushed her back into the group, and they continued to beat her. Later we walked up to the Comfort Inn. Everyone was talking about the fight like it was a big rush," she said, as if disgusted by their callous pride.

"Who was the most aggressive during the fight?" Adrian Brooks asked her, for all the previous witnesses had told the jury she was the main aggressor.

"I believe Dusty was the most aggressive," Kelly said, primly. "Dusty seemed to be punching her hardest, with the most force."

She told the jury her version of the murder of Reena Virk:

On the bridge, she'd seen Dusty and Josephine. They told her to leave. She walked away and saw Reena, a girl walking away from her attackers, a girl on the bridge.

"Reena, are you all right?" she had screamed helpfully.

"Fuck off! Leave me alone," Reena had replied.

She'd wandered about for a bit then. Dusty and Josephine clearly didn't want her around, and she'd wandered to the Mac's and used the bathroom, and then she'd wandered to the bus stop and talked to Laila and some friends.

Suddenly, as she was heading home, under the streetlights, she'd heard a boy calling her name.

"Kelly," Warren Glowatski called, emerging from the darkness, standing alone, just above the Gorge. The boy was smoking and he said he had something "important" to tell her.

He told her this: "We went back after her. We followed her. Josephine and me beat her up some more. Dusty was just watching."

There was moonlight on the pavement, the red embers of the small boy's cigarette. The black waters of the Gorge glimmered with the reflection of the moon, below them both.

"Is she okay?" Kelly asked him. "Is Reena okay?"

Warren told her to look down at the black abyss. He told her the girls were still down there with Reena, in the water.

She looked down to the black water.

"I couldn't see anything," she told the jury.

Warren walked off then, with only this stern warning: "If Syreeta asks you about the blood on my pants, tell her I beat up a Native guy."

He left her then. He left her "without even saying good-bye."

Alone, she'd walked to her father's house. The night was very dark, and perhaps she was troubled and stressed out by the story of the second beating in the darkness near the old white schoolhouse. Perhaps this was why she'd told Billy, the fireman's son, that "they beat up a girl and she was put in the water." She'd gone home and changed into her pajamas, and gone outside to say good-night to her stepmother and Tammy, drinking wine in the warm water of a hot tub. In the morning, she met up with Dusty and Josephine. "We talked about the fight. Josephine thought it was funny. Dusty was bragging." She didn't mention Warren's story "because I didn't want Warren mad at me."

And then, at Shoreline, every unpopular girl's worst nightmare unfolded: she had become the scapegoat, the patsy. Rumors floated and reeked. "They said that I had gone back after Reena, and I was denying all of this. I was saying, 'No. No. It was not me!'"

Kelly cried for the first time as she recalled the way she was tormented in juvie. "They called me all kinds of names," she said, while pulling at the sleeves of her sweater. How must that have felt? To be a normal schoolgirl and then to be in prison with heroin addicts and hookers? "Lily told me I was sick. She gave me dirty looks all the time. I said to her, 'It's not fair that everyone is blaming me,'" Kelly said, crying at the memory of her persecution.

"Did you kill Reena Virk?" Adrian Brooks asked her.

"No," she said, shaking her head, rapidly.

"Did you tell anyone you had killed Reena Virk?"

"No!" she said, while her mother wept and the judge looked down at her with what seemed a great and obvious sympathy.

Ruth Picha stood up to cross-examine Kelly. She was not a seasoned prosecutor, and Adrian Brooks would later admit to being quite startled that she, not Prevett, stood up to handle the most important part of a murder trial.

"All these people have come forward and told us that you said you killed Reena. Why would they do that?"

"I don't know," Kelly said, genuinely hurt at the long list of accusers.

The judge looked down at Kelly now, as she had looked down at Richie D., Lily, Dusty, and Tara. When the defense lawyers brought up their previous crimes or past lies, she often seemed truly dismayed.

And now, she looked down at Kelly.

Meanwhile, Ruth Picha's listless cross continued. "Well, were they collectively conspiring against you?" she asked, sarcastically.

"I don't know," Kelly said primly, as if she was reluctant to speak badly of her former schoolmates.

"Was there anything about you that makes you important to frame in this murder?"

"No," Kelly said, with the sadness of a true martyr.

• • •

"This case is based entirely on rumor," Adrian Brooks said, with great conviction, in his closing statement. "The Crown has given you no DNA, no fingerprints, and no bloodied clothing. There is no evidence to put Kelly Ellard at the scene. Rumor plus rumor still equals zero. Zero plus zero still adds up to zero. Ladies and gentlemen, throw this all out. It doesn't mean anything."

Judge Nancy Morrison cautioned the jury once more: "There are no witnesses who have seen the accused kill Reena." She asked them to consider the witnesses very carefully. "Was that witness annoying?" "Did they have their own motive?" "Did some have their own agendas?"

Before finding Kelly Ellard guilty, she cautioned from her perch above, "Be sure. Be very sure."

• • •

The jury began deliberating Wednesday at 11:45 and returned with a verdict on Friday at precisely 4:00.

"She's going to walk," a feminist advocate monitoring the trial whispered, bitterly.

"It's April Fools day in India," her friend replied, with pessimism.

She's going to walk, the youth of View Royal predicted as they waited by their TVs. At Brady's Fish and Chips, Syreeta told Diana, "I always told you they wanted Kelly to walk and Warren to fry."

Rushing into the courtroom, Mark Jetté and Adrian Brooks buttoned their cuffs and straightened their white collars. Derrill Prevett's gown was ripped under the arm. Judge Nancy Morrison looked deeply pained. Kelly's father chewed his lip, and the veins on his neck were livid and engorged. Six sheriffs entered the courtroom and lined the doorway, warily, like some nervous cavalry.

The words, when announced, seemed to hover in the air and not resonate as truth for several seconds. Everyone in the courtroom seemed held by disbelief.

"Guilty."

Nevada let out a loud shriek, while Kelly herself gasped.

A chorus of the word rose from outside the courtroom as twenty reporters simultaneously announced the verdict to their editors and producers. "Guilty! Guilty! Guilty! Guilty! She's guilty! It's guilty! Guilty!"

Kelly's mother remained in her seat, pale and broken and weeping.

Mukand tried to call his daughter, Suman, but he was not sure how to use the cell phone a stranger had lent him.

Kelly's mother remained still and sobbing, and Reena's grandmother, noticing this, walked over to her slowly and held her hand to the crying woman's heart.

• • •

On April 20, 2000, Kelly returned to the courtroom to face Judge Nancy Morrison. She now wore a blue sweatshirt with the name of her prison emblazoned across the back. Her hair was lank, and a certain heaviness caused her every feature to look protuberant.

The newspapers had nicknamed her "Killer Kelly." The boys in her prison mocked her with this catchy adage.

On this day, Honorable Madame Justice Morrison would set "how many years Kelly Ellard must serve in prison before she is eligible for parole." She noted that "if the decision depended only on the brutal murder of Reena Virk . . . then a decision would be a very easy one: seven years." The minimum was five years.

Judge Morrison stated her intent to "take other factors into consideration as well." She must, she said, "view the accused as an individual and look carefully at her age and her character." She noted "Kelly Ellard has an extraordinary network of family and friends, a large and loving close extended family.

"She has a way with the elderly and with children. There is a lack of racism in her makeup. She no longer associates with her former peers, and there is no suggestion that she is attempting to reunite with those persons. . . . She's making a commitment to better herself. She's achieved good marks. She's spoken and demonstrated remorse for this terrible event. There is no history or signs of violence before this event or after. She has always had and remains having an overwhelming love of animals, gentle and caring with them."

She then sentenced the "fifteen-year-old with no record, and an otherwise good character" to "the lower number of five years."

The judge looked directly at the young girl. "Kelly, you are young, intelligent, and you have a wonderful family. They believe in you, and I can only say that you must never let them down and, more importantly, you must never let yourself down again. I think you owe it to Reena Virk to live a life that is exemplary. And now you owe that to yourself." Her last words were a wish.

"I hope you do well."

ANOTHER CHANCE

Kelly in a low-cut red top revealing the curve of her breasts, Kelly being chased, Kelly, Kelly, Kelly! Kelly, with the cameras all about her. A stranger might have thought she was a movie star, for the cameraman chased her and the man with the microphone called her name. Kelly was in the parking lot, rushing toward her mother's car. Flashes and screams. "Kelly! Killer Kelly!" The look on her face could only be described as "tremendously pissed off."

Why she wore such a furious look, one could not be sure. Perhaps the chase of the adults bothered her, for they moved so close to her body and their name-calling was so hostile. But, surely, she should have been happy, for on this day, February 4, 2003, Kelly Ellard was freed. The verdict of guilty might never have been uttered. She would have a new trial. She would have another chance.

Kelly had been freed once before. Sixteen months before. Almost immediately after her verdict of guilty, Mark Jetté announced he would be filing an appeal, and a judge, saying, "Ms. Ellard poses no threat to society," allowed Kelly to go back home to View Royal and live under house arrest until the Supreme Court reached a decision on whether she would receive a new trial. Kelly's family provided a $50,000 surety. Her father mortgaged his home in View Royal.

"I think it's a gross injustice to allow her to go home," Suman Virk said. "We've got Glowatski's testimony that Kelly committed the murder and she gets all the breaks. It's really unfair. It's also unfair to the young people who testified at Kelly Ellard's trial. The message is that if you have money and get a good lawyer, you get all the good breaks."

Marissa and Tara were working behind the counter at New York Fries in the mall when they saw Kelly. The mall was alight with Christmas decorations, and past the beaming Santas and cavorting reindeers, the two girls spotted Kelly wandering about with her mother. An emotion close to panic was followed by a dark and volatile outrage.

"How can that be?" Tara wondered. "How can she be walking around a mall? It made me feel that everything I testified to in court, and giving a police statement, was a waste of time because this girl is walking around Christmas shopping. Me and Marissa were freaking out. I went and told the security ladies. I told them, 'This girl is here!' And then I felt something on my back. It was Kelly. She bumped into me. I couldn't see her. I just felt this person bumping against my back, and when I turned around, she was walking away."

• • •

Mark Jetté spent "many, many" hours on the Factum, the document of appeal. Warren too had tried for an appeal of his conviction, which had been dismissed in 2001. Kelly's appeal was presented before three judges, named Lambert, Rowles, and Donald. Kelly sat in the witness box, seemingly oblivious to or disinterested in Mark Jetté's complex and comprehensive attempt to save her and set her free.

Of the presentation before the Honorable Three, Mark Jetté would write:

> The appeal went ahead and the court reserved judgment. They are particularly interested in our argument that Ruth's cross-examination of Kelly was improper, unfair, and deprived her of a fair trial. It would seem that this is the only ground of appeal which has caught their interest. The Crown has conceded that this was improper cross-examination, but argues that the Judge's charge to the jury cured the problem, a kind of "no harm, no foul" pitch. This is a close call, but we are definitely in the ballpark, and may succeed in getting her a new trial.

• • •

Judge Donald stood and read his reasons for ordering a new trial: "The Crown's questioning of Kelly Marie Ellard was unfair and improper, in particular the questions like: 'What reason would these people have to frame you?' Such questions could induce a jury to analyze the case on the reasoning that if an accused cannot say why a witness would give false evidence against her, the witness's testimony may be true. The risk of such a course of reasoning undermines the presumption of innocence and the doctrine of reasonable doubt."

Interesting was the subtle denunciation of the youth of View Royal evident in the judge's statement. "The milieu in which the Crown witnesses moved, and the influences, peer and otherwise, may have affected their testimony."

"There is no doubt," Justice Donald wrote, "that most of the witnesses were exposed to rumor, gossip, and news reports surrounding the disappearance and the homicide of the victim."

The "significant media attention" would be another reason the highest Court ruled in Kelly's favor. "The revulsion of community to the circumstances of the crime was palpable. It was therefore incumbent on the Crown to proceed with special care that the appellant receive a fair trial. Unfortunately, the cross-examination by the Crown on the question of motive crossed the line. The Crown's tactic makes a new trial necessary. For these reasons, I would set aside the guilty verdict and order a new trial."

Kelly, brought to Vancouver and held in a cell in the bowels of the courthouse, learned of the decision from Mark Jetté. "She wasn't very excited," he observed, thinking she must be "stunned. She's shut down."

That evening, a journalist who'd attended all the trials recounted Kelly's apparel to a friend: "She had on this horrible outfit. This red top, it was like lingerie. It showed her entire cleavage. Her breasts were just hanging out. She's got dyed black hair now. She's way bigger than she was at her trial. She's taller. I couldn't get over that top! It was so low-cut. You couldn't take your eyes off her breasts. She plunks in her car. She tells her mom, 'Let's get the fuck out of here!' That top she had on, it was all satiny and shimmery. It was so extremely low-cut. She was walking so fast; she was bouncing. She was really mean looking, she just kept glaring at us all, with her dead eyes."

In View Royal, Tara watched the constant footage of Kelly's walk to her parents' car. The improperness of the outfit did not arouse her wrath. She was upset far more by the decision of the Honorable: "I flipped! I was right pissed off," she recalls. "My first reaction was, 'Great. We've got to go through another trial again.' I had thought her first trial was the final chapter for us. And then, to know she's getting another chance. . . ."

• • •

Warren received the news, well Warren saw the news, while in Ferndale Institution, a minimum security prison he'd been transferred to in 2003. It was not easy to get into this prison, the Harvard of prisons in a sense—one needed an immaculate record and numerous recommendations and an exhibited degree of responsibility and good intentions.

"Your co-accused is pretty hot," a fellow inmate told him, as the footage of Kelly's stroll in her red top was played, and replayed, and played once more.

Though he'd taken a million courses in anger management ("It's best, when one is angry, to try and discuss your anger. Tell the other person about it. Have a dis-

cussion. 'I'm feeling very hurt by what you just said.'")
Warren couldn't help but feel something stronger than
anger as he watched Kelly walk with her family out to
her car, on her way back to her home, back to View
Royal.

He had been incarcerated since November 14, 1997.
His only time outdoors had been when he was getting
into the sheriff's van or working in the garden of the
walled and gated grounds. *Everywhere I go, it will be
there. I'll never get away from it.* He'd somehow managed
to turn the institution into a makeshift academy. "I
never did any homework until I got to prison," he
would later recall. He studied with a criminology professor who often came to discuss the justice system with
the men inside. He hung out with another young
inmate who was studying empire (as in *The Decline and
Fall of the Roman Empire*), and this young guy gave him
a few books to read, one being *The Art of War.* Not that
Ferndale was pleasant, for it most surely was a *prison*
above all. But sometimes he thought he never would
have learned all he was learning if he'd stayed in View
Royal. "I probably would have just been some two-bit
drug dealer."

When he heard of Kelly's new chance, he went to his
room so he would not have to find himself in a possible
confrontation. He expressed his thoughts in a letter:

> I am doing all right, I guess, as good as can be ex-
> pected. I really have not done much thinking
> while I am here about where I will go if I get pa-
> role. I'm hoping to go for work release to Chilli-

wack. They are starting a program there, and I would be working with elderly men who have been in prison for twenty to thirty years. I would like to go to Simon Fraser University, and earn a B.A., but in what, I still do not know.

I have been pretty lonely since my arrival to this place, but I have gotten used to that feeling. It goes with the territory. It is not a big thing for me anymore. Sometimes life can be just another boring, sluggish, aging day for me. I don't want to grow old.

As for Kelly's shit dragging on endlessly, well, she is playing the system, and the system is falling for it, ultimately hurting and re-victimizing the Virk family.

I personally don't agree with all of the system's antics, as well as Kelly's. I don't want to comment because it is not my place. I would probably be discredited anyway.

Keep in contact a little more often if you can.

P.S. Lots of care and respect,

Sincerely,

Warren P. Glowatski

• • •

Kelly was pretty sure that lady took her cell phone.

Her mom had given her the cell phone because she was living in Vancouver now. Big deal. She was still under all these rules, and stupid rules they were. Rules were easy to break, especially if your boyfriend was a member of the Triad, a hard-core Asian gang, and you'd been inside Wilingdon Detention Center since you were just sixteen. Killer Kelly, what a stupid name. That lady took her cell phone. Danica was just wasted. She'd been throwing back Buds since two in the afternoon. Danica was pretty pregnant, so that was going to be one messed-up baby. That lady stole her phone! The halfway house was run by the Elizabeth Fry Society. She was supposed to learn "life skills."

"Danica, call that lady over here. She stole my fucking phone!"

Danica screamed, "Hey lady!"

Danica's hair was black, little pixie bangs, and she wasn't even at the Elizabeth Fry Society. Kelly met her one day on the street, and Danica was just hanging about, the way she and Nevada and Josephine used to hang about Marton Place hoping to get some weed or attention from Colin Jones. She and Danica would just wander over to this park and drink some beer and hope a cute guy would walk by, even though Kelly already had a boyfriend in the Triad. Do you know what that is? The Asian mob! Don't fuck with me. Nobody better even try.

Her bail conditions said she shouldn't be drinking beer in a public park at 2:30 in the afternoon. Life skills. She didn't even know what that shit was all about. Her mom gave her the phone just in case she ever got lonely or needed to talk or had some kind of emergency.

The lady came over.

"What's your name?" Danica asked.

"June."

"June, sit down and have a beer."

June sat down. She was fifty-eight.

"Hey, lady. Where's the cell phone?"

"I don't know—"

"Listen, lady!" Kelly screamed. "I've done some weird shit."

"She stole the phone!" Danica screamed, and she hauled off and began to hit June in the face. When the cops found June, her lips were bleeding and there was a bruise on her face.

"These two girls," June said, and she described them, though she had no idea one of the girls was the notorious Killer Kelly.

Kelly denied taking part in the assault and she denied drinking beer. "They're just trying to get her back in jail," her mother mused.

The Crown filed a motion for Kelly's bail on the murder charge to be revoked, and thus Kelly found herself before Associate Chief Justice Patrick Dohm of the Supreme Court, the same judge who had relaxed her bail conditions two months before, releasing her from house arrest so she could look for a job.

How many courtrooms had she been in? How many judges had she stood before? She might have counted as she waited for the judge to announce his decision. Her fingers moved through her hair, black with red streaks, and she clenched her palms and did not turn to look at her mother. She was dressed as so many girls dressed, in cargo pants and a loose sweatshirt. Judge Dohm revoked her bail and ordered Kelly back into custody. She would have to stay in jail now for at least four months, until her second murder trial in June. After that trial, she would face an assault trial for the incident in the park. Another trial, another courtroom.

For now, she was back on television and on the front pages of newspapers. Many were surprised to discover that she'd been out of jail for months, no longer under house arrest. In View Royal, people would shake their heads and say their banker or their Realtor had told them they'd heard Kelly was a vicious child who decapitated her Barbie dolls. A friend of a cousin of a friend said they'd heard that when Kelly went to her mother's wedding to George Pakos, the soccer star, she signed the guest book "Jeffrey Dahmer."

Kelly's mother bristled when she heard such tales. "It's all false," she said. Asked what Kelly was really like as a child, she said, "Kelly rode horses. She was a Brownie. She wasn't an abused child. We're honest, hard-working parents. And Kelly was just like every child. She had curfews. She came home on time. She never defied us.

"Before all this happened, she was just a regular girl."

CALIFORNIA CATHY

The pretty blonde woman surprised the boys of View Royal. In the courtroom, she wore the black gown, but she seemed so friendly and cheerful, and they were surprised when she'd turn on them suddenly, though they should not have been surprised, for she was their adversary.

Catherine Murray, a Crown prosecutor, had once been Don Morrison's protégé. Her life amid criminals could not have been foreseen. She was from the comfortable neighborhood of West Van, she'd grown up with trips to Hawaii, she had been head cheerleader for four years, received a new car at sixteen. Before she went to law school, she spent her vacation in California. She entered law school with a tan and a cheerful demeanor and fellow law students dubbed her "California Cathy."

First as a criminal defense lawyer and now as a major crimes prosecutor, Catherine Murray maintained her sunny, hopeful manner despite her constant dealings with horrible acts of violence.

While the attorney general debated whether it was worth the time and great expense to retry Kelly Ellard, Catherine faced some of the more troubled youth of View Royal.

"I did a bunch of Crips cases," Catherine recalls. Many

of Warren's high school friends had grown up and now, as young adults, still held onto their adolescent fantasy. Only the gang was real now, no longer "wannabes."

They would often engage in sudden and vicious attacks on respectable strangers waiting for taxis on the wrong street on the wrong night. They also managed to gain access to the occasional firearm as well as crystal meth and cocaine. The police, in response, formed a special gang unit, and, after months of surveillance, arrested at least fifteen young boys, for crimes ranging from possession of stolen property to aggravated assault. It was Catherine Murray who won convictions, mainly because she was able to convince the often reluctant and frightened girlfriends to testify against their boyfriends. "She's just really good with kids," her superiors observed. Unlike Ruth Picha or Derrill Prevett, or even Don Morrison, she did not prefer the vagaries of DNA and legal precedents. She was said to be: a "people person."

Her string of Crip convictions culminated with a boy with the unlikely name of Harry Hiscock. The twenty-one-year-old ringleader and avowed lifelong thug was charged with beating a young man into a comatose state, a young man who had been carrying flowers for his girlfriend on the wrong street at the wrong time. Despite being represented by Kelly's skilled lawyer, Adrian Brooks, Harry Hiscock was found guilty by a jury. The police were pleased by his eight-year sentence as he was "a major leader of the group, somebody that the younger people looked up to. Now, with him out of circulation, a lot of the other Crips, with too much heat, have simply moved on."

With both police and her superiors impressed by her dealings with the Crips, it was perhaps not surprising that Catherine Murray was asked if she would like to handle the second trial of Kelly Ellard. "I'd be very interested!" she told her bosses, and she agreed to junior alongside Stan Lowe.

After the debacle of the last trial, everyone in the Crown office, from the deputy chief to the paralegal, thought the only way Ellard would be convicted was if Warren Glowatski testified. He was the only eyewitness. Word was that he was in good shape, "doing really well," "a pretty good guy." Yet no one knew how he could be convinced to testify. He owed no favors to the Crown. ("They never believed what I said the first time around, so why should I say it again?") And would he want to even meet with Stan Lowe, the one who brought in Syreeta, brought her to tears? The one who thrust Reena's clothes in his face and sent him away to live in a place with no girls or swans.

Several months before Christmas, Catherine went to visit Warren at the minimum security prison where he now resided. The prison was on lush green grounds, and inmates were free to wander on the field of grass with picnic tables and a view of a Benedictine monastery.

When Warren walked into the room, Catherine was surprised and not surprised, for as a defense lawyer, she'd learned that supposed criminals could be likable and polite. But Warren was unlike many of the accused Crips, who were brutish and surly. "He was cute," she noted. "He looked like he could be my son."

She was surprised by all the progress he'd made. He'd been editing a documentary video and working as a volunteer for a restorative justice program. The prosecutor and the convicted murderer hit it off. ("We just got along right away," they both would later say.) Warren asked her if she was thirty-five, and she laughed. "You're my new best friend," she said. They talked for a long time about a lot of things besides Kelly Ellard. He couldn't bear to tell her he wasn't going to testify against Kelly—not just because he didn't want to cooperate with Stan Lowe but because he didn't want the trauma. He didn't want to die from a shiv in his back; he didn't want to talk about that night again and again and once more.

He was hoping she'd come back and visit him, so he told her he'd think about it.

"I promise you one thing," she said. "I'll never bull-shit you."

He hadn't asked for any kind of deal, although his parole date was looming. He didn't even have a lawyer. ("I've had my share of those guys. They never did anything for me.") It seemed to him that he was doing so well after so much struggle to emerge from whatever nightmare he'd been in. To get up on the stand and talk about the night under the bridge and over the bridge would put him back seven years, traumatize him all over again, open him up to all kinds of slings and jabs, the least of which would come from inside. They would come from all the forces of the world—the media, the defense lawyers, those with a kind of influence he'd never known. He'd known only the opposite in that brief moment when the cop in Estevan had said, "Glowatski. Oh, another one of them." Now he knew where he stood, despite all his studies and change. "Society pretty much sees me as a scumbag."

Marissa wrote him sometimes. "I really hope you testify," she said. "Otherwise Kelly is just going to get away with it again."

He did not write to Syreeta anymore. Gregory, her stepdad, had said they'd appreciate it if he stopped calling. Syreeta was trying to get on with her life, that's what he'd heard.

Catherine came to visit him a few more times, and she never put any pressure on him. They just talked about his life before this all happened and where he saw himself going, and he told her some theories he had about why kids like Harry and Carter were still acting like fools.

By December, just before Christmas, and once again against his dad's advice, he'd decided to testify as a witness for the Crown. "You think you'll come back before that?" he asked Catherine Murray.

She said, sure she would. *I promise you I'll never bullshit you.*

A REUNION, OF SORTS

The second trial of Kelly Ellard began on June 14, 2004, and it was a reunion of sorts, a strange camaraderie inevitably forming between the Virk family, Kelly's family, and the media, who had spent so many hours together, years before, in this very modern gleaming courthouse. Stan Lowe was not on the case. ("I got a triple murder. I had to handle that."), so Catherine Murray would be lead, and she chose as co-counsel a young woman named Jeni Gillings. Jeni, with the intelligent beauty of a French actress, was "so organized." Catherine could not believe the boxes and boxes and files and transcripts involved in the Virk case. Jeni as well had a scathing sense of humor and shrewd instincts. Without Jeni, she wouldn't have convicted all those Crips. "She's the brains behind the operation," Catherine would often say.

Kelly sat blithely in the prisoner's box, with her hair newly cut in trim bangs, no longer black, but a pale brown with auburn highlights. In the prisoner's box, she would write copious notes, and she would hand these to her fourth lawyer, a woman named Michelle. Michelle was both partner and girlfriend of Kelly's main lawyer, Robert Claus. Robert Claus, like Adrian Brooks before him, was well respected and known for victory.

• • •

The trial was a remake of sorts, a production with the same actors as the original, all only more noticeably older now.

Dusty, looking vaguely as if she'd wandered in from a Gauguin painting, seemed the most transformed. Softer, prettier, her voice now seemed to suit her at last, and as often as she could, she interspersed her testimony with mentions of her daughter, the fact that she was a single mother, and in school.

"Let's talk about what kind of teenager you were," Catherine said to her warmly.

"I dropped out of school in grade 8," Dusty said, comfortable, for she'd talked with Catherine so many times. They'd just had a smoke together, and even her older sister Destiny thought Catherine was "pretty awesome."

Dusty said, "I lived in Edmonton, Windsor, Maple Ridge, Thunder Bay, Vancouver. I didn't want to follow the rules. I was put in Seven Oaks. It's a house where they put kids who didn't want to follow the rules."

"What was the secret bond with Warren?" Catherine asked her.

"We all have one," Dusty said softly. "We all did it together. We were all involved. That's not going to change."

"Did you kill Reena Virk?"

"No," Dusty said, and she began to cry, and the jury looked at her with sympathy, for when talking of her life to Catherine, she seemed likable, even redeemed.

• • •

"This lawyer," Reena's dad said of Kelly's representative, "is it just me or is he very irritating?"

Bob Claus was a very tall man with a constant scowl. Throughout the proceedings, he would often call for a mistrial. His first one was in regard to his client's lack of medication.

"Your Honor, my client has been unable to get her anti-anxiety medicine and she cannot contribute to these proceedings in any meaningful way if she is suffering from anxiety, and I am going to have to request a mistrial at this time."

He would often produce an exhibit known as "the dark photos." He would show these to every witness in an effort to establish that you can't see anything on the bridge in View Royal during the darkness of evening. "You'll agree with me that it is impossible to make out who is on the bridge in photo 14?"

"Yes," the kids would say, half-bewildered, half-amused. While showing the "dark photos," Bob Claus did not refer to the presence of a full moon in the sky on that certain dark evening.

The judge, Selwyn Romilly, originally from Trinidad, sat through the days with a wry look. Occasionally, he seemed near laughter or lecture, but he kept his expression both amiable and stern. On the lunch breaks, he changed into shorts and sneakers and jogged for many miles.

*

If the young witnesses were more remorseful and polite, less sullen and defensive, it was perhaps because over time, they had come to understand the horror of what had truly happened. Most often they would cry when describing how Reena was kicked and punched, and most often they would not try to minimize their own role.

They were savvier as well, so used to the process of interrogation by now.

Billy politely told the court of how he "just bumped into Kelly on the Old Island Highway." Her pants were "soaking wet" and she said, "I just killed someone. I held her head under water. What should I do?"

"Did you not say before that Kelly might have said, 'Her head was put under water'?" Bob Claus asked, hopefully.

"I said that last time," Billy said, "because the lawyers tricked me."

This seemed to startle Bob Claus, and he flipped through his notes for a few seconds. "Did you not say before that you thought Kelly was just making a joke? That it was all a big joke?"

"Yes, I said that," Billy agreed. "Because," and here he shot a disgusted look at Kelly, "you just don't think someone you know is capable of doing something so terrible. I just didn't believe it. I didn't think somebody could do that to another person."

"No further questions," Bob Claus said, his voice heavy with temporary defeat.

•   •   •

"Tell us what you were like in 1997," Catherine said to her star witness.

"I was trying to find my place in the world," Warren said. "I was basically very directionless. I was living two lives. One was with my girlfriend where I didn't have any emotional turmoil, and then, in the other, I was trying to be a tough guy. I hung around with the Crips, they accepted me, and just feeling accepted was good enough for me."

"How did you feel about violence?" Catherine asked him.

"It got my blood flowing."

In her box, Kelly began to fidget about.

"I want to take you to that night—November 14th."

"Some kind of rocket went across the sky. I think it was a shooting star," he said before describing the fight under the bridge—all the girls hitting Reena, the way he'd kicked her too.

"There was a shimmer from the moonlight," he said. "Kelly asked me if I wanted to go see if Reena was all right, but the way she said it, I knew that was not what she meant. She had a smile on her face.

"I knew I was going to do more of what I did before. Beat on Reena. We caught up to her on the other side of the bridge, near the white schoolhouse. Kelly asked her if she was going to rat out. She said no. Kelly asked her to take off her shoes and jacket."

He sighed, for here was where his telling would begin to change from all the tales he'd told before.

"Kelly started punching her, and I jumped in. We were both kicking and punching. She eventually hit the ground. We continued to beat on her." He began to cry, and his voice was almost imperceptible, particularly as the microphone in the courtroom had been broken for days. It did not amplify the sound, so people had to lean forward and listen to the words of the boy they'd never listened to before.

"We were kicking and stomping on her. All over. All over her body. On her head. We both grabbed Reena by the legs. We took one leg each. Reena was unconscious. We dragged her to the Gorge waterway. She was face down. We took her to the water's edge."

In the utterly quiet and transfixed courtroom, Kelly began to cry. She leaned forward as far as she could, her head hanging over her knees; she clasped her own ears. She cried as if something was lifted from her, something she'd held on to for so long.

"I saw a military police car go by. I stopped. Kelly took her into the Gorge waterway. She became semiconscious. She started mumbling words. She started struggling. Kelly was holding her head down. Kelly held her head under water. She struggled a bit. Kelly gave her a chop to the throat. Kelly stuck her head under water until red stuff floated to the top. Kelly started walking out of the water." Here Warren stopped talking, but from the corner of his eye, he saw Kelly, her long hair set across her face, now pale and tear-stained.

"Reena was floating," he said, and then he was silent.

"What did you think of Reena's state?" Catherine asked.

"That she was dead," Warren said, with a kind of horror at his own words. He put his head down for the first time.

"Me and Kelly told each other not to talk about it. She asked me for a cigarette. I gave her one."

"What was her emotional state?"

"I can't really describe it—she was. . . ." He paused, thinking of the word while the sheriff handed Kelly a tissue. *Blank*. That was the word he finally chose. He said she was "blank."

• • •

"It's beyond comprehension," Manjit said to his wife. "How could a woman have so much ruthlessness?"

"It takes real guts for Warren to admit a mistake," Mukand said to his wife. "Only a gentleman or a nice person will admit they made a mistake, but Kelly is not a nice person. She has been a brat all her life. I don't think she will change. She will stay that way all her life. I hope the judge puts her away for a long time. There's no doubt in my mind that she'll be found guilty."

Warren made a single request of Catherine: don't make me ride in the sheriff's van. In this way, he found himself escorted to the courthouse by the very man who had once yelled at him, "You're going down big time!" It was a reunion with his interrogator, Sergeant John Bond.

"He was so meek and mild," John Bond says. "I didn't even recognize him. I thought when I got to the prison, I'd have to go through all kinds of security and he'd be all locked up, but when I got there, he was just standing outside, waiting for me, by himself. I think he was surprised I handcuffed him. He's been so used to not being cuffed."

The men drove away from the town of Mission, past the cattle farms and fields of gathered hay. Bond, now the head of the Strikeforce, a covert operations unit, also looked rather different than he had seven years ago. If Warren was more clean-cut, Bond was in his undercover mode; his hair was long and scraggly, his mustache was a mess, and he looked more the prisoner than Warren did.

"I've got a lot of respect for the guy," Warren thought of Bond, though he wasn't sure why. There was just something about him he liked, and both men thought, on their own, that if they had met under different circumstances, they would have liked to grab a beer and just shoot the shit. In this way, it was an easy drive from Mission. They were forbidden to discuss the case, and so they talked of this and that.

"What do you think of restorative justice?" Warren asked Bond.

"I think it's a fad."

"You think it's a fad?" Warren said disbelievingly, and they debated the merits of the program, which involved offenders meeting face to face with their victims.

They talked about mortgages and motorcycles, and when Warren grew suddenly quiet, Bond realized it was because they were driving by the cliffs, and Warren was smelling the ocean for the first time.

"His whole face just changed," Bond saw, and he said nothing, but unrolled the window, silently.

• • •

Catherine finished with Warren in the morning, asking him only about Kelly's jacket. "Calvin Klein, black," Warren recalled.

"You refused to give evidence before. Why are you now?"

"I feel I have an obligation to the Virk family—to tell the truth. I've had time to think of what they were going through. Before, I didn't care at that time."

"And now?"

"I care a hell of a lot," he said, and several of the jurors were crying.

Bob Claus, when he started with Warren, seemed suddenly charged with a new energy.

He began with Warren's jacket, the jacket he'd worn to court yesterday.

"You were wearing that jacket yesterday as part of your little theater? To make you look small?"

"No," Warren said, surprised by the misinterpretation. He did not volunteer that it was hard to get a respectable jacket while you were in prison and so he'd borrowed one from a larger friend.

"Now, you're eligible for parole next year, and *of course,* to get parole, you have to admit participation, and you have to show that you have some caring for the Virk family. So your testimony here is all about your parole opportunities. You want out of prison. It's about getting Warren out of jail."

"It has nothing to do with that, sir."

"Well, to get parole, you have to say you have remorse for your crime?"

"I think you have to be genuine."

"Well, speaking of genuine, when Sergeant Bond and Sergeant Bruce Brown first interviewed you about this missing girl, you swore on your grandfather's grave that you had nothing to do with it. You swore on your grandmother's grave."

"I was messed up. I was quite the sleazeball then."

"Yes, you said you were really into violence yesterday. It gave you a rush."

Warren nodded while Bob Claus leaned back slightly, folded his arms across his chest, and sighed, as if the boy before him was an irascible student and he was a very disappointed teacher.

"You testified at your trial that you told Kelly to stop. And that was a lie?"

"Yes," Warren admitted.

"Your whole testimony was a pack of lies, just like your statement to the police. And you're still saying you're not really guilty of murder. Kelly did it all."

"By not stopping her, that's how I'm guilty of murder," Warren said.

"You did the drowning! That's why your pants were wet."

"No, I wasn't wet, sir."

Warren hung his head while Claus appeared to search for more questions on his pad.

"I'll suggest to you that you saw Kelly on the other side of the bridge, and you showed Kelly where Josephine and Dusty were drowning Reena."

"Wrong, sir. That's absolutely untrue."

Claus went on for a while, doing his best to provoke Warren into revealing himself to be belligerent, to scream, to swear, to show himself to have the nature of a killer. But this did not happen, and at 4:00 P.M., Warren returned with Bond to prison where he noticed that he had broken out in hives and his body felt suddenly heavy, as if a concrete weight was placed on his heart. "I know what hell feels like," he thought, and he could hear all the accusations in his head for a long time and he thought of the cell under the courtroom. There were yellow lights in that little cell, and he thought the lights were far more ugly than any other lights he'd seen.

Mr. Glowatski, you got teary in here. You were crying. Did you cry when you were kicking Reena? Did you cry when you killed her? Did you cry when you were telling Syreeta? Did you cry when you bleached blood off your pants? You never cried for Reena Virk. You want out of jail. *You drowned her. You drowned her. You drowned her. You.*

• • •

Kelly's mother did not understand the media or the Virks. "Why do they say they respect Warren?" she wondered. She wanted to smile at Mrs. Virk, to say hello, but she would always lose the nerve and look down at the floor instead. It was just terrible walking by her, day after day, never having the nerve to say hello. And then one day, Mrs. Virk smiled at her, and she just wanted to rush over and hug her. It had meant so much to her, the mother's smile.

George, her husband, was getting fed up with the media, and he nicknamed one reporter, named Catherine Pope, "Catherine Dope." He went right up to her: "You said on the news last night, the jacket Kelly was wearing on the night of the murder, well, it's the *alleged* jacket she was wearing."

It bothered Kelly's mother when the media described Kelly as emotionless. They said she showed no remorse. How did they know? They couldn't even see her in the prisoner's box. She'd cried all through Warren's testimony. How was that emotionless? Sue just didn't understand. None of it made sense. Warren's story made no sense. It was Dusty who was mad at Reena because Reena was wearing Jack's jacket. She often thought of Mark Jetté saying: *There's something under the surface here.* Kelly had given her back a lipstick she'd bought and said she didn't like the color, so Sue now rushed from her hotel, the Four Seasons, to a department store and tried to find a color Kelly would like. She would cry, remembering that Kelly once hoped to become a makeup artist on movie sets, and now, whatever happened, her daughter's life was basically ruined.

With the new lipstick for Kelly, Sue rushed back to the courtroom, as this afternoon her daughter was going to take the stand.

• • •

"Don't think you'll get her to just confess," Stan Lowe advised Catherine over the phone. "She's not going to just say, 'Okay. I did it. I killed Reena Virk.' You've got to chip, chip, chip at her. Chip away. . . ."

• • •

There was a kind of frenetic energy in the courtroom, and, because all the seats were full, several Japanese schoolgirls sat cross-legged on the floor. The microphone was still broken ("What is this, Romania?" the journalists complained), and so as Kelly told her story, in a very soft voice, even those in the front row moved forward, and were almost falling out of their seats as they strained to hear.

Catherine was scribbling rapidly. There were Post-its and ripped pieces of paper and notes from yesterday, all forming a messy union on the table. It was Michelle, not Bob Claus, who stood to ask Kelly about the evening.

Kelly told her story of the evening and as she spoke, her voice took on a clipped, precise tone, both prim and concise, and occasionally it seemed she was using a British accent.

After the fight, Kelly saw Reena walk up to the top of the stairs. "Her hair was all messy," she recalled. "She was walking really, really slow."

"I was about to head to the parking lot with everyone else, and I saw Dusty and Josephine standing at the start of the bridge. Dusty told me to go away. I pretty much got impatient, and so I crossed the street. I went to the parking lot, and I saw some guys, and then I walked with Laila and her cousin to the bus stop. I then was just about to walk home but I decided to stop in the Mac's to use the washroom. I got to the intersection where the light is. There's a cement island there. I heard my name being called behind me. It was Warren. He told me to come across the street."

"He told me it was important." Then as she had said in her previous trial, Warren told her that "himself, Josephine, and Dusty had gone back after the girl, and him and Josephine beat her up some more. He told me he had sobered up and just stopped beating her up. He said he left, and the last time he looked, Dusty and Josephine were in the water with her. He pointed over to the schoolhouse area. I just took it as drunken babble. He asked me to walk home with him and then he just took off. He didn't even say good-bye."

"And we've heard from Billy Schilling at this trial that you had a conversation with him. Can you tell us about that?"

"Actually," Kelly said, "I asked him if he had a smoke and he reminded me that he did not smoke. He commented that I looked nervous and upset, and so I told him about the fight and what Warren had told me. I said, 'We beat up a girl and I think she was put in the water,' or something to that effect. He just said, 'Whatever,' quite rudely, and he walked ahead with his girlfriend."

"You heard him tell the court that you were saying, 'What do I do? What do I do?' Did you ask him that question?"

"Uh, no."

"You've seen Exhibit 15 in this trial—the black nylon jacket with the Calvin Klein logo."

"That's my stepsister's jacket."

"Did you tell Jodene that you held Reena's head under water?"

"At no time did I ever say anything about drowning her. I didn't even know anything about her being dead or drowned. It was just she was put in the water, and that happens a lot at parties we go to—someone is thrown into the water as a way to humiliate them, so I just thought that was what Warren was talking about."

Kelly said that by Thursday, the wellspring of rumors was causing her to become very "cautious and scared." Soon after, Warren told her she was being a "bitch" and should "keep her mouth shut."

Then with a series of loud no's, she denied beating Reena, throwing her head into a tree. No. Telling anyone she killed Reena Virk. No. Killing Reena Virk. No, she said, and that was the end of her evidence in chief, Kelly saying no.

*

Catherine Murray was already asking questions before she was on her feet.

Her voice was staccato and sudden, so different from the voice she had used with her own witnesses.

"Why were you so worried about protecting Josephine Bell under the bridge?"

"Well, she's small and dainty."

"So?"

"Well, she was one of my good friends. I didn't want her to get hit."

"You knew full well at the beginning of the night that you and your friend Josephine had cooked up this little plan to get Reena to go out with you and beat her up, didn't you, Miss Ellard?"

"No," Kelly said primly.

"Well, I put it to you that you were well aware that there was a plan that night, and you were part of the plan."

"Um, actually, no, I wasn't," Kelly said, less primly. "Or I would admit that right here. I would not lie about it."

"You and your friend Josephine Bell had talked earlier that week about digging a hole and burying Reena alive, correct?"

"No," Kelly said, grimacing.

"You find that distasteful?"

"Yeah, quite," Kelly said, and her tone had now veered from British nanny to sullen Valley Girl.

"Reena wanted to go home. You knew that."

"Obviously," Kelly snarled.

"Well, we weren't there. What was obvious about it?"

"She wanted to use the phone and go home."

"You knew she didn't have any friends there. You knew she was an outsider. The atmosphere under the bridge was a very unfriendly one toward Reena Virk. She was not being treated well. And you, of all people, are very sensitive to not being treated well, correct? You're a sensitive person, aren't you?"

"Where did you get that from?" Kelly said. And then, as if sensing the trap, she quickly interjected. "I am. I am sensitive. Somewhat, yes."

"Now, all this yelling is going on. Laila is yelling at her. Laila's a tough girl. Dusty is mad at her. And she's a big girl. And Reena is scared, and that's when you think, 'Oh my God. Reena Virk, who doesn't have any friends here, is going to hurt my friend, Josephine Bell, the dainty girl?'"

"I don't know," Kelly said, and it was at this time that court was adjourned for the lunch break.

• • •

Later people would wonder what occurred in those minutes between 12:30 and 2:00, for when Kelly returned to the courtroom, it was as a different girl—nothing like the girl on the stand in the morning. "She just looked like she hated Catherine," a courtroom observer noted. With her eyes flashing and her head tilted in an arrogant, *don't fuck with me way,* Kelly marched to the stand.

"Could you show us how you punched Reena?"

Kelly swung up her hand, easily and suddenly, and several journalists raised their eyebrows, surprised at the natural way her fist rose, like she wanted to smash the air.

"Why didn't you just grab Reena to prevent her from getting to Josephine? How does that punch help?"

"It obviously doesn't. I told you already! I didn't know what I was thinking. It was stupid."

As if she had not heard the answer, Catherine contemplated out loud, "What I don't understand is—"

"I already told you," Kelly screamed, suddenly. "It obviously doesn't make sense!"

"Well, let's move on," Catherine said, as if oblivious or unconcerned with the impending tantrum. "You said while the fight was going on, you were just standing there, watching Reena. Why were you watching Reena?"

"Maybe I just wanted to watch."

"You like watching people get beat up?"

"No," Kelly said, and she glared at Catherine, as if offended by the insinuation.

After a few more questions about the fight, she began to cry.

"Is it the recollection of Reena getting beaten that's causing you distress?"

"You, and her, yeah," Kelly said, pulling at a tissue.

"Do you want to take a break until you stop crying?"

"No, keep going," Kelly barked.

"Eventually, Reena came flying down a couple of stairs, right into you. I imagine with some force. She's a big girl, we've heard, 180 pounds, but she doesn't knock you down?"

"I almost fell. She almost knocked me over, but I did not fall, and that's my answer."

"So you pushed her back into the crowd, where she got punched some more. Do you want another break?" Catherine said tauntingly, as Kelly was in tears once more.

"No, keep going. I want to get this over with," Kelly replied, as if to say, *I can handle you, bitch.*

"Do you recall Laila telling people to stop? And most people listened, because Laila was pretty tough."

"I don't know her. I just met her once before at Shoreline. She came to visit."

"Oh, was this at one of those gatherings where someone was thrown in the water?"

"Yes," Kelly said haughtily, "that happened quite often."

"Did it?" Catherine said gleefully. "Regularly?"

"At parties. It happens."

"So *party* to you is kind of a loose term? It doesn't mean a happy gathering?"

Unaware of the trap she'd wandered into, Kelly snapped back, "Not all parties are happy. Bad things happen sometimes. Kids are cruel."

"Mm-hmm," Catherine said.

"You heard what I said," Kelly snapped, once more irritated by the steely derision of her opponent, this blonde. "You heard what I said. Kids are cruel. They can be cruel."

"*You*, Kelly Ellard, can be cruel," Catherine noted, seizing the implication.

"I used to be," and realizing, too late, the trap she'd fallen into, she quickly added, "sometimes."

"You were cruel on this night."

"But I didn't kill Reena Virk."

"We'll get to that."

"How many times do I have to say it?" Kelly sighed.

"Now, after Laila stopped the fight, you say Reena is in a heap in the mud. She's crying. That was upsetting, to see her like that?"

"Obviously. I'm not a monster."

"But at this point, you're still concerned about Josephine Bell, not Reena Virk."

"You keep wasting time!" Kelly suddenly screamed. "I just want to get this over with!" She then told the prosecutor: "Quit repeating yourself, please!"

Again, Catherine appeared oblivious to the outburst. "Did Reena say anything to you?"

"You know what?" Kelly said, with an exaggerated air of exasperation. "I don't remember. It's seven years ago. Do you remember what you were doing seven years ago?"

"Well, unfortunately, here, I get to ask the questions, and you have to answer them. You saw Reena wasn't well. Did you ask her if she needed help?"

"Not at that time."

"You stayed back to take some extra shots at Reena Virk. You were the main aggressor in that first beating. Your story is that you were an onlooker?"

"I was the first one to punch her, and I pushed her back into the group. That's all I did."

"Well, I say you did a lot more than that."

"You're very wrong," Kelly retorted, and she seemed to revive, and the woman and girl battled on. The prosecutor, who seemed utterly content and even blasé yet full of vigor, tried to get the accused to "pinpoint when exactly you started to care about Reena Virk."

"When I saw her hunched over and she looked humiliated," Kelly said.

"But after you've had a number of occasions to help her, you don't do anything until she's halfway across the bridge, and then you yell out, 'Reena, are you going to be all right?'"

Several of the onlookers laughed out loud then.

"Did you really care about her at that point?" Catherine said with a laugh of astonishment.

"Is that funny to you?" Kelly said. "Of course, I cared."

"Did you go to the Mac's to call 911?"

"Obviously, I didn't and it was stupid and I'm sorry."

"You didn't care."

"I did care! I did. Say it as much as you want. My story is not going to change."

"So you crossed the street, and you were mad because your friend Josephine was ignoring you, and so you left. That's your story?"

"That's the truth, actually."

"How long were you at the bus stop talking to the three guys?"

"Fifteen minutes."

"Okay. Now, when you saw Warren, you say he calls you over and tells you these things. Now, my question is this: If Warren had a secret or a problem, was it *you*, Kelly Ellard, that he'd seek out?"

"No."

"But on this particular night, he called you. He said,

'I was just on the other side of the bridge. We went back and beat up that girl some more.' And didn't that cause you concern?"

"I didn't believe him."

"Was he wet and muddy?"

"I don't recall."

"Do you remember at the bus stop Rich asked you if you were wet?"

"*You'd* like to think that, but, no, I was not."

"You weren't wet?" Catherine said, as if fighting back the urge to break into laughter. "That's your evidence?"

"I was not wet," Kelly said, and it was at this point that she leaned forward and her eyes narrowed, and she glared and glared at the blonde woman who was moving closer to her now.

"*You* were wet and you told Laila you'd taken care of Reena so she wouldn't rat."

"You are 100 percent wrong, and I was not wet. I did not say that. You're just making suggestions. My story is not going to change."

"You call your evidence a story?"

"Well, you referred to it as a story, but it's my truth," Kelly said, and she seemed to weary, and then rallied, rolling her eyes at the next question about evidence that she was wet. She then let out a torrent of words, although her lawyers had likely told her to only answer with yes or no.

"If what you're saying is true," she said, loudly, "I would have had hypothermia by the time I got home."

"Have you had hypothermia?" Catherine said, clearly enjoying the escalating battle.

"Yes, I have," Kelly sulked. "When I was twelve. I was in the hospital." She began to talk very fast, and most of the reporters had stopped taking notes, too riveted by the conflict between woman and girl.

"Well, if you weren't wet, why did you change your clothes when you went home?"

"You can say whatever you want but everything that comes out of your mouth is going to be wrong because I did not change my clothes. I was not wet. And I did not kill Reena Virk."

"You called Maya, and you told her you killed Reena Virk."

"I did not call her! You are wrong!"

"You called Dusty and Josephine and you took them to the Gorge and you found Reena's shoes."

"You are just merely making suggestions. I did not have any such conversation," Kelly said, and her British accent returned with her more formal language.

"You do have protective instincts toward Josephine Bell? You'll admit that?"

"Yes."

"And yet you don't tell her that Warren is saying she was in the water with Reena Virk?"

Kelly rolled her eyes and raised her elbow to her forehead, melodramatically.

"Here you sit on the swings with your best friend and you do not tell her that such terrible things are being said about her."

"She was not my best friend!" Kelly screamed. "My closest friend was Kyla!"

"You know they called Reena's home because you'd

been telling them you killed Reena Virk, and they did not believe you so they called her mom."

"No, that's not true. I will swear on anything that I'm not the killer. I am not the killer!" She began to cry and threw her head down on the witness stand before her, near the Bible and the box of tissues.

"You said to Maya that you were happy you killed her."

"I did not say that!" Kelly screamed, her voice louder than anyone's voice had yet been. "I am not a monster!" She beseeched Catherine Murray then: "Please stop!" she screamed, and the sheriff, a white-haired man with a rich tan, looked at the young girl sympathetically. It seemed then that Catherine might stop, for she'd pushed the girl for so long, days, but Catherine did not stop and seemed still utterly unfazed.

"Let's carry on with what you said to Willow. You said to her that you broke Reena's arms and legs and held her under water. You told her that you felt that you had to go back and finish everything, otherwise Reena would rat everyone out."

It seemed then that Kelly must have stood up, though she remained seated, and yet her voice was so loud and forceful as she screamed: "I did not kill Reena Virk and I will repeat it and repeat it and I will stick with that until the day I die! I don't care how much jail time I do, I did not kill Reena Virk. I will still say I did not kill Reena Virk until the day I die. I don't care if I get another life sentence but I did not kill Reena Virk!"

Kelly's mother had her head in her hands, much the way she did on the night of her daughter's arrest. The jurors had long ago stopped taking notes and looked alternately disgusted and transfixed. The judge said, "Let's take a break," for a break was clearly needed. Some of the onlookers refused to move, however, and the sheriffs had to come and pull them from their seats.

At the end of the long hallway, far away from reporters, Catherine asked Jeni, "How much longer should I keep this up? Do you think the jury is feeling sorry for her?"

Just then Michelle walked by in her high heels and long black robe. "End the pain," she said to Catherine. "Please. End the pain!"

The reporters were all on their phones, dictating tomorrow's headline: ELLARD: I AM NOT A MONSTER.

After the break, Bob Claus again asked for a mistrial, citing a newspaper article about his prior request for a mistrial. "It's irresponsible," he pleaded. "I renew my application for a mistrial."

"Motion denied!" Judge Selwyn Romilly boomed. "Get the jury in here!"

"You were doing a lot of bragging about killing Reena Virk. Was that week your moment of glory?"

"No."

From then on, Kelly's voice stayed monotone, but she began to repeat the same sentence over and over, like a mantra, and with the repetition, she seemed closer to unhinged.

"Let's talk about Jodene. She says you told her you put your foot on Reena's head."

"Jodene is lying," Kelly intoned. "I did not kill Reena Virk. I did not say any of those things. Keep going."

"Can you listen to the question?"

"I did not kill Reena Virk," she said, now robotically.

"And you held Reena's head under water and that's how she sucked up those pebbles."

"I did not kill Reena Virk."

"You were carried away with your own self-importance. You told Dimitri you finished her off."

"I did not kill Reena Virk."

"You told Lily you held Reena's head under water for five minutes."

"Lily's a liar. She's not trustworthy. I would not have said such a thing!"

With this, she closed her eyes, folded her arms, and began to rock back and forth, up and down.

"Do you remember what Reena was wearing?"

"I did not cross the bridge."

"You and Warren continued to beat on her."

"I did not cross the bridge."

"Kicking, stomping, jumping all over her."

"I did not cross the bridge. I did not kill Reena Virk."

This went on for a while. Every statement met with: "I did not cross the bridge."

Kelly said this twenty-three times.

I did not cross the bridge. I did not cross the bridge. I did not cross the bridge.

She began to cry.

"Warren and you took Reena to the water's edge and then you dragged Reena all the way in."

"I did not cross the bridge."

"She started struggling when she was in the water! There was a bit of movement."

"I wouldn't know. I did not cross the bridge."

"So you karate chopped her to the throat. Do you remember that? And then you held her head under water."

"I was a fifteen-year-old girl! I'm not a monster! I did not cross the bridge!"

"Well," Catherine said, and she moved forward, and she put her finger directly in front of Kelly's face. "Then why does your jacket have saltwater on it?"

"There could be a number of reasons." She became defiant again. "I put the jacket on the ground at the beach. I often did that."

Catherine Murray then pulled the jacket out of a bag, and walked over to Kelly, and placed the jacket right before her, with her hands on the white lines of salt.

"You were wearing this jacket the night you killed Reena Virk."

"You can stop!" Kelly screamed at her. "You've got what you wanted. I'm obviously going to be convicted. My life is over." She put her head in her hands, and began sobbing, and for several seconds, short seconds, there was only the sound of her tears and ragged breath.

"This jacket has salt all over it," Catherine said, holding the jacket up toward the jury. "This jacket tells the story, doesn't it?"

"I didn't kill Reena Virk," Kelly said one last time, while covering her face with her hands.

"This jacket tells the story," Catherine repeated once

more, and then she left the girl alone at last, and the girl kept her head in her hands.

In his office, Andy Ivens of the *Vancouver Province* reworked his story. "Kelly Ellard predicted her own demise," he'd written, but then his editors called and said they weren't so sure about the word *demise*.

He looked in the thesaurus. "Perdition, downfall, ruination. Hey," he said to his editor, "how about predicted her own Waterloo? Predicted her own perdition? Too highbrow. Yeah, I agree. Okay, *downfall*, then. Use *downfall*."

Reporters swarmed Catherine Murray, begging for an interview.

"Talk to Jeni," she told them. "She's the brains behind the operation."

To the reporters, Suman said, "Kelly seems to be a very sad and frustrated person. She doesn't seem to have any hope for herself. I see her as a very pitiable person."

Manjit was more succinct. "She's just incorrigible," he declared.

• • •

What was taking the jury so long? For three days they'd been deliberating. Catherine and Jeni went shopping, and Jeni bought only practical clothes and Catherine teased her that she should get married in a gown of khaki.

As the hours went on and on, Catherine kept thinking to herself, *I pushed Kelly too hard. I should have done, what should I have done, what could I have done differently?*

*

More hours went by. The weekend passed.

"This is trial by exhaustion," Bob Claus declared. "I ask for a mistrial."

The atmosphere in the courthouse in which the families and media sat around from early morning to 10:00 P.M., waiting, began to resemble the sudden bonding of those aboard a sinking ship. Suman Virk brought in doughnuts and offered them about. Newspapers were shared. Mrs. Virk asked Kelly's mother if she was "hanging in there," and soon the two women began to talk.

"I don't know what happened that night," Suman said. "It was like evil took over everyone."

"Maybe it was just peer pressure," Susan said, "just teenagers. . . ." Her voice trailed off, and she began to cry. Her husband wore a blue stone around his neck, a good luck charm he'd picked up in his days as a soccer star, on tour in Florence. "I don't think it's doing me much good," he remarked.

After five days of deliberations, the jury finally announced, on a Sunday afternoon, that they'd reached a decision. Reena's mother and Kelly's mother had been talking privately in a corner when they heard the news. The two women looked at each other and hugged suddenly.

"We are unable to reach a unanimous decision," the jury wrote. "Eleven are for conviction. One is not. The past days have been extremely difficult and emotionally devastating for all of us. We have exhausted all avenues of deliberation and have reached an impasse that cannot be resolved by ANY further discussions."

"I have no choice but to declare a mistrial," the judge said, with a resigned sigh.

"This is unbelievable," Suman said outside court. "I can't believe this is happening. I was prepared for guilty or not guilty, but this never entered my head."

Catherine Murray, surrounded by cameras, tried to pull Jeni up to the literal spotlight with her, but Jeni dashed away.

"The Crown is prepared for a third trial," Catherine announced, though she had not heard whether this was the case. "One juror was thinking with their emotions rather than their head. This was one juror. *One* juror."

"Are you prepared to put all those witnesses through another trial?"

"It's not a case of putting anybody through anything. This was a brutal murder, a brutal, brutal murder. These witnesses, they are never going to forget," she said. "They'll never forget."

THE COST OF MEMORY

The mistrial is an outrage," declared Nancy Upton of West Vancouver. "Why do we let twelve people with no experience make life-changing decisions? Now, all this time and money and stress must be repeated, and Kelly Ellard must be held accountable for her actions."

This sentiment—the mistrial is an *outrage*—was voiced by many in coffee shops, taverns, and on talk-radio shows. ("All you need to do is take one look at her to know she's pure evil," a caller said on Victoria's C-FAX radio.) The mystery of the holdout juror, dubbed the "rogue juror" by the media, also intrigued many. Who was this person? What had been his or her reason for believing, clearly, very strongly that Kelly should be found not guilty? The answer would never be known, for in Canada, jurors are strictly forbidden by law to discuss deliberations.

Nonetheless, outrage seemed even to rise to the highest levels of power. Shortly after the mistrial was declared, the province's attorney general mused publicly about national reforms to the jury system: "We should perhaps reduce the number of jurors from twelve to eight" or maybe remove the "requirement of unanimity." "I think we've got a situation where we've got to look at reform," he offered, amid the public outcry over the mistrial.

It might have seemed an unlikely turn of events—a single schoolgirl creating talk of legal reform. Yet Kelly, on the advice of her lawyers, offered no opinion on her many trials and the lack of a verdict. Had she answered questions, she might have screamed to her interrogators, as she had screamed on the night of her arrest: "Quit asking me questions! I can't take it anymore. I just want to go home. You can make me stay in my room for the rest of my life."

• • •

After a brief vacation to California, Catherine Murray returned to her office in the Victoria courthouse, across from the Cherry Bank Inn. The boxes of transcripts, police reports, and witness statements cluttered the hallways and were stacked to the ceiling. Now they would have to be reopened, reread, rather than sealed up and sent to the archives. There would be new transcripts arriving, thousands and thousands of pages, and these voluminous pages, marked Ellard #2, would have to be organized, analyzed, and memorized in preparation for Ellard #3.

Had she been a sigher, she might have sighed. Her cheerful fortitude might have been diminished by the prospect of a return to the prosecution of the girl who had screamed at her, "You're wasting time! You ask too many questions!"

Kelly had a new lawyer, her third prestigious and skilled defender.

Catherine wondered and worried as she faced the

precarious mountain of cardboard boxes. *I did the best I could last time,* she thought. *I don't know if I can do it any better this time.*

The youth in View Royal were approaching adulthood. ("I hope now that they've grown up, they'll start telling the truth," Kelly's mom said to a reporter.) New witnesses might be called who were not battle-scarred and exhausted by the often ruthless pummeling they withstood on the witness stand. There were kids who had told the police about the braggings of Kelly Ellard, kids who spoke with her on the night of the Russian satellite. There were her confidantes and girls who'd joined her in the first beating—girls like Laila and Eve and Josephine. Yet, these potential witnesses were perhaps aware of the cost of memory, and so they refused to speak out in the courtroom, telling the Crown they just couldn't, or wouldn't, for yes, they'd told the police this and that, but now they'd forgotten. It was so long ago. They'd blocked out the evil memory. Of a girl in wet pants, a girl confessing murder, they couldn't, so sorry, too bad, unfortunately, just could not remember anymore, not at all.

And so, drafting her trial plan, Catherine Murray would ask for assistance from the same witnesses: Dusty, Billy, Lily, Marissa, Tara, Maya, Warren, and others who did not run from memory and were willing to tell what they knew about the murder of Reena Virk. It seemed unreal to all of them, as if the night continued to linger, to hold them in some kind of fierce embrace. It seemed as if Kelly Ellard, once a girl, now possessed an almost superhuman power to remain unvanquished and triumphant. But they told Catherine, with sighs of resignation, that, yes, they would testify once again.

These witnesses are so courageous, she thought, knowing they were reluctant, frightened, weary, busy. She held no cynicism or uncertainty when it came to the moral goodness of the youth of View Royal. *These witnesses,* she thought, with her cheer returning, *are just amazing.*

PART V

The Adulthood of View Royal

"Stories do not end."

—Anais Nin

THE VISITOR'S FORM

Warren saw, on the pale blue envelope, a name in a familiar girlish scrawl, two words in the top left corner, two words that still caused his heart to catch and rise like a tuned guitar string: *Syreeta Hartley.*

More than two years had passed since he'd heard from Syreeta. He could still remember, with a faint sting, the voice of her stepfather informing him that it would be best if he called the home no more.

"I'm really sorry for testifying against you," Syreeta wrote from a new address, for she and her mother no longer lived in View Royal.

She told him she was studying to be a legal assistant, and hoped to one day do something in the legal field, though exactly what, she wasn't quite sure. "I don't want to defend the guilty and prosecute the innocent." She said her mother said hello and wished him well. How are you doing? she asked. How are you?

She said only one thing about the night of the Russian satellite. "Life would have been different if I'd let you walk me home."

"Don't apologize for anything," he wrote back, for he was, in fact, rather stunned by her apology. ("I would have understood if she told me she hated me.") He told her about his work with restorative justice and alternative-to-violence programs, how he was busy organizing meetings and working on a documentary. He told her he was going up for parole soon, and he thought maybe he'd get day parole soon, and if so, he'd move to a halfway house in Cowichan.

"Don't apologize for anything," he wrote. "I have so much respect for you and your mother." Then he wasn't sure what else to say. He wrote down one of his favorite sayings, a quote from Gandhi: "If you want change, you have to be the change." He wasn't sure if he should include the saying, and he thought about erasing it, but left it there, on the edge of the white paper.

There was something else: he wondered if he should include it, but did not have time to decide for he had to return to his cell. In his room, on the wall, there was no longer the photo of Syreeta beside him, with her eyes closed and her smile and her braces, and his arm on her shoulder. A hole from a pin remained under a piece of tape, for in all his different cells, when he was young, he'd kept the photo up high so he could look at her when he needed to remember the time he had loved and been loved. He did not retrieve the photo from a box, but instead took a certain piece of paper from a file on his desk. The sounds of the jail could be so constant and metallic, the clanging of keys and doors. He was silent but could hear the noise clamoring closer with the routine of incarceration. Head count. Every night at 10:00, the guard would say, "Name," and he would answer, with little enthusiasm, "Glowatski."

He took the Visiting Application and Information

Form—composed of boxes for "information on applicant" such as given name, relation to inmate ("specify type and length of relationship"), and questions: "Are there at present any outstanding charges against you?"—and folded it into a neat square, then placed it in the envelope with his letter.

Maybe, he thought. Maybe Syreeta would walk in here, past the herons and convicts and slow, aging days, past the barbed wire, and locks, and grim and steady routine.

Head count. Name? *Glowatski.*

• • •

"You got a letter from Warren," Syreeta's mother said, and Syreeta nodded, reaching into the refrigerator for some apple juice. Syreeta did not have a boyfriend in her new home. In high school, she had always had a boyfriend. Now, after her classes at community college, she would work at Brady's or another restaurant, and nights, she would sometimes go dancing with Diana, to "the club"—a dark place downtown near a wharf. ("Yeah, it's a dirty club, but it plays good music, and we see people we know and have a good time.") Syreeta would twirl around, laughing, her hands on her hips, her body raised by a pair of stilettos. She and Diana had even gone to Vancouver for a Christina Aguilera concert. Men would often hit on her, but Syreeta was indifferent to the attentions and desires of strangers. ("I can go out and I can get hit on, but who can't? That means absolutely nothing to me.")

When she met someone new, she felt obligated to reveal her past, for what if the person discovered it later and felt she'd been keeping it a secret? With her blunt and self-possessed manner, she would assert, "My boyfriend killed Reena Virk, and I'm the one who sent him to jail." Then, seeing their startled gaze, their disbelief, she would change the subject.

After dinner, she and her mother settled on the couch. In his letter, Warren had sent a DVD entitled *A Healing River*. She knew little about restorative justice, and she watched the film because he had asked her to, and he'd said he worked on it, helping to edit and file footage. After some of the experts spoke ("We need to see crime not as merely a broken law, but as harm done to people, and we need to ask, 'Who was harmed?'"), Warren appeared on her television screen.

He looked the same, only his hair was now cropped short, and there were circles under his eyes, which looked slightly startled, as if he'd witnessed something he had never wanted to see. His eyes seemed tearful, and yet he was not crying.

"That's Warren," Syreeta said to her mother, with some astonishment. "Wow. That's exactly him."

After the film ended, she and her mother remained curled up on the couch. Syreeta held a pillow on her lap and touched the embroidered threads.

"Would you see him again?" her mother wondered, for she knew Warren had sent Syreeta a visitor's form.

"I guess so," Syreeta said. "I'm not angry at him. A lot of people think I should be, but I'm not. That would be kind of a selfish thing, to be angry at him. I mean, obviously, he's going through a lot worse."

"Where is Ferndale?" she asked her mother.

"I think it's near Mission, about an hour or two from Vancouver. You'd have to drive."

"I'd probably get lost," Syreeta said, thinking of the towns and valleys that were across the water, not on her island. "I wouldn't mind seeing him though," she continued. "I don't need him in my life as a constant person, but I guess. . . ."

Her voice trailed off. She was thinking about the young man in the film, how he was now and how he had been. "It was so weird seeing that film," she thought to herself, "especially hearing his voice. Just to hear his voice," because of course, "I hadn't heard him talk in so long."

DAUGHTERS AND A DREAM

I saw Syreeta the other night at the club," Marissa says. "She looks great. We all kind of went our own ways after we graduated, but I still see her now and then, and we always have a blast."

Marissa is seated at the Starbucks in the Hillside Mall, dressed in a navy pea coat. Her hair, which has been blue, gold, red, black, and blonde, is now cut in a bob and tucked behind her ears.

When she thinks of her role in the tragedy and trials, she believes: "It made me grow up really fast." The girls of View Royal often say this. They say they don't like fights because they know where fights can go. They say they leave if trouble starts because they never want to be a witness again. And they say they don't stress over small stuff, like a car breaking down or a botched job interview, because they know "worse things can happen." Far worse. "Someone can lose their life for no reason at all."

At thirteen, Marissa had been the youngest girl under the bridge. ("I was just a baby!") She had fled from the fight and later provided some of the most crucial evidence at the trials of Warren and Kelly. ("I saw Reena on the bridge. She was staggering. She looked really light-headed. I saw Warren and Kelly follow her.") And yet she wonders why "the media portrayed us as the bad ones when we were the innocent ones." The "media pissed me off a lot," she says now, with a sanguine giggle. "I've had a lot of times where I've had my little breakdowns, where I'm freaking out, thinking, *Oh God, I've done something so wrong.* The media said, 'You girls were there. You didn't do anything to help Reena Virk.'" But, she says, sighing, "People can all say what they want. I know what happened."

Sometimes Warren calls her home. He wants to hear where she went last night, who she saw. He wants to hear the names, the familiar names of The Five: Syreeta, Tara, Felicity, Diana. . . . Of their new loves, of their lives, for it's as if he can still live in View Royal, still be part of that world, if she evokes it for him.

"When I talk to him, he wants things to be the same as they were when he was out, but it's just so hard to explain to him that it's not the same anymore. The Five of us don't talk anymore. We've all grown up. He still calls me his little munchkin. I'm not that little girl anymore! I still love him, though. My parents pay for his calls, but I'm not home very much, so usually when he calls, I'm not there and I haven't talked to him for a while."

Despite her sweet nature and delicate features, Marissa has often had to reflect on the moment after she left, a moment so gruesome and terrible, the moment a girl was brought to a dark place and pushed into the water until her breath was no more. She can't see anything, though, when she tries to imagine this, for how could she know what truly occurred below the white schoolhouse?

"Obviously Warren had something to do with it if he is where he is. But for the most part, I don't think he did." She avoids the use of words like *prison*, like *murder*. "And he promised us that once he gets out, he'll tell us what happened, once it's all over with, but to this day, I don't believe that. . . ." Her voice stops. She still cannot say the word and laughs softly, as if willing some moment of joy, or hopefulness, back into the sentence she cannot complete.

• • •

The youth of View Royal do not know the facts of the Karmann Ghia. Never had they noticed the yellow car, such a rare and treasured thing, speeding through their streets. Never had they seen Reena Virk in the passenger seat, laughing, with her hand out the window, the blue nail polish and black platforms, the new accoutrements of belonging, singing about every breath you take. Teasing her uncle Raj about his affection for Bryan Adams, asking him to take her down streets where she might see her new friend, her glorious friend, a blonde, slim, white girl with the name of Josephine.

The tremors and pains in Raj's body only intensified after Reena's murder. The doctors diagnosed him with MS, and soon after Warren's trial ("I don't care what happens. He'll get more justice than Reena got, that's all I know."), he'd found his limbs like stones, useless, offering only betrayal. It was not the MS that caused him to park his car in the garage where it began to rust and decay. He'd loved it so much, painted the once-cherry-red car a brilliant yellow. Yet he could not drive the car, for it was too full of memories. The car had taken him through View Royal, those days when he'd been searching for Reena, hoping to find her hiding out at a friend's, hoping she'd emerge laughing, and say, "Raj, I'm sorry. Let's go get that teddy bear." He told his parents he would *never* again drive the Karmann Ghia.

Almost eight years later, nobody wonders who is driving the car, weaving through the streets of falling petals.

• • •

The driver might have noticed the silver cross was gone. A mysterious stranger one night, soon after the murder, mounted a metal cross on the railing of the bridge. For a while, near the bouquets, a tiny cross of sticks rose up, with the backdrop of the Gorge, the watery grave. Tiny and makeshift, the cross was precarious and resembled something one might find in a pueblo. Handwritten were the words: *the Reena Virk bridge*. Rain washed away the words; wind tossed the cross to the site where Reena's diary page had been discovered so unexpectedly. But the second cross would not be lifted and would not fall, for the anonymous builder had constructed it with a view of stability. "It was welded on to the railing," Reena's grandfather, Mukand, explains, with astonishment. "Someone put a lot of work into it. It was about four feet tall, and silver."

A year or so after the murder, Mukand had received a call in regard to the second cross.

"Do you mind if we take it down?" the police officer asked him. "We want your permission. You can be there when we remove it." Mukand agreed, though he did not attend to see the officers take the cross from where it stood as a makeshift memorial.

"Kids were scared to cross the bridge," Mayor Bob Camden explains. "We had to take it down." Camden, a former accountant and volunteer fireman, did not want a permanent memorial on the bridge, as, "The problem with memorials is once you start putting them up, everybody wants one."

Understandably, the mayor was concerned about the tarnishing of his town's image. Around the world, the town was now associated with violence, death, gangs, cruelty. Yet the town was full of hard-working families, of close friends, of good, normal folks.

"The school felt unfairly tarred," he says. "It wasn't a Shoreline issue. It was a foster care issue. It was really unfortunate, really sad, but most people in View Royal do feel it was an isolated incident. This may sound callous, but I don't think too many people in the town think about it too much anymore."

Had there been calls for renewed youth programs, for better schools, for a community center? Yes, some antiviolence programs and antibullying measures had been put in place, but for the most part, the mayor observed, "as long as people's toilets flush when they want them to flush, they don't complain."

After all, the murder was an isolated incident. It revealed nothing about the mores or manners of an average Canadian town. "Kids have been partying and hanging out since the dawn of time. There's no way you could predict a gathering of girls would turn out so ugly. Most police would see a group of girls and think nothing of it." How could anyone have known such Furies would arise?

Mayor Camden was, in the years after the murder, concerned with improving the civic life and value of View Royal, and to this end, he considered applications from Home Depot and The Great Canadian Casino.

The latter promised a great source of revenue. "Ten percent of the casino's gross revenue would go to the town, and so if they earn $2 to $3 million a year, that would double our revenue and we could spend it on capital projects. That could be spent on things like a youth center or sidewalks. Sidewalks are expensive."

The driver of the Karmann Ghia would, by 2005, have noticed the 35,000-square-foot casino not far from the Gorge. Inside are state-of-the-art slot machines with names like "Big Bang Piggy Bankin" and "Mermaid's Gold Magic Lamp." By 2005, the casino had provided over $7 million to the town of View Royal, but no plans for a youth center currently exist.

The detectives still drive through the town in their unmarked cars. Not far from the pay phone at the Mac's, where Reena had last called home, Sergeant John Bond, now head of the Strikeforce, apprehended a murder suspect. The victim was a fifty-four-year-old barber. ("Nice guy," Bond says. "Just couldn't beat the dope. Years ago he cut my hair.") Krista Hobday dealt with a man who beat his girlfriend to death—beat her so badly her face was unrecognizable. Sergeant Ross Poulton apprehended an arsonist who'd torched buildings and watched the flames rise, proud of his handiwork. Bruce "Brownie" Brown retired and was feted for his long-term career as "an officer and a gentleman." Sergeant Gosling returned to the Dive Unit, searching for marijuana or missing fishermen, not for the body of a missing girl.

Never again did the Saanich station witness an evening like the one on Friday, November 21. Never again were the cells full of girls with ponytails and braces and platform shoes. How strange that night seemed in retrospect. All those girls, some suspects for murder, some with information about a murder, in the station after being pulled off the green field, sobbing to the older men, sassing off the detectives, crying for their boyfriends, saying they saw nothing, saying they heard it but *did not believe.* Girls with their names like brands of perfume. Chandelle and Laila, Syreeta and Marissa, Eve and Melody. Some of the girls had been stunningly beautiful, with soft hair and softer skin; some had been burly and rude, with heavy bodies and rough eyes. But they'd spoken of broken arms and whispers and lurings and blood in the water.

The presence of so many girls in their station remains simply a truth, an anomaly, a rather bizarre and unlikely event. A complete mystery. "I guess it was socioeconomic," Poulton offers. "The group dynamic," Bond suggests. "The mob mentality. It was definitely unusual to see so many young females involved in an incident," Hobday observes. "The kids in the beating and murder, not one of them came from an intact family." Of the witnesses, she says, "They were just your typical girl next door."

In the exhibit room, marked pieces of property remain in boxes. Willow's yearbook. Josephine's Nivea cream. A shard of glass from the bottle of Polo Sport perfume. Maya's pillowcase with daffodils and a tiny blood stain. Kelly's drawings of decapitated bodies and bullets flying at an officer going, "Oink, oink, oink." Adidas, Nike, Calvin Klein. A white sock recovered from Seven Oaks Group Home. A letter Dusty wrote to Warren in juvie. ("Hey hon, whad up. I have a lot of questions I need answered.") A Shoreline yearbook with inscriptions such as, "Call me baby, let's party all summer long. Love ya forever." Josephine's notebook of phone numbers recovered from Reena Virk's home. Like a poem or a trove, the real clues might have been uncovered here—some clues to the lives and dreams and lack thereof, some sensations and longings, some meaning in these seized possessions of adolescence. But the exhibits remained sealed, kept from the public while, in the parlance of the police, "legal matters remain pending."

Principal Frances Olsen left View Royal and now lives on a houseboat reachable only by kayak or canoe. Her former school, Shoreline, is no longer a school for teenagers who memorize war poetry. *Short days ago we lived, felt dawn, saw sunset glow. Loved and were loved.* The school is now a middle school for those in grades 6 to 8. The purpose of this transition was not to obliterate a site where a murder may have been planned but to accommodate, according to the school board, a change in the population.

Seven Oaks is also no longer a "receiving and assessment home." A former worker explains that after the murder, "We were shut down by the Ministry. The girls went home to their families, if they had them, and if not, they were put into foster homes. The Reena Virk murder had a huge, huge effect on all those girls. They were really traumatized."

When speaking of Nadja, the woman from Seven Oaks softens her voice. In the town, no one has ever learned of Nadja's actions. Her heroism and determination are known only by those involved in the investigation. "If the Russian sisters hadn't come forward, there's a chance we might never have learned about the murder," a detective admits. Perhaps the body would have drifted for weeks on end, been discovered rather than searched for, ruled death by accident or death by suicide. Perhaps. Nobody could say for sure, in retrospect.

"After they shut Seven Oaks down, all the girls left, except for Nadja," the care worker recalls. "She had nowhere to go. She stayed with us until Christmas. The day she left was one of the toughest days of my life. She had to leave. And she was crying. I was crying. It was horrible. She's just an amazing girl, and when she left, she was at the highest risk she'd ever been."

Of Nadja's current status, she says only, obliquely: "She's taken a turn for the worse, unfortunately."

Anya, like her sister, seemed to vanish from Victoria, as if absorbed by the endless clouds and forests of evergreen.

Warren's father lays pipeline in the Rio Grande. He is near sixty now, his face weather-beaten and still ruggedly handsome. In the high heat, he recalls the "horrendous" times with Warren's mother, the "bottles of vodka under the bed, in every drawer." He is not unaware of his own mistakes, but insists he did not "abandon" Warren. "My lawyer told me to get out of town because Warren's mother was trying to get all my money. I was going to get set up in California, and Warren would have come down at Christmas. My wife wanted him there. It all would have been fine. It would have been fine." He visits his son when his health and time permit, and he plans to go to Warren's parole hearing. He's not one to cry, but now and then, tears come to his eyes when he thinks of the places he's been—the deserts and the red suns, these places Warren will never be able to see: Tunisia, Libya, Las Vegas, the Rio Grande.

Grace Fox moved away from the lane of swans and herons. Josephine's mother moved to Asia. Mrs. Smith, the beloved school counselor, moved off the island to a smaller, quainter town.

Amy, Reena's counselor, still works with troubled young girls, but the budgets are always being refined, reduced, and the program she's now with is said to be removed soon, so the girls Amy deals with will be on their own.

Maya is not in View Royal anymore. There are too many ghosts for her there. The ghost of her dead father, the ghost of Reena. She says, "I put this all behind me when I turned nineteen," and she talks to few people from her past. In 2002, her best friend, Willow, passed away suddenly. Willow had once written to Warren, "I miss being able to talk to you and have you understand. I am here for you and always will be." The coroner had found that Willow's unexpected death was a result of "an arrhythmia, an irregularity or loss of rhythm of the heart," and Willow's death was classified as natural.

Eve has moved away as well, and says the night under the bridge is one she cannot recall. Laila can be seen on downtown streets, still with her long hair and Cleopatra makeup. She has lost interest in kickboxing, and her body is softer, fuller now, less taut and powerful. Her philosophy on life is, generally, "What's in it for me?" She has refused to cooperate with the Crown. For a while, she lived with a man who was known to the police, described in their files as "armed and dangerous."

Of all the girls, Dusty is the most likely to recall the night under the bridge. "I think of Reena all the time," she says, with her voice still strikingly melodic and lovely. Once she was a "dangerous young lady," but her run-ins with the law ceased soon after she was no longer a teen. "I kind of feel at fault for what happened to Reena," she admits. "If it wasn't for me and Josephine, she wouldn't have been there that night." She does not speak of a wish for closure or putting it behind her. "I can't heal. I can't get over it. Reena was really hurt, and I was part of the beating. Even if she'd survived that, she would have had real damage. And then, a life was taken. I don't think I'll ever get over it."

Of the justice system, Dusty believes, "We should have got more time. We were monsters. We did a terrible thing."

Of her mother, Dusty is forgiving. "I don't put the blame on anyone for my behavior back then. It sucked. My mom couldn't control me, so she just said, 'You're gonna do it anyway. Go ahead.'" Dusty laughs at media reports that Reena's demise was tied to their shared love of Jack Batley. "He was just a typical boy who thought he was the best thing since sliced bread. I never slept with him. I was a little kid. I didn't know what love was."

Now twenty-three, Dusty has two daughters of her own. It is her daughters who changed her, she believes.

("I got to do whatever I wanted when I was a kid, and that's not going to happen with my daughters.") The presence of two little girls softened her, saved her and makes her all the more admiring of the Virks. "Reena's grandmother hugs me at the trials. I wouldn't be able to hug someone who did that to my daughter."

"We did a terrible thing," she says again. "There's nothing we can do about it now. I want to make my kids be civil and nice. That's my job. That's all I can do."

• • •

Here is the person driving the Karmann Ghia: Reena's little brother, Aman.

At fifteen, he began to resurrect his uncle's car, cleaning off the spider webs, scraping away the rust. The car became his passion, and he himself slid under it, examining the intricacies of motor and brakes. He buffed it endlessly, shone the windows, washed away the silvery mazes of webs. When he turned sixteen, and not a day after, Aman began to drive his car past the street named Earl Grey and to the strip mall that housed the Salvation Army. Once, in Brady's Fish and Chips, Aman commented to his friend on the beauty of the dark-haired girl behind the counter.

"He had no idea who I was," Syreeta says, wistfully. "The Virks were never rude to me. In fact, they were the only people who ever treated me like I wasn't a bad person." She wished she could say something to the young boy, but what could she say? She would only smile at him, and think again, "I should have let Warren walk me home."

Aman might pass the truck owned by Kelly's father.

No longer does the logo bear his last name of Ellard, but simply his initials, "L.E."

Aman drives to visit his grandparents. Mukand and Tarsem have observed Reena's brother and sister grow up, without incident or even rebellion. Both children, they see as reserved and quiet. The murder of Reena is not spoken of, for the subject is incomprehensible, too shattering, and instead they speak of classwork, of travels, of jobs, of friends.

The television is often on at the Pallans' home, and the screen presents reruns of old American sitcoms and news stories of abductions or forest fires. When speaking of the trials of Kelly Ellard, Mukand can grow feisty and scathing, despite his polite nature. "Judge Nancy was so lenient." He says of the rogue juror, "Maybe she knew Kelly or was very, very stupid."

Reena's grandmother, a Jehovah's Witness still, finds her hope in the thought of seeing Reena again. "I'll see her again," she insists.

Her husband, tending to the fireplace, says with a resigned sigh, "You'll never see her again."

Tarsem shakes her head, smiles, refuses to engage in an argument, for her faith is strong. She feels the possibility of goodness whenever Aman comes over, with the car, brought back, revived. He is so happy, speaking of the new brakes, and how he placed them in the dark shell underneath and she thinks, tomorrow. *Tomorrow I will give him the note.* It is a note she wants him to see, a note she's been saving to give to him. He'd written it when he was a child, when Reena was at the Kiwanis shelter. He had written: "Reena, please come home."

*

One night, Marissa and Tara see Syreeta at "the club" and hug her, before explaining they are running off to crash a friend's bachelor party at The Fox, the strip club in the Red Lion Inn. Syreeta and Diana often thought of going to The Fox just to see why guys liked it so much, but when it came time to enter the club, they'd lose their nerve. ("We just couldn't go through that door.")

At the strip club, Tara and Marissa wander past the tables of men in baseball caps and flannel shirts. On the television screens, dirt bikes soar into the sky, performing feats of impossible gravity. The stage is circular and raised high above the men. A country and western song is playing, and the girl on the stage is dancing slowly, taking off a leopard-skin bra, roaming about in black leather chaps.

The next girl on stage moves in a more arrogant and harder way. Marissa thinks she looks familiar, the blonde girl on stage, and she nudges Tara. "Is that Josephine?"

The girls both look up at the blonde girl above them, in the center of the dusty spotlight. Her blonde hair is down to her shoulders, and she wears black leather boots with seven-inch heels, a black leather vest, and a bra of white lace. But her face is the same, with full lips and dimpled chin, the same taunting smile that seems at odds with the features, both classic and innocent.

Josephine sees her former friends and schoolmates, and as she struts close to the edge of the stage, she waves at Marissa and Tara, with a slight awkwardness, as if aware that, unlike the men, they know exactly who she is.

Marissa waves back halfheartedly, but Tara turns away with disgust.

The men gaze at and long for the girl on the stage, for they know nothing of her beyond her willing postures and arching body. They do not know that she once lured Reena Virk out on a moonlit night with a promise of a party. They do not know that her mother told police of a conversation in which Josephine spoke of graves and burials. They have no idea that the near-naked girl on stage once thrust a burning cigarette into a lonely girl's forehead, and the next day threw a dead girl's shoes in a trash can.

Josephine, despite efforts of police and Crown, has never once appeared in a courtroom as a witness. She has never betrayed Kelly, despite hearing the tapes of Kelly's accusations. She has instead toured the strip clubs of the land, taken the money thrown at her, danced, and been told of her beauty.

Marissa and Tara now walk away from the stage while the men continue to stare up at Josephine, and she reaches down to collect all of their money, and then saunters off, to the applause, toward the back of the stage where she is no longer illuminated but back in the ordinary darkness.

November in View Royal is now, as it was then, a gray season, with a constant fog that seems suspended in heavy clouds, like a sheath, over the mountains and above the firs. The town falls under this weather of melancholy, accustomed to the way the rain blurs their vision as they drive, turns the firs of the tall trees a particularly vivid shade of green. No Russian satellite has fallen from the heavens ever again. No mysterious explosion of brightness and falling fire causes the youth of View Royal to turn their eyes upward. Every year on the anniversary of Reena's death, flowers appear at "The Reena Virk Tree," a maple sapling planted in her honor. Every year, articles are written about "teen bullying" and proclamations that "Reena Virk will live forever in our memory."

But in the summer months, the clouds lift and the Gorge turns again into a site of such remarkable beauty. A park for children now is near the water's edge, so the very young children of the town play in sandboxes and on slides, filling the air with exuberant noise. Kayaks cross the Gorge, their passengers paddling slowly, turning their faces to the sun, then lifting, with oars, the waters, which seem full of gold. Swans float slowly by the shore, as if unbothered by the presence of a young couple on the green grass, wrapped in each other's arms, staring out at the light on the water.

The boy in the Karmann Ghia drives home. He passes his sister's room and hears her singing to a song on the radio. He walks upstairs and smells the scent of cardamom in his mother's tea. His father is in the living room, with a green singing lovebird on his shoulder. His father now works as an interpreter in courtrooms, helping lawyers translate Punjabi into English and English into Punjabi. His father does not tell his son of the dream.

The dream is this. A dream of Reena, the first since her death, so long ago.

In the dream, Reena has returned home and she wanders into the house and hugs her mother.

Her mother says, "Aren't you going to hug your father?"

His daughter then holds him. They embrace. In the dream, Manjit is "crying profusely." He turns to his daughter, with the tears still in his eyes, and in the dream he says to her:

Reena, where did you go?

He says, "Reena, *where have you been?*"

AFTERWORD

On April 12, 2005, after deliberating for thirty-six hours, a jury found Kelly Ellard guilty of second-degree murder. The third trial presented much of the same evidence as the prior two, only this time, Kelly Ellard did not take the stand on her own behalf. After the verdict, Judge Robert Bauman sentenced her to life imprisonment and handed down the maximum period of imprisonment to be served before parole eligibility—seven years. His decision was based on the fact that "this was a deliberate murder, not one committed in the heat of the moment," and that "Ms. Ellard's conduct after the murder shows her utter disregard for the life which she has taken."

In assessing her character, the judge also reviewed a huge volume of prison records—records that depict Kelly as a less than stellar inmate. According to logs and incident reports, she has written threatening notes to guards, planned and participated in assaults on other inmates, been found in possession of cocaine and other drugs (as well as the odd contraband of "eleven brand-new toothbrushes"). She's often heavily medicated, on what she herself describes as "massive doses" of anti-anxiety medications, tranquilizers, and sleeping pills. She shows little interest in redemption, as one log notes: "Inmate has no ambition to attend any programs, yard, or school." "You guys made me like this,"

Kelly complained to a guard. "Why should I do anything?"

Citing Kelly's prison conduct, Judge Robert Bauman noted that he "did not see any progress towards rehabilitation," and chastised the young woman for blaming her predicament on others. "Ms. Ellard, *you* alone are responsible for your situation, and until you reach this elementary conclusion, you will be forever stalled in this nightmare which you have created."

After her sentencing, Kelly was sent to a federal prison in Nova Scotia, almost 4,000 miles from her home. But this March, the maximum-security unit of the Fraser Valley Institution, a new women's prison outside of Vancouver, opened, and Kelly was moved back to the milder climates of British Columbia. She is said to be in contact with several male prisoners whom she met while in co-ed remand facilities, including "Shy-Lox," an aspiring rapper incarcerated for the murder of his young girlfriend. Her lawyer has said he plans to appeal her conviction, asking for an acquittal or new trial. If the appeal is dismissed because of time served, she will be eligible for parole in 2009. At that time, she will be twenty-seven years old.

At the time of her former best friend's sentencing, Josephine Bell was dancing at Vancouver's Number Five Orange ("Canada's Finest All-Nude Strip Club"), and while dancing there, she was contacted by Peggy Holter, a producer for the evening news program, *Dateline*. Holter asked Josephine if she would be interested in appearing on a forthcoming episode about *Under the Bridge* and the Reena Virk case. After much negotiation and discussion about the quality of lighting and hotel accommodations,

Josephine agreed to fly to Los Angeles. Her hotel of choice was the Chateau Marmont, a $375-per-night hotel favored by starlets and rock stars.

On television, Josephine wore red lipstick, smoked Newport Lights, and appeared nonchalant and sanguine. "I'm not responsible for the murder in any *way, shape,* or *form,*" she said, emphatically. Asked again if she felt at all responsible, she shrugged her shoulders. "I wasn't there. I didn't kill her."

After the interview, she checked out of the Chateau Marmont and went to the Shara, a motel on Sunset Boulevard where she stayed for three weeks, before returning to Vancouver. Today, she says she is no longer dancing and feels sympathy for the Virks. "I never wanted any of this. I love Kel, and it kills me she's in a bad place," she says. "When I think of Kelly, I remember when we were kids and we would dress up like Courtney Love and go to the store. I can't hate her no matter what she does. I miss her every day."

While Josephine appears unscathed, the other girls who were under the bridge and part of the swarming against Reena Virk continue to struggle with guilt, poverty, and misfortune. Eve, said by lawyers and reporters to be "pretty as a model," is now literally scarred for life, with a large, red welt across her forehead, the aftermath of a car accident she was in one night when her boyfriend was driving. Dusty has been close to homeless, moving from subsidized motels to government homes to her sisters' houses, a kind of vagabond with two young daughters. Maya, now married, wrestles with her weight and bouts of depression. She refuses to get counseling and hasn't told her husband or boss about her role in the crime. She keeps this a painful secret, just like the silence she's long kept about her own father's murder, which she witnessed as a child.

In fall 2006, a pig farmer named Robert "Willy" Pickton is scheduled to stand trial for the murder of twenty-six women, many of them prostitutes and runaways in Vancouver's roughest neighborhood, known as the Downtown Eastside. Many of the adults involved in the Reena Virk case now play roles in this latest sensational case. James Williams, who successfully prosecuted those accused of assault against Reena Virk, was appointed to the Supreme Court of British Columbia in 2004 and will be the judge in Pickton's trial. Derrill Prevett, Crown prosecutor in Kelly's second trial, will represent the Crown against Pickton, while Adrian Brooks, one of Kelly Ellard's most able defenders, is a member of Pickton's large legal team. Catherine Murray is still a prosecutor in Victoria, though since there are so few murders in the town, her caseload is mainly composed of rapes and assaults. Recently, she prosecuted a case in which the victim, a self-professed vampire, lived in a coffin and sported a set of fangs.

In September 2005, Syreeta Hartley was invited to speak on teen violence to students at Nightingale-Bamford, a prestigious private school on Manhattan's Upper East Side. "A lot of these girls who got involved in the fight were like you," she said to a rapt audience of teenage girls. "They were beautiful and had things going for them, and had good families." She encouraged them to study the case, to learn something from "what happened to us." The schoolgirls were fascinated by the fate of her first love. They wanted to know if Warren was angry with her for testifying against him, if the two still kept in touch by mail. "I've got a boyfriend now," she said, "a job, a life. I don't have time for a pen pal. We have nothing in common anymore. I've moved on."

Warren Glowatski has also moved on, though he remains in prison, without the usual acquisitions of adulthood: a bank account, a driver's license, keys to his own home. He has a spotless prison record and, due to his good behavior, has been granted dozens of escorted temporary passes that allow him to leave the prison, albeit with a guard. He remains active in Restorative Justice programs, which unlike the Western idea of punishment and penalty, draw on Aboriginal principles of healing and community. It was through the Restorative Justice programs that one of the more hopeful and surprising developments in the Virk case occurred: a face-to-face meeting between Warren and Reena's parents, Suman and Manjit. Though many parents would find it hard to meet with the man convicted of killing their daughter, the Virks decided to listen to what Warren had to say, and, in turn, "make him realize what he's done, the damage he's done to our family." They found the direct meeting a more cathartic experience than the hours of time in the courtroom, where "you never have any control or power over what's happened." After the meeting, Suman Virk, Reena's mother, felt that Reena's death was "more real to Warren now. He understands the impact on others. At the time, [when he was sixteen] he was just thinking of himself."

Relatives of the victim, by law, have the right to attend parole hearings and most often show up to argue against release. But, on July 18, 2006, the Virks were at Warren's parole hearing in Mission, B.C, and instead of opposing Warren's request for unescorted temporary passes, they spoke with great kindness: "I am thankful and grateful you have taken responsibility for your actions. You have to go forward. I hope you stick to your path and prove that you have learned from your experiences and will truly love and respect others for the rest of your life." On his own behalf, Warren asked the board for "a chance." "I would like to be out in the community," he said. "I want to take the next step."

The board voted in favor of his application, giving him the chance for more freedom, stating that he'd demonstrated a "sound understanding of his crime," as well as "remorse and empathy."

Since 1997, no young girls have been murdered in Victoria. Reena Virk's name and story are constantly spoken of in high schools across Canada—in drama classes, where plays are performed about the case, and in numerous anti-bullying programs that have been put into place since the crime.

A maple tree was planted in memory of Reena Virk soon after her murder. The tree still stands, without the supporting wooden guides that held it in place when it was first set in the ground. Behind the tree are the waters of the Gorge, but the leaves grow and fall in Kinsmen Park, close to the place of Reena's murder, and closer still to the place where she played when she was a little girl.

-July 2006

ACKNOWLEDGMENTS

I am very grateful to the many people portrayed here who shared their experiences with trust and generosity, particularly the Virk and Pallan families. Thank you also to David Rosenthal and Iris Tupholme for believing in this book seven years ago, and Denise Roy, for being the dream editor. I am indebted to Barbara McLintock, a wise and insightful guide and friend, to Ellen and Dave Godfrey for everything, to Aaron Rose, Fi Campbell, Janet Johnson, Juliette Consigny, Diane Williams, and Holley Bishop for inspiring, Samuel Godfrey and Paul LaFarge for reading and improving early drafts, and to Yaddo, The Canada Council, Djerassi Resident Arts Program, and the Allen Room at the New York Public Library. For endless patience and help, thanks to (the wonderful) Emma Parry and all at Fletcher & Parry, Annie Orr, Jim Gifford, Katie Rizzo, David Kent, and the legal counsel of Kai Flankenberg and Alison Woodbury. For their kindness in Victoria and Vancouver, thanks to Pamela Hutchison, Dean Melanson, Catherine Snowdon, Marilyn Bowering, Matt Pollard, and the journalists: Jane Armstrong, Greg Joyce, Roger Stonebanks, Andy Ivens, Neal Hall, Amy Carmichael, Murray Langdon, Daniel

Girard. Great thanks also to Lydia Wills, Zoe Wolff, Stephanie Savage, Heather McGowan, Ken Dornstein, Phyllis Beren, Michael Turner, Jeff Rogers, Evan Bernard, Patrick Li, Brigitte Lacombe, Christine Schutt, and Beatrice von Rezzori.